To Dana —
Continue to
impact students
in your amazing
way!

ENHANCING STUDENT LEARNING THROUGH COLLEGE EMPLOYMENT

Edited by Brett Perozzi

Cite as:

Perozzi, B. (Ed.). (2009). *Enhancing student learning through college employment.* Bloomington, IN: Association of College Unions International.

Association of College Unions International
One City Centre, Suite 200
120 W. Seventh St.
Bloomington, IN 47404-3839 USA

This edition published by
Dog Ear Publishing
4010 W. 86th Street, Ste H
Indianapolis, IN 46268
www.dogearpublishing.net

ISBN: **978-159858-978-8**

Library of Congress Control Number: Applied For
This book is printed on acid-free paper.
Cover design by Andrea Langeveld
Printed in the United States of America

CONTENTS

ACKNOWLEDGMENTS

I would like to thank Elizabeth Beltramini, director of communications for the Association of College Unions International. Her skill is unsurpassed, her kind yet direct communication is cherished, and her friendship valued. We shared a dream of creating a groundbreaking publication for higher education in record time, and were able to go from idea to print in fewer than 16 months.

The authors of this publication have given tremendous time to their chapters, despite other, demanding presses in their jobs and family life. I thank them all for the sacrifices made to revise and re-revise manuscripts with such professionalism and timeliness. You made this dream a reality through your diligence and aplomb.

I also would like to thank Jan Winniford, vice president for student affairs at Weber State University. Her generous support of my professional development and this project is deeply appreciated.

Finally, I would like to thank my life partner, my wife, Teri Bladen. Thank you for sharing almost every weekend for a year with this project, putting up with the late nights and the early mornings at the computer. I so appreciate your love and support.

INTRODUCTION

As one of the first edited volumes dedicated to student employment, this book provides scholar-practitioners with pertinent information about many aspects of working during college. It is intended for those working in higher education who have responsibility for student employees. Given the breadth and depth of the chapters included in this publication, that audience may range from vice presidents and deans to students in supervisory roles. The book has utility for academic colleges and departments, student affairs divisions, auxiliary services, foundations, libraries, and facilities—essentially, all areas of the academy that employ student workers.

Student employment in college

While the numbers and percentages of students working during college vary slightly from source to source, it is appropriate to report that well over half of all undergraduate students work during college. The most recent data available from the National Center for Educational Statistics (2009) show that an average of 79 percent of all undergraduate students work at least one hour per week while enrolled. Students' reasons for working are numerous, but a prevalent reason is to afford college-related expenses (Baum, 2005).

The U.S. federal government recognized the social and economic need for college employment in the early 1960s. At that time, the national Job Corps was created, and the work-study program was institutionalized in the Higher Education Act. The act has had significant revisions over the years and the federal government now provides almost $1 billion in funding each year to more than 3,400 participating institutions to support students in the federal work-study program (U.S. Department of Education, n.d.).

In addition, most college students who work on campus hold non-work-study positions (Perna, Cooper, & Li, 2006). Think for a minute about the resources any single institution invests in student employees outside of work-study. While no research currently tracks the aggregate figure, surely that number would be staggering. Horn and Nevill (2006) reported that 70 percent of all undergraduates at four-year institutions work and do so at an average of 26 hours per week. This adds up to billions spent annually.

Students work both on and off campus, full-time and part-time. Some students are full-time employees taking classes and others are full-time students working part-time. Employment of students, particularly on-campus employment, is relevant and germane to the student experience, yet the academy rarely embraces employment as a means to education and student development. Interestingly, many other countries (including the two featured in Chapter 8) refer to most of their on-campus employment experiences as "casual" employment. While on-campus employment in the United States is not referred to in this way, that is essentially how the concept is treated.

INTRODUCTION

Previous research on student employment has tended to focus solely on the negative implications of working while attending college. Ford and Bosworth (1995) found that the majority of students employed while in college indicate that their academic endeavors faced negative consequences directly due to their employment. These negative consequences included reduced time to study, missed assignments, and missed lectures. Perkins and associates (1999) found that GPA dropped 0.03 points for every $1,000 earned while working in college for students ages 18 to 24.

Additional research has indicated that working during college can become detrimental to academic achievement if students spend too much time on the job during their college experience (Furr & Elling, 2000; Hood, Craig, & Ferguson, 1992; Van de Water, 1996). Furr and Elling (2000) found that students who worked more than 20 hours per week during their undergraduate careers felt that their occupational workload interfered with their academic performance. In general, students working more than four hours per weekday, despite total number of hours worked per week, were found to achieve lower mean GPAs than students who worked fewer hours or did not work at all (Hood, Craig, & Ferguson, 1992). Further, Astin (1993) found that working full-time during college implies a strong negative association with completing a bachelor's degree, earning a good college GPA, preparing for graduate school, and graduating with honors.

Other researchers have described the relationship of number of hours worked to academic success. Van de Water (1996) reported that student grades tended to improve as students worked more hours per week, up to a total of 20 hours per week. After 20 hours of work, the number of hours worked had a negative relationship with GPA. In addition, students who worked 10 to 20 hours per week performed better academically than students who worked fewer than 10 hours, more than 20 hours, or not at all (Van de Water, 1996). Hood, Craig, and Ferguson (1992) had similar findings to Van de Water's (1996) in establishing that moderate participation in employment (defined as 2–4 hours per weekday) led to higher GPAs. Students who were not employed or worked more than four hours per weekday had, on average, lower GPAs (Hood, Craig, & Ferguson, 1992). And Astin (1993) suggested that, in general, part-time, on-campus employment has positive effects on student development: higher GPA, faster degree completion, and more frequent self-reported cognitive and affective growth.

Many of the positive academic effects are attributed most directly to on-campus rather than to off-campus employment (Astin, 1993; Furr & Elling, 2000; Pascarella et al., 1994). Astin (1993) found a positive association between on-campus employment and attaining a bachelor's degree, self-reported cognitive growth, and improvement in GPA. These positive effects on academic achievement are believed to occur for on-campus employment because students are more likely to work in roles that relate to their academic field (Stern & Nakata, 1991) and to interact more frequently with the campus environment, fellow students, faculty, and administrators (Astin, 1993; Pascarella et al., 1994).

Interestingly, off-campus employment yields many negative academic results similar to those of working too many hours, regardless of the amount of actual time spent working at the off-campus site (Astin, 1993). Pascarella and associates (1994) established that employment off campus has a negative influence on year-to-year persistence in college and in completion of a bachelor's degree. In addition, students employed off campus tended to study less than their counterparts who were employed on campus or who were not employed (Pascarella et al., 1994).

In any case, students are working during college. If students are going to be employed, administrators have an obligation and an opportunity to ensure experiences are meaningful, intentional, promote cognitive growth, and complement—rather than interfere with—students' academic pursuits. Acknowledging the available research about potential negative aspects of working during college, part-time, on-campus job opportunities and employment programs are the primary considerations of the following chapters. While off-campus employment is certainly not ignored, this publication focuses on foundational concepts and proven solutions to support practitioners in creating educational and engaging student employment programs on campus.

Student learning

Student learning is an underlying assumption of this publication. All chapters emanate from a perspective of supporting and encouraging student growth through college employment. Student learning need not be mysterious or haphazard; indeed, the current tenor of American higher education calls for the opposite: obvious and measurable added value. Providing information for viable programs to measure students' gains as a result of their employment is a foundation for the publication.

The authors in this book advocate making learning overt and incorporating learning outcomes into the fabric of employment programs. Development, cultivation, description, infusion, and evaluation of student learning outcomes through the higher education employment setting are all facets of a theme throughout the chapters.

Student learning is an objective around which all members of the higher education community can rally. And it is a point of identification that unites the academy. The concept of students gaining valuable knowledge and skills cuts across academic and student support areas. The growth of students is a galvanizing point for most facets of higher education and provides islands of clarity for working together toward the common goal of helping students become educated, contributing members of a global society. All members of the academic community share the desire for students to acquire broad-based learning outcomes such as becoming servant-leaders, skilled problem-solvers, clear communicators, etc. With this level of agreement about the core function of higher education and the demonstrable value of the collegiate experience, it makes sense that student employment be embraced as a central tenant in students' development.

About this book

College and universities provide myriad types of employment for students. From clerical work to research assistants, an array of opportunities is available to students during their college careers.

While this publication focuses on students who receive remuneration from the institution, there also are abundant unpaid opportunities for students to gain the same types of skills and knowledge, and many of the concepts discussed here also are relevant to those settings and students.

Employment is conceptualized as students who are paid by the institution and officially report to a supervisor, as opposed to students who may be in a role where they receive a stipend or other remuneration for their service, time, or leadership role; for example, many of the traditionally volunteer positions on student governments and programming boards. While unpaid positions such as internships, practica, and some undergraduate research roles would not fall within this definition, most of the principles can be extended and applied to these other categories of student workers. Several chapters address the broader context of employment during college, especially as it relates to student success. The majority of concepts embraced in this publication do not include employment opportunities such as externships, student teaching, medical-related rotations, and other forms of student employment required for an academic degree. However, many of the concepts discussed here are applicable in those realms as well.

The chapters flow together as a single work on student employment, yet references have been retained at the end of each chapter so that each is able to stand on its own. Most chapters within this book appeal to multiple audiences. Some readers may seek information on student employment, yet others may have an interest in the chapter's secondary aspect. For example, the first chapter is a tidy précis of student development theories, from classics to contemporary, which a range of scholar-practitioners is likely to seek. And because the desire was to promote chapters' individual merit, duplicate information is minimized and in-text references to other chapters have been inserted so that readers can further explore concepts that are embraced in depth elsewhere in the publication.

One challenge or difference in thinking is addressed in multiple chapters and worth mentioning here: The concept of measuring student growth, particularly along stated learning outcomes, and how that is incorporated with, or separated from, other, more traditional measures of employment continues to be controversial. Many secondary questions cloud the primary issue. For example, whose responsibility is it to teach and whose is it to learn? Is learning assessment a critique to improve organizational functioning? If so, where is the onus placed if students are not learning what is hoped or what the institution says they will? Is it appropriate for students to be or not to be given raises or promoted to higher-level positions when they do/do not demonstrate proficiency on specified learning outcomes? And, how is employment the same or different from expectations faculty have of students in the classroom? These vexing issues are not necessarily solved in this publication, but they are addressed and data and discussion are presented in an effort to move the discussion forward, allowing readers to draw conclusions and add to the debate.

In an effort to meet the needs of busy higher education scholar-practitioners almost every chapter in the book concludes with suggestions, implications, or recommendations for study or practice. This format helps the publication cohere as a unit, and also allows for each chapter's utility. This consistent approach provides the reader with specific and demonstrated integration of data and discussion ready for use and adaptation in new or existing student employment programs.

About the chapters

"Enhancing Student Learning through College Employment" is organized into three sections: foundational principles, demographics and special populations, and administrative considerations. There are four chapters per section, providing a nice symmetry and balance to the book.

Foundational principles

Section I prepares readers for the publication's focus on student development and learning outcomes. Kate M. Boyle's synthesis of student development theories covers massive territory in minimal pages, providing readers with a breadth of developmental theories unparalleled in the higher education literature. This lead chapter is a must-read for many segments of the academy, especially graduate students and those seeking a progressive summary of contemporary theories and the foundational bases for them. Boyle masterfully provides an overall rubric for classifications of theories and presents cogent and succinct summaries of individual theories.

This backdrop of student development theory is followed by a review of research that uses these theories as a platform for measurement of student growth and individual gains through college employment experiences. Ryan Padgett and David L. Grady wade through a significant volume of research to piece together meaningful results and implications for administrators, institutions, and students. From academic achievement to degree completion, the authors ameliorate data from a variety of sources, relying heavily on Pascarella and Terenzini's (2005) meta-analysis of the literature and drawing conclusions about the personal growth students demonstrate and the impact of work during college.

Addressing learning outcomes directly, Jonathan S. Lewis and Sebastian Contreras Jr. present the results of a recent study of student employees. The authors' research included the integration of learning outcomes into position descriptions, and the findings point to positive impacts along several outcomes measures. The chapter also demonstrates how scholar-practitioners can use their everyday organizational reality to study learning and modify practice based on results.

Integrating student learning outcomes into the fabric of student employment programs is the focus of last chapter in this section. Brett Perozzi, Janelle Kappes, and Deborah Santucci review relevant considerations when grounding an employment program in learning outcomes. They provide useful background information for institutions that have established employment programs about how such programs can be reconceptualized to embrace learning outcomes as a core component. They also offer strategies and processes for scholar-practitioners who are starting, or would like to establish, a new employment program. The chapter takes the reader through a series of considerations and nuances for both creating and enhancing student employment programs based on learning outcomes.

Demographics and special populations

Section II of the book focuses on demographics of students and special populations. This section brings to life current realities of student employment on college campuses, both in the United States and abroad. Disparate models, paradigms, and approaches are presented for consideration. This is a unique look at the varied populations associated with student learning and employment, and demonstrates the significant differences between institution types, cultures, and support for education and employment.

The section begins with a study using the vast National Survey of Student Engagement databank. The scope of these data is tremendous. John V. Moore's and Melanie Rago's literature review leads them to queries exploring pertinent aspects of employment on U.S. college campuses. The focus of their study is squarely on the critical and emerging topic of student engagement, and they embrace both on- and off-campus employment as well as students' motivations.

Larry Lunsford focuses on underrepresented students in his chapter addressing unique needs of this rapidly growing population. In his mini-study, he is able to combine a significant literature base with qualitative research conducted with current student employees from various ethnic backgrounds. These students' direct quotes and experiences underscore employment's relevance during college. The chapter is both informative and compelling, and provides higher education administrators with data on critical and burgeoning student populations.

The third chapter in this section is a multiple case study that explores the intricacies of two California universities where student self-governance is practiced. The difference in governance and paradigm is a stark contrast to what most higher education administrators encounter on a daily basis. The history, significant milestones, and organizational structure of these student-led entities provides an intriguing platform for the study of student development and how it impacts student employment, attention to learning, and leadership. Lessons learned and implications of this unique environment are explored in relation to student-administrator interaction for success. Jerry Mann, Nadesan Permaul, and Perozzi are able to provide nuance and detail of this environment based on their intimate and auxiliary-veteran experiences.

The final chapter in this section departs from U.S. higher education to explore student employment in Ireland and Australia. Linda Croston and Andrew O'Brien artfully depict aspects of their higher education systems. They include funding schemes, information about organizational structures, and the conventional ethos around students working while attending college. The data provide great insight into differences and similarities related to U.S. student employment. This chapter is attractive to those interested in comparative higher education as well as student employment concepts.

Administrative considerations

The concluding section of the book is the most approachable and practitioner-based; however, it draws heavily on existing literature within the higher education and student affairs cannon, as well as from other disciplines. For the reader who is looking to readily gather information and put it into practice, this section is essential. From critical administrative considerations to measuring learning, this section provides information to help any institution create a solid base for its employment program, while also offering excellent advice on maintaining the program and looking toward the future.

Z. Paul Reynolds begins the section by addressing crucial administrative concepts for both the novice supervisor and the seasoned professional. Aspects of human resource management are considered and reminders presented that can save valuable time and resources. The chapter also addresses organizational philosophy and alignment for employment programs' continued success.

The second chapter in this section is a ground-breaking exploration of student development's potential prominence in employment roles within services that higher education increasingly outsources. Maggie Towle and Denny Olsen use their own experiences as a point of departure as they investigate the possibilities presented to higher education through relationships with third-party vendors. The unique aspect of working with these companies to help students learn and achieve the learning outcomes is a compelling read. They provide data and suggestions that can assist with this integrative process from initial requests for proposals through the continuation of long-term contracts.

Training and the provision of ongoing developmental opportunities for students is the focus on the publication's penultimate chapter. Keeping students motivated, using existing structures to train students, and infusing current pedagogy are themes of this critical chapter. Eve Scrogham and Sara Punsky McGuire convey purposeful approaches grounded in relevant theory and best practices. They provide "how-to's" as well as examples for immediate implementation into employment settings.

The book's final chapter is an eloquent presentation of current methodological considerations for measuring student learning. Jessica Hickmott adroitly captures relevant data from contemporary literature and explains often complicated concepts in a simplistic and approachable manner. The issues and methods included are critical to student employment, and many options are presented so that individual institutions can make the best decisions for their current environments. The presentation of this information is well-suited for graduate students starting in the field, practitioners looking to create an assessment plan for their student employees, and senior administrators wanting to gain additional knowledge about methodological considerations as they relate to student employment in higher education.

This publication is among the first of its kind, addressing student employment during college from a learning perspective. The innovative chapters have utility for many constituencies within the academy. It is hoped that this pioneering book will provide scholar-practitioners, faculty, external service providers, post-graduate employers, and others with the tools and knowledge base to continue to develop students in their employment roles, with a particular focus on learning. Helping students become educated, engaged citizens of a global society will require the attention and keen acumen collected from all members of the higher education community.

References

Astin, A. (1993). *What matters in college? Four critical years revisited.* San Francisco: Jossey-Bass.

Baum, S. (2005). *Financial barriers to college access and persistence: The current status of student reliance on grants, loans, and work.* Paper prepared for the Advisory Committee on Student Financial Assistance, Washington, DC.

Ford, J., & Bosworth, D. (1995, June). Part-time work and full-time education. *Studies in Higher Education, 20*(2), 187–203.

Furr, S.R., & Elling, T.W. (2000, Winter). The influence of work on college student development. *NASPA Journal, 37*(2), 454–470.

Hood, A.B., Craig, A.F., & Ferguson, B.W. (1992, September). The impact of athletics, part-time employment and other activities on academic achievement. *Journal of College Student Development, 33*, 447–453.

Horn, L., & Nevill, S. (2006). *Profile of undergraduates in U.S. postsecondary education institutions: 2003–04: With a special analysis of community college students* (NCES 2006184). Washington, DC: National Center for Education Statistics.

Kuh, D., Kinzie, J., Schuh, J.H., Whitt, E.J., & Associates. (2005). *Student success in college: Creating conditions that matter.* San Francisco: Jossey-Bass.

National Center for Educational Statistics. (n.d). NEDRC tables: student employment. Retrieved January 6, 2009, from http://nces.ed.gov/das/library/tables_listings/nedrc_table.asp?sbj =student%20employment

Pascarella, E., Bohr, L., Nora, A., Desler, M., & Zusman, B. (1994, Summer). Impacts of on-campus and off-campus work on first-year cognitive outcomes. *Journal of College Student Development, 35*, 364–370.

Pascarella, E.T., & Terenzini, P.T. (2005). *How college affects students: A third decade of research* (Vol. 2). San Francisco: Jossey Bass.

Perkins, G., Pitter, G., Wijesinghe, H., Howat, C., Whitfield, D. (1999). *Relationship of financial aid, work and college performance.* AIR Annual Forum Paper.

Perna, L., Cooper, M.A., & Li, C. (2006). *Improving educational opportunities for students who work.* Paper prepared for the Indiana Project on Academic Success, Bloomington, IN.

Stern, D., & Nakata, Y. (1991, January/February). Paid employment among U.S. college students. *Journal of Higher Education, 62*(1), 25–43.

U.S. Department of Education. (n.d.). Federal work-study program. Retrieved January 2, 2009, from http://www.ed.gov/programs/fws/gtepfws.pdf

Van de Water, G. (1996). The effect of part-time work on academic performance and progress: An examination of the Washington state work-study program. In R. Kincaid (Ed.), *Student employment: Linking college and the workplace* (pp. 57–67). National Resource Center for The First-Year Experience and Students in Transition. University of South Carolina University.

SECTION I

FOUNDATIONAL PRINCIPLES

STUDENT DEVELOPMENT THEORY AS A BACKDROP FOR EMPLOYMENT

by Kate M. Boyle

A gap exists between the academic discipline of higher education and student affairs administration and the applied practice of the field. Academicians often prioritize learning theory as primary to understanding practice. Faculty in student affairs preparation programs review theories and research relevant to applied practice, and many of these professors try a variety of exercises (e.g., case studies and role plays) to help graduate students see connections and put them into practice. Practitioners supervising graduate students recognize college students cannot be neatly fit into theoretical frameworks. Many college and university staff members find they must prioritize time to respond to the most urgent crisis. Thus, professionals often challenge graduate students about how, when, and where to use theory appropriately.

Knowledge about college student development, characteristics of diverse college students, campus environments, and organizations increases annually. Theories continue to grow in number and have become well defined (Evans, Forney, & Guido-DiBrito, 1998; Hamrick, Evans, & Schuh, 2002; Stage & Kuh, 1996; Strange, 1994; Torres, Howard-Hamilton, & Cooper, 2003). College and university professionals expect application of this knowledge. Yet many professionals struggle with linking theory and practice (Caple & Voss, 1983; Parker, 1977; Plato, 1978; Stage, 1994; Upcraft, 1994, 1998). An area in which student affairs practitioners can examine the linking of theory and practice is when employing students within various work sites around campus.

Using theory

As students arrive at work, their primary focus may be on tasks and responsibilities placed in front of them. Yet, when working with student employees, student affairs practitioners need to carefully consider issues and concerns students bring with them to the work setting. These particular employees are developing as they progress through their academic years—moving away from parents and other authority figures' ideas (of who they are and what they think) to gain a greater understanding of their own identity. As they experience training and intentional development seminars or discussions, student employees may be able to understand better their personal preferences or the way in which they make sense of the world. Practitioners and administrators need to be aware that even when a student is simply "clocking in and out" of their place of employment, development has not stopped and can still be a part of practitioners' interactions with these employees. Practitioners can assist student employees by improving their own understanding of the ways in which students develop, change thought processes, and make sense of their world throughout their collegiate years.

In an effort to make sense out of life, people develop theories (Evans et al., 1998). *Why would he react that way? What motivates her? How could we help this group connect better?* Student affairs professionals develop "informal theories" from ideas about the needs and concerns of students. Individual value systems, backgrounds, and experiences influence the development of personal, informal theories. However, these informal theories are not self-correcting (McEwen, 2003a; Parker, 1977).

Research-validated, formal theories provide a way in which professionals can support their internal perceptions of individuals and situations. A theory is a conceptual representation composed from "potentially infinite specific and concrete variations of a phenomenon" (Strange & King, 1990, p. 17). Rodgers and Widick (1980) defined formal theory as "a set of propositions regarding the interrelationship of two or more conceptual variables relevant to some realm of phenomena. It provides a framework for explaining the relationship among variables and for empirical investigations" (p. 81). According to McEwen (2003a), practitioners can think of theory as "interrelationships among concepts and constructs" (p. 165). A researcher or several researchers develop hypotheses regarding human development, environmental dynamics, and organizations, which evolve from the collection of data. Theory often simplifies the complex—it organizes what seems to be chaotic and connects what appears to be random (McEwen, 2003a).

A profession's foundation is theoretical. Knowledge, expertise, and practice explored in the field of higher education and student affairs administration is based on theory and thus supports the field's professional standing (McEwen, 2003a). When student services professionals know and understand theory, a medium for communication and understanding exists. Theory provides a common language within a community of scholars-practitioners (Knefelkamp, 1982; McEwen, 2003a).

This chapter provides a review of theories. What follows is a thumbnail sketch of theoretical categories and brief insights into each of the more prominent theories. Although an array of theories is provided, practitioners must seek out more details on theories they believe relate to their specific situation and employees.

Theory and higher education and student affairs administration

Evans and her colleagues (1998) presented perhaps the most comprehensive examination of college student developmental theory to date. Building on Knefelkamp, Widick, and Parker's (1978) work, Evans and associates identified three primary areas of developmental theory: psychosocial and identity development, cognitive-structural, and typology theories (Evans et al., 1998). Other theoretical areas explored in the academic discipline of higher education and student affairs administration include: person-environment interaction and campus ecology, learning, spirituality/faith, and organizational (Baxter Magolda, 1992; Chickering, Dalton, & Stamm, 2006; Hamrick et al., 2002; Torres et al., 2003). Beginning with psychosocial/identity development theories, this chapter explores each of the three theoretical foundations proposed by Evans et al. (1998) along with a brief exploration of a few person-environment interaction theories. Further exploration of the theoretical premises within the field of higher education and student affairs administration is highly encouraged (see Baxter Magolda, 1992; Braxton, 2003; Chickering et al. 2006; Evans, 2003; Evans et al., 1998; Hamrick et al., 2002; King, 2003; Kuh, 2003; McEwen, 2003a, 2003b; Strange, 2003; Torres et al., 2003).

Psychosocial and identity development theories

As higher education and student affairs administration emerged as a profession in the mid-20th century, student development theory arose from the fields of psychology and sociology (Evans et al., 1998; Hamrick et al., 2002). Human development—in particular college student development—is critical to understanding the issues and concerns students bring with them to the work setting. Although day-to-day interactions may not present opportunities to explore individual developmental patterns, these developmental processes are occurring within the students and may be apparent within the work setting. "Psychosocial theorists examine the *content* of development, the important issues people face as their lives progress, such as how to define themselves, their relationships with others, and what to do with their lives" (Evans et al., 1998, p. 32). Individuals who successfully develop appropriate coping skills resolve developmental tasks effectively (Evans et al., 1998).

Identity development

Psychologists such as Erikson (1950, 1968) proposed that human development occurs over the life span. Development occurs, according to Erikson, through individuals' resolution of compelling questions. Transitions of childhood to young adult and young adult into adulthood rely on resolving identity and intimacy questions (identity versus identity diffusion and intimacy versus isolation) (Erikson, 1950, 1968).

Models presented by Marcia (1966) on ego identity status and Josselson (1987) on women's identity development expanded upon Erikson's (1950, 1968) concepts. These lifespan models of development relied on interacting variables of crisis and commitment: *diffusion* – lacking crisis and commitment; *foreclosure* – committing to an identity without a crisis; *moratorium* – searching for an identity and/or having identity conflict; and *achievement* – breaking from childhood and creating an identity (Josselson, 1987; Marcia, 1966).

In 1969, Chickering (revised by Chickering & Reisser, 1993) built on these researchers' concepts by focusing on traditional college students' development throughout the critical transition into adulthood. Chickering recognized identity formation was central during the college years. Chickering and Reisser identified seven "vectors of development"; each vector possesses "direction and magnitude—even though the direction may be expressed more appropriately by a spiral or by steps than by a straight line" (p. 8). Revised vectors include: developing competence, managing emotions, moving through autonomy toward interdependence, developing mature interpersonal relationships, establishing identity, developing purpose, and developing integrity (Chickering & Reisser, 1993). Collegiate environmental factors influenced these developmental tasks: institutional objectives, institutional size, faculty-student interaction, curriculum, teaching practices, diverse student communities, and student affairs programs and services. Chickering and Reisser (1993) suggested three principles support these factors: integration of work and learning, recognition and respect for individual differences, and acknowledgement of the cyclical nature of learning and development.

Between the 1960s and today, several researchers challenged Chickering's concepts of development, in particular noting theoretical applications may differ for students from various backgrounds. A number of theorists published different views of identity development based on ethnicity, race, and sexual orientation (Atkinson, Morten, & Sue, 1989; Baldwin, Duncan, & Bell, 1992; Cass, 1979; Choney, Berryhill-Paapke, & Robbins, 1995; Cross, 1971, 1995; D'Augelli, 1995; Ferdman & Gallegos, 2001; Gay,1984; Hardiman, 2001; Helms, 1990, 1995; Horse, 2001; Ibrahim, Ohnishi, & Sandu, 1997; Jackson, 1976, 2001; Keefe & Padilla, 1987; Kim, 2001; LaFromboise, Trimble, & Mohatt, 1990; Maekawa Kodama, McEwen, Liang, & Lee, 2002; Phinney, 1990; Robinson & Howard-Hamilton, 1994; Torres, 2004).

Ethnic/racial identity theories

Atkinson, Morten, and Sue (1989, 1993) and Phinney (1990) often are referred to as authorizing theories of ethnic development. Atkinson et al. created a minority identity development model and later renamed the racial/cultural identity development model. Within the model, individuals move from conformity (valuing the majority culture above self) to integrative awareness (strong sense of self) (Torres et al., 2003). Phinney posited a theory building upon Marcia's (1966) concepts with three stages of diffusion-foreclosure (unexplored feelings and attitudes), moratorium (awareness and exploration of ethnic identity), and identity achievement (healthy bicultural identity).

African American/black racial identity theories

Cross (1971) developed a theory of black identity development or *nigrescence* (a French word meaning the process of becoming black). Development occurs through the five stages involving pre-encounter (low-salience attitudes toward being black), encounter (valued world view is flawed, move towards nigrescence), immersion-emersion (pro-black, anti-white), internalization (acquired inner peace, cognitive dissonance dissipated), and internalization-commitment (identities formed of black nationalist, biculturalist, and multiculturalist—comfort with blackness). Stages focus on psychological and behavioral characteristics of African Americans based on their interaction with oppression (Cross, 1971, 1991, 1995; Torres et al., 2003). A revision of his theory took into account cultural, social, psychological, and historical changes that occurred in the years between his initial model and his later model, particularly issues of language (Torres et al., 2003).

Two other theorists developed black identity development stage theories similar to Cross (1971, 1991, 1995). In the mid-'70s, Jackson (1976, 2001) suggested that individuals moved through five stages: naïve, acceptance, resistance, redefinition, and internalization. Another theorist exploring black identity development, Gay (1984), proposed a three-stage model based on socioracial identity and consciousness: pre-encounter, encounter, and post-encounter.

African paradigms also were used in developing theories. Two core components compose the African self-consciousness construct proposed by Baldwin, Duncan, and Bell (1992): African self-extension orientation (spirituality) and African self-consciousness (direction and purpose). Robinson and Howard-Hamilton (1994) looked to psychological health and interpersonal relationships in their theory of development focusing on the Afro-centric resistance paradigm and Nguzo Saba principles (the seven principles of Kwanzaa): unity (*umoja*), self-determination (*kujichagulia*), collective work and responsibility (*ujima*), cooperative economics (*juamaa*), purpose (*nia*), creativity (*kuumba*), and faith (*imani*). Individuals engage one principle at a time or all seven collectively.

Latino, Chicano, and Hispanic American racial identity theories

Keefe and Padilla (1987) examined Mexican American or Chicano racial identity through cultural awareness (awareness of Mexican culture and people), ethnic loyalty (attitudes and feelings about Mexican culture), and ethnic social orientation (preference for interacting with others of Mexican descent and for ethnic foods). Generational differences were noted and the researchers created five types ranging from Type I (unacculturated and identifying as Mexican) to Type V (extremely Anglicized and having little knowledge or identity with the Mexican culture).

After interviewing self-identified Latino and Hispanic college students, Torres (2004) suggested three conditions influenced their ethnic identity: the environment where they grew up, family and generational influences, and self-perception of status. Torres found when students experienced conflict with culture or a change in relationships within the environment they experienced identity change. "As students find congruence between their old learned beliefs and new beliefs, they establish relationships that better match this new identity. This change in relationships can be positive (if congruence is found) or negative (if conflict is not resolved)" (Torres et al., 2003, p. 57).

A model of Latino identity development developed by Ferdman and Gallegos (2001) suggested six orientations: *Latino integrated, Latino identified, subgroup identified, Latino as other, undifferentiated/denial,* and *white identified.* Each orientation possesses a different lens, preferences, and views. The model focuses on all Latino groups; however, and does not elaborate on development or how lenses are developed.

Native American racial identity theories

More than 481 tribes are recognized by the U.S. government. Each tribe potentially possesses different language and customs (Torres et al., 2003). "Among Indians, identity development begins with the family, extended family, kinship, or clan affiliation" (Horse, 2001, p. 94). Tribal sovereignty history and government-sanctioned oppression connect with the developmental issues of American Indian college students (Torres et al., 2003). "Factors that influence our individual and group consciousness as either tribal people or as American Indians" delineate the identity (Horse, 2001, p. 100). Five factors influence consciousness: grounding in native language and culture; valid genealogical heritage; a worldview that derives from old traditions; thinking of self as American Indian; and being officially recognized as a member of a tribe. A person might meet four of the factors and still not be recognized as a member of a tribe. Tribes function as sovereign nations and have the power to determine who is or is not recognized as a member.

LaFromboise, Trimble, and Mohatt (1990) categorized American Indians in three ways: residential patterns, level of tribal affiliation, and extent of commitment to tribal heritage. Five categories composed the authors' concept of "Indianness": *traditional* (little English, observe "old-time" traditions and values); *transitional* (speak both English and the native language, question basic traditionalism and religion, and yet cannot fully accept dominant culture and values); *marginal* (may be defensively Indian but are unable, because of their ethnicity, to live the cultural heritage of their tribal group or to identify with dominant problems); *assimilated* (for the most part, have been accepted by the dominant society and have embraced dominant culture and values); *bicultural* (for the most part, have been accepted by the dominant society, yet also know and accept tribal traditions and culture—can move either in direction with ease).

Health, rather than deficit, was at the center of the conceptualization of acculturation proposed by Choney, Berryhill-Paapke, and Robbins (1995). Four areas of human personality are in harmony "with the domains of the medicine wheel (a uniquely Indian means of conceptualizing the human condition based on four essential elements)": *behavioral, social/environmental, affective/spiritual,* and *cognitive* (p. 85). Within each area are concentric circles representing different levels of acculturation: *traditional, transitional, bicultural, assimilated,* and *marginal.* One level of acculturation is not valued over another; one dimension of personality is not emphasized more than another. The nonlinear approach allows for an individual to maintain four different levels of acculturation corresponding to the four personality domains.

Asian American racial identity theories

As Kim (2001) studied Japanese women, she found five sequential and progressive stages. The stages are similar to other racial identity theories: *ethnic awareness* (being Japanese), *white identification* (different from others), *awakening to social political consciousness* (sees self as a minority and loses white-identified ideals; self concept becomes more positive), *redirection to Asian American consciousness* (embrace Asian American identity and immerse self in Asian American heritage), and *incorporation* (healthy, secure balance with self and others) (Kim, 2001).

When applying the Atkinson, Morton, and Sue (1993) minority identity development model, Ibrahim, Ohnishi, and Sandu (1997) discovered differences for immigrants from South Asia. South Asian immigrants do not experience a *pre-encounter* or *conformity* stage because they desire to be a part of the dominant culture. Additionally, this group agreed with the "American dream that hard work will overcome all difference" (Ibrahim et al., p. 42). The *dissonance* stage comes when immigrants discover that hard work is not enough. Within the current American culture it is not easy to overcome cultural differences. Once South Asian immigrants become aware of this they enter into *resistance and immersion*, rejecting the dominant culture and going back to their Asian heritage and culture. Immigrants then move to *introspection* where they begin to question dogmatic beliefs and recognize some positive elements of dominant culture. Asian American immigrants develop a strong sense of self-worth and individuality in the *synergistic* stage. At this point, they can accept or reject other cultural values (Ibrahim et al., 1997).

Maekawa Kodama, McEwen, Liang, and Lee (2002) posited a model of Asian American identity development that addresses dominant U.S. culture as well as traditional Asian cultures. *Identity* is in the center of an axis, representing the college student between two domains (U.S. and traditional Asian family and culture).

> For some students the distance between the two ends may be great, representing much incongruence between the dominant society and the values of their family. For others, the distance may be short, particularly if the student is relatively acculturated and feels little conflict between the domains of family and society. (Maekawa Kodama et al., 2002, p. 49)

The researchers identified five developmental tasks influential with regard to identity and enhanced the model: *emotions, competency, interdependence, relationships*, and *integrity*.

White American racial identity theories

Hardiman (2001) initially conceptualized a white identity model in the early 1980s and then amended her ideas throughout the 1990s. Five stages construct the model: *naïve about race* (no social consciousness of race), *acceptance* (begin to accept or internalize a sense of superiority due to prevalent covert and overt messages of white privilege), *resistance* (realization dominance of one group over another is wrong, question and resist racist messages), *redefinition* (personal interest in fighting racism, redefining whiteness), and *internalization* (raised consciousness, awareness of racial and social injustices) (Hardiman, 2001; Torres et al., 2003).

Originally, Helms (1990) proposed a model of white identity comprised of seven stages. In the most recent version of this model presented by Helms and Cook (1999), the focus is on two primary phases: giving up a racist identity and creating a nonracist identity. Helms and Cook identified seven statuses (as opposed to static stages, statuses are dynamic): *contact* (unaware of racist nature and happy with the status quo), *disintegration* (experience dissonance as becoming aware of whiteness and implications of some of their actions for other racial groups), *reintegration* (prejudicial acts and belief in white superiority), *pseudo-independence* (committed to white group "and subtle superiority and tolerance of other socioracial groups" [p. 92] as long as they work to conform to white standards), *immersion* (seek out information about other groups in an effort to redefine what it means to be white), *emersion* (pride in developing a new white identity and interacting with others who are like-minded), and *autonomy* (internalized multicultural perspective).

Sexual orientation identity theories

Clinical work with gays and lesbians in Australia led Cass (1979) to develop a homosexual identity model. Cass defined identity formation as "the process by which a person comes first to consider and later to acquire the identity of 'homosexual' as a relevant aspect of self" (p. 219). Six stages encompass the model: *identity confusion* (initial awareness of homosexual thoughts, feelings, and attractions), *identity comparison* (acceptance of the possibility of being gay or lesbian), *identity tolerance* (acknowledge probably gay or lesbian and seek out others to reduce feelings of isolation), *identity acceptance* (positive connotation with being gay or lesbian), *identity pride* (focus on gay issues and activities and minimize contact with heterosexuals), and *identity synthesis* (individuals judged on personal qualities rather than sexual identity, less dichotomy between homosexual and heterosexual worlds).

D'Augelli (1995) proposed a lifespan model of lesbian, gay, and bisexual (LGB) identity development. This model suggested individuals not only react to environments, but also shape them. Three sets of interrelated variables are involved in the formation of identity according to D'Augelli: personal subjectivities and actions, interactive intimacies, and sociohistorical connections. D'Augelli suggested six interactive processes (not stages) involved in lesbian, gay, and bisexual development: *exiting heterosexual identity, developing LGB identity status, developing an LGB social identity, becoming an LGB offspring, developing an LGB intimacy status*, and *entering an LGB community.*

Meeting the challenge of multiple identities

Higher education and student affairs professionals need to be aware that each student possesses a unique story, recognizing that few people link themselves to only one identity and no one theory matches all of the components of individuals' identities. Multiple identities of race, class, gender, and sexual orientation combine to form an individual's comprehensive identity. Multifaceted identities often are immersed in oppression and may subordinate their "status in an array of either/or dualities" (Collins, 2002, p. 472). Theory and research are beginning to address how various dimensions of identity may interact with one another and whether they are salient to an individual and under what conditions (for additional information see Jones, 1997; Jones & McEwen, 2000; Reynolds & Pope, 1991).

Other psychosocial theories

Addressing college students' psychological and social needs does not always revolve around identity development. At times individuals look to their peer group to establish a sense of belonging within their new college environment. Two theorists who address these psychosocial concerns are Schlossberg (1989) and Tinto (1975, 1986, 1993).

Theory of marginality and mattering

According to Schlossberg (1989), having a sense of belonging is critical in college students' development and success. New experiences and roles can lead to individuals feeling marginal, particularly when they question their abilities. Not fitting in, or marginality, may lead to feelings of insecurity, irritability, and/or depression. Schlossberg recognized that students who identify as minority group members view themselves as outsiders throughout their college years. Meanwhile, other students may experience temporary marginality (new students or transfers who are members of a dominant group).

A sense of not mattering can result from feelings of marginality. Schlossberg (1989) defined mattering as "our belief, whether right or wrong that we matter to someone else" (p. 9). Schlossberg characterized five components of mattering: *attention* (an awareness of being noticed by others), *importance* (an impression of being cared about), *ego extension* (believing another empathizes with one's successes and failures), *dependence* (a sense of being needed), and *appreciation* (recognition efforts are valued by others).

Interactionalist theory

In Tinto's interactionalist theory (1975, 1986, 1993), he suggested college students separate from those with whom they formerly were associated (high school friends, family, etc.). Transitioning into a new group becomes their focus. College students look to their peers to establish normative values and behaviors. A student's interaction with the college as an organization determines the student's departure or retention at that institution.

Tinto posited that students enter college with various individual characteristics (*family background* – socioeconomic status, parent's education, and parental expectations; *personal attributes* – academic ability, race, and gender; and *educational experiences* – characteristics of secondary school, high school achievement, and social attainments of the student). Initial commitment to the college or university and initial commitment to the goal of graduation influences the level of an individual student's integration within academic and social systems of an institution of higher education. Academic and social integration need to occur to retain the student (Braxton, 2003; Tinto, 1975, 1986, 1993). Braxton (2003) suggested Tinto's (1975, 1986, 1993) theory "enjoys paradigmatic status among theoretical perspectives on college student departure (i.e., considerable consensus around the potential validity of the theory)" (p. 326).

Transition theory

Schlossberg, Waters, and Goodman (1995) suggested that significant individual events (marriage, birth, and death) and cultural events (war, economic conditions, and social movements) shape a person's life. In their transition theory, Schlossberg and her colleagues posited that how an individual makes sense of a transition depends on the *type, context,* and *impact* of said transition. A type of transition could be anticipated (graduation), unanticipated (divorce/death), or a nonevent (expected but does not occur). Context of transitions refers to the individual's relationship to the transition (personally affected or happens to a significant other) and the setting in which it occurs (work, personal relationship, or within community). Determining the degree to which the transition alters one's life sets the impact of the transition. Transitions, according to Schlossberg and her associates, are a process. Successfully coping with transitions involves four sets of factors: situation, self, support, and strategies.

Summary

Identity formation is an important, if not critical, process throughout the college experience. Additionally, establishing a sense of belonging and a peer group is essential for many students' adjustment to the college experience. As students explore their own ethnic and racial backgrounds and sexual orientation, create a space in which they matter, and set up a group with whom they identify, they also have entered into a quest to make meaning out of their lives. Another important area of development that theorists explore is students' cognitive or thought process.

Cognitive-structural theories

Cognitive-structural theories assist practitioners in explaining ways in which college students' thought processes changes throughout their collegiate experience. These theories describe the process of intellectual development during collegiate years; in other words, how people "think, reason, and make meaning of their experiences" (Evans et al., 1998, p. 124). People adapt to and organize their environments via sets of assumptions or structures (referred to as schemata by Piaget [1952], positions by Perry [1968], and stages by others). Structures, stages, positions, or schemata serve as filters or lenses for determining how individuals perceive and evaluate events and experiences. As a person develops, structures expand, change, and increase in complexity. Although stages always progress in the same order, regardless of cultural conditions, the "age at which each stage occurs and the rate of speed with which the person passes through it are variable" (Evans, 2003, p. 187). Stages build upon each other—each incorporating aspects of the prior stage—and become qualitatively different and more complex than the proceeding stage (Wadsworth, 1979).

According to cognitive-structural theorists, assimilation and accommodation bring about change (Evans et al., 1998). Taking new information into existing structures, adjusting them, and contributing to their expansion creates a process of assimilation or quantitative change. Altering existing structures or establishing new structures that incorporate stimuli that will not fit into existing structures generates a process of accommodation or qualitative change (Evans et al., 1998; Wadsworth, 1979). "Equilibrium, a balance between assimilation and accommodation, is necessary if the person is to interact efficiently with the environment. Disequilibrium, or cognitive conflict, occurs when expectations are not confirmed by experience" (Evans et al., 1998, p. 124).

Cognitive-structural theories support higher education and student affairs professionals by providing insight into ways in which students view situations they are experiencing (Evans et al., 1998). This, in turn, allows practitioners guidance in constructing effective communication strategies to work with students. Recognizing students "interpret experiences differently, depending on their level of intellectual development can help student affairs professionals understand the variations in feedback they receive from students about activities, classes, and other experiences and will assist them in advising students about available options" (Evans et al., 1998, p. 125).

Cognitive and intellectual development

Perry's theory of intellectual and ethical development

Throughout the 1950s and into the 1960s, Perry and his associates (1981) researched ways in which students understand and make meaning of the teaching and learning process. He described "the typical course of development of students' patterns of thought" (Perry, 1981, p. 77) and "unfolding views of the world" (Perry, 1968, p. ix). Evans and her colleagues (1998) referred to Perry as a "somewhat reluctant theorist" (p. 129). He proclaimed, "Our intent was purely descriptive, and not even systematically so" (Perry, 1968, p. 6).

Perry (1968) referenced "forms" of intellectual and ethical development or structures that shape how people view their experiences. A continuum of development in which an individual moves through nine "positions" is the foundation for Perry's (1981) theory. Four key words labeled the nine positions: *duality*, *multiplicity*, *relativism*, and *commitment*. Duality, multiplicity, and relativism represented essential differences in the process of making meaning. Commitment was an important schematic concept (Evans et al., 1998). Perry (1981) suggested positions were static with development occurring during transitions between them; "Perhaps development is all transition and 'stages' only resting points along the way" (p. 78).

Dichotomous perspective of the world is fundamental to *dualistic* meaning makers: good/bad, right/wrong, black/white (Perry, 1981). Students view quantitative knowledge (facts) and authorities as having right answers. *Multiplicity* meaning makers honor various views when "right" answers are unknown. All opinions are equally compelling, conceptions of learning shift and students think more independently and analytically, and peers become more legitimate sources of knowledge (Evans et al., 1998). Recognition of the need to support opinions moves students to *relativism*. All opinions are no longer equally valid; some may be of little value and individuals can legitimately disagree. "Knowledge is viewed more qualitatively; it is contextually defined, based on evidence and supporting arguments" (Evans et al., 1998, p. 132). Students' choices, decisions, and affirmations— made from the vantage point of relativism— create the *commitment* process. Individuals make choices in a contextual world and involve ethical awareness and development.

Women's way of knowing

Belenky, Clinchy, Goldberger, and Tarule (1997) suggested women derive their most valuable life lessons from relationships, crises, and community involvement versus formal education. The authors' intent was to share observations regarding "alternative routes" for women's intellectual development. Belenky and her colleagues referred to five perspectives and cautioned that these perspectives do not portray unique and complex aspects of individual thought processes.

In the perspective of *silence*, women know and view the world as obedient, voiceless, and mindless—subject to the whims of external authority. In the *received knowledge* perspective, women listen to the voices of others and lack self-confidence; a fundamental belief is that one can receive and reproduce knowledge from authorities but cannot create it on one's own. With the perspective of *subjective knowledge*, views radically change and truth resides in the self; eternal knowledge is inferior to internal knowledge. Often this perspective occurs for women when a male authority figure has failed. In the perspective of *procedural knowledge*, women learn and apply objective procedures for receiving and conveying knowledge via two approaches: separate knowing and connected knowing. Critical thinking is the core concept for separate knowing; believing is at the core of connected knowing (Belenky et al., 1997; Evans et al., 1998).

Both feeling and thought (subjective and objective knowledge) integrate within the *constructed knowledge* perspective. Belenky and her associates (1997) suggested when women sort out pieces of the self and search "for a unique and authentic voice," they reveal all knowledge is constructed and each knower is an intimate part of what is known (p. 136). Women operating from a constructed knowledge perspective are articulate, caring, concerned with separation and connection, self-aware, struggling to find balance in their lives, and fighting to find their own voices (Belenky et al., 1997; Evans et al., 1998).

Baxter Magolda's model of epistemological reflection

"Understanding college students' intellectual development is at the heart of effective educational practice," according to Baxter Magolda (1989, p. 3). Influenced by Perry's (1968) work with men, Belenky and her colleagues' (1986) work with women, and Kitchener's and King's (1981, 1990) work with both genders, Baxter Magolda was intrigued by gender similarities and differences within intellectual development. In her five-year longitudinal study of more than 100 Miami University students, Baxter Magolda identified four stages of intellectual development: *absolute knowing*, *transitional knowing*, *independent knowing*, and *contextual knowing*.

Students view knowledge as certain in the first stage of *absolute knowing*. Authorities (instructors) have the answers. In the *transitional knowing* stage, some knowledge is uncertain. Students realize that authorities are not all-knowing. *Independent knowing*, the third stage, brings about a view of knowledge as mostly uncertain (Baxter Magolda, 1992). The first three stages each have patterns of knowing that tend to be gender-specific. The final stage shows a "convergence of previous gender-related patterns" (Evans et al., 1998, p. 156). In the final stage of *contextual knowing* (rarely experienced by undergraduates), knowledge claims are examined and determined legitimate contextually. Individuals construct a point of view, yet the perspective requires supporting evidence (Evans et al., 1998).

Kitchener and King's reflective judgment model

Kitchener and King (1994) posited their reflective judgment model in response to the question, "How do people decide what they believe about vexing problems?" (p. 2). Viewing reflective judgment as "a neglected facet of critical thinking," the researchers suggested "one of the most important responsibilities educators have is helping students learn to make defensible judgments about vexing problems" (p. 1). The reflective judgment model consists of seven stages with a "distinct set of assumptions about knowledge and the process of acquiring knowledge," with each set of assumptions resulting in "a different strategy for solving ill-structured problems" (Evans et al., 1998, p. 162).

The seven stages cluster into three categories: (1) *pre-reflective thinking* (no acknowledgement or recognition that knowledge is certain; no use of evidence in reasoning toward a conclusion); (2) *quasi-reflective thinking* (recognize ill-structured problems exist and knowledge claims regarding these problems include uncertainty; identify some problems as authentically challenging); and (3) *reflective thinking* (claim knowledge must be actively constructed and claims of knowledge must be understood in relation to the context in which they were generated; assert judgments must be based on relevant data and conclusions remain open for reevaluation) (Evans et al., 1998; Kitchener & King, 1994).

Moral development

Kohlberg's stages of moral reasoning

Central to Kohlberg's (1976) work was the concept of how people make moral judgments. Moral development was "more than gaining increased knowledge of culturally defined values" (Evans et al., 1998). Determining what is viewed as right or necessary arose from "the transformations that occur in a person's form or structure of thought" (Kohlberg & Hersh, 1977, p. 54). Kohlberg (1972) identified justice as the central principle in the development of moral judgment. He defined justice as "the primary regard for the value and equality of all human beings, and for reciprocity in human relations, is a basic and human standard" (p. 14). According to Kohlberg (1976), moral development occurs in six stages grouped into three levels. In Level I, or the pre-conventional level, individuals are focused on themselves and do not have an understanding of societal norms, rules, or expectations. The conventional level, or Level II, is the "member-of-society" perspective. Individuals recognize the rules and expectations of others—in particular authorities. Level III is the post-conventional or principled level or "prior-to-society" perspective. Individuals base decisions on self-chosen principles, not on the rules or expectations of others. Each level has two stages in which people make decisions based on external or internal ethics (Evans et al., 1998; Kohlberg, 1976).

Rest's modifications of Kohlberg's model

Intrigued with Kohlberg's approach, Rest (1979) used his model to examine people's thinking regarding knowing and sharing societal expectations regarding rules. He also was interested in how individuals viewed balancing interests. His stages of moral development included obedience ("Do what you're told"), instrumental egoism and simple exchange ("Let's make a deal"), interpersonal concordance ("Be considerate, nice, and kind, and you'll get along with people"), law and duty to the social order ("Everyone in society is obligated and protected by the law"), social consensus ("You are obligated by whatever arrangements are agreed to by due process procedures"), and non-arbitrary social cooperation ("How rational and impartial people would organize cooperation is moral") (Rest, 1979, pp. 22–23).

Gilligan's theory of women's moral development

Women's experiences were not seen as worthy of psychological study by human development theorists prior to the success of Gilligan (1982/1993). Kohlberg generalized his research on males to both genders and claimed women were unable to reach the same developmental height as men (Gilligan, 1982/1993). In examining women's experiences, Gilligan suggested that people reason in different ways. Kohlberg's model focused on a "justice voice" and moral orientation that males use when making decisions, whereas Gilligan conceptualized that women had a "care voice," a pattern observed in women contemplating abortion (Evans et al., 1998).

In her text "In a Different Voice," Gilligan (1982/1993) clarified "different voice" as the themes of justice and care, not to distinguish gender. Gilligan (1982/1993) suggested relationship and interpretive frameworks were central to women's thinking. Attachment to others is at the core of her care orientation (i.e., relationships with others is equally weighted with care for self when making moral decisions). A different view than Kohlberg's (1969) concepts of progressing "from lower order to higher order moral thinking in which autonomy is prized and universal justice is the goals" (Evans et al., 1998, p. 191). Women's moral judgment moves through three levels and two transition periods (Gilligan, 1982/1993; Evans et al., 1998).

At the first level, *orientation to individual survival*, self-centeredness and preoccupation with survival characterize the individual (Gilligan, 1982/1993). Relationships do not meet expectations for most women at this level and at times women isolate themselves intentionally in an effort of self-protection. The first transition, between Level I and Level II, *from selfishness to responsibility*, focuses on attachment and connection to others. *Goodness as self-sacrifice*, Level II, brings individuals from an independent, self-centered perspective of the world to a view of greater involvement with and dependence on others. During the second transition, *from goodness to truth*, women question why they continue to put others needs prior to their own. In Level III, *the morality of nonviolence*, women view nonviolence as an overriding principle governing moral judgment and action. At this third level, the individual raises to the principle of care by "transformed understanding of self and a corresponding redefinition of morality" (Gilligan, 1977, p. 504).

Summary

Knowledge of students' reasoning process assists student affairs professionals in understanding students' decision making (for themselves and during their interactions with others). By knowing students interpret their experiences differently, practitioners can make better-informed decisions. Feedback from students regarding activities and other experiences will vary with students' level of intellectual development. Structure may be important for students at lower levels of cognitive-structural development, whereas autonomy may be important for those at higher levels.

Typology theories

When working with student employees, typology theories assist practitioners in understanding how students approach their worlds via individual stylistic differences. Typology theories are not actually developmental; students do not progress through these theories in stages (Evans et al., 1998). Rather, these theories build upon Jung's (1923/1971) theoretical concepts of inherent differences in mental functioning bringing about variations in human behavior. Apparent in many areas of students' lives, differences appear in activities in which they are involved or interested, learning style preferences, ways in which they process information, and how they prefer to spend their time. Typology theories provide frameworks for development to take place—whether psychosocial or cognitive-structural—and influence how students address their development (Evans et al., 1998).

Holland's theory of vocational personalities and environments

As a vocational counselor, Holland (1985/1992) began to notice that individuals with whom he worked seemed to fall into broad categories with regard to behavior, interests, and personality traits. He founded his six scales of the Vocational Preference Inventory (Holland, 1958) on his observations and Linton's (1945) and Lewin's (1935) concepts of person-environment interaction. A more recent publication, Holland's (1971) Self-Directed Search assessment instrument, has held up under extensive review and critique (Evans et al., 1998).

Holland (1985/1992) suggested that people match one of six personality types with varying degrees. "The more similar they are to a particular type, the more they exhibit the behaviors and attitudes associated with it" (Evans et al., 1998, p. 227). At the same time, six environments correspond with each of the personality types' qualities and attributes. According to Holland, individuals pursue environments in which they can express their values and attitudes and use their talents (i.e., environments comprised of individuals similar to themselves). Similar to Lewin (1935), Holland posited behavior results from person-environment interaction (Evans et al., 1998; Holland, 1985/1992).

Attitudes, behaviors, and specific interests define Holland's (1985/1992) six personality types: *realistic* (prefer working with objects, machines, and animals); *investigative* (prefer systematic investigation in science and mathematical areas controlling biological, physical, and cultural); *artistic* (prefer creative, spontaneous, unregulated activities leading to a variety of art forms); *social* (prefer working with others to enlighten, cure, inform, or educate); *enterprising* (prefer working with others toward achievement of material outcomes and organizational goals), and *conventional* (prefer working with data in orderly, systematic, explicit ways) (Evans et al., 1998, pp. 228–229). Holland identified that individuals have one dominant type and two subtypes. Environments have similar characteristics to the personality types. In turn, individuals seek out congruence between their own preferences and the environments in which they work (Evans et al., 1998; Holland, 1985/1992).

Myers-Briggs adaptation of Jung's theory of personality type

Perception and judgment are central to personality type theory. Based on Jung's personality types, Myers (1980) identified personal preferences for perceiving environments (taking in and processing information) and making judgments (drawing conclusions) about what they perceive. Jung's (1923/1971) personality type theory, later built upon by Myers (1980), proposed eight preferences exist along four bipolar dimensions: extraversion-introversion (EI), sensing-intuition (SN), thinking-feeling (TF), and judging-perception (JP).

Combinations of these preferences present 16 different personality types. Each of these types results from their dominant functions of being directed outward (extroverted) or inward (introverted) and modified by their auxiliary (or secondary) preference: SN, TF, or JP. Myers and McCaulley (1985) conjectured "people may reasonably be expected to develop greater skill with the processes they prefer to use and with the attitudes (extraversion or introversion) in which they prefer to use these processes" (p. 3).

Professionals in various fields use the Myers-Briggs Type Inventory extensively to assess personality type. Although the instrument evokes strong responses (both positive and negative) regarding reliability and validity, evidence suggests it is a popular and helpful personality measure

(Zemke, 1992). Many student affairs professionals have used the Myers-Briggs Type Inventory in a variety of settings with various applications (Evans et al., 1998).

Kolb's theory of experiential learning

Kolb (1984) characterized learning as "the process whereby knowledge is created through the transformation of experience" (p. 38). Four stages cyclically composed the learning process: *concrete experience* (feeling), *reflective observation* (watching), *abstract conceptualization* (thinking), and *active experimentation* (doing). From individual preferences for one of the polar opposites (concrete experience/abstract conceptualization; reflective observation/active experimentation), four individual learning styles become apparent: *accommodator, diverger, assimilator,* and *converger* (Kolb, 1981, 1985).

Accommodators are action-oriented, at ease with people, and prefer trial-and-error problem-solving (Kolb, 1984, 1985). These individuals are good at carrying out plans, open to new experiences, and easily adaptable to change. Divergers are both people-oriented and feeling-oriented. Imaginative, they are aware of values and good at generating and analyzing alternatives. Assimilators place an emphasis on ideas versus people. Their strengths lie in integrating observations, creating theoretical models, and reasoning inductively. Convergers are technically oriented, preferring tasks over social or interpersonal interactions. These individuals excel at decision making, practical applications, and problem solving (Kolb, 1984, 1985).

Summary

Typology theories help provide higher education and student affairs professionals with important information about students with whom they work. Assessment of individual preferences potentially guides training sessions or workshops, aids in making work assignments, explains interpersonal interactions, assists with conflict resolution, and provides insights regarding sources of support and challenge for students who are otherwise developmentally similar (Evans et al., 1998). The non-evaluative nature of typology theories (no good or bad types, only identified as different), allows professionals to show each type as contributing something to any situation.

Person-environment interaction/campus ecology theories

Person-environment interaction theories

Person-environment interaction theories in the field of student affairs build upon Lewin's (1936) premise of B = f (P x E): behavior is a function of the interaction between an individual and his or her environment. Student characteristics (academic ability, educational background, socioeconomic status, developmental level, and personality type) and college environment (social climate, physical surroundings, organizational structure, and the human aggregate) offer important components of this premise; however, most importantly, the interaction between person and environment is critical in Lewin's conceptualization.

Sanford's theory of challenge and support

According to Sanford (1966), three conditions augment student growth and development: *readiness*, *challenge*, and *support*. He suggested individuals could not change until they were willing to do so. "Readiness results from internal processes associated with maturation or from beneficial environmental conditions" (Hamrick et al., 2002, p. 82).

Additionally, Sanford (1966) observed student growth could not occur without environmental challenges. Furthermore, finding an optimal level of challenge was critical for development to occur. If the level of challenge was too high and students experienced high levels of dissonance, they could fall back on unhealthy coping strategies (i.e., escaping or ignoring the challenge). Yet if the level of challenge was too low, development and learning are not likely to occur (even though students feel comfortable). Support must balance challenge in order to address dissonance within the environment. The ratio of challenge and support depends on the individual backgrounds and personalities (Sanford, 1966).

Astin's theory of involvement

Active involvement in the college environment is essential for learning to occur. Astin (1984) built his theory of involvement on this premise. He defined involvement as "the amount of physical and psychological energy that the student devotes to the academic experience" (p. 297). Stressing that involvement must be both quantitative and qualitative in nature, Astin referred to the amount of time a student devoted to an activity and the seriousness applied to that experience. He hypothesized that "the amount of student learning and personal development associated with any educational program is directly proportional to the quality and quantity of student involvement in that program" (p. 298). Educational practice or policy effectiveness is directly connected to the capacity of that practice or policy to increase student involvement (Astin, 1984).

Campus ecology theories

Campus environments invariably affect students' learning and outcomes (Hamrick et al., 2002). Physical components, human aggregates (subcultures, typologies, and styles), person-environment interactions, organizational structures and designs, environmental presses, social climates, and campus cultures each influence students' learning experiences (Hamrick et al., 2002; Strange, 2003). "Each campus can ensure an excellent education for a student, but the manner in which that education is obtained depends on what the campus offers" (Hamrick et al., 2002, p. 81).

Pace and Stern's theory of environmental press

Pace and Stern (1958) were among the first researchers interested in the impact of the college environment on the individuals within it. The authors explored the interaction of environmental press (characteristics, qualities, and pressures exerted by the environment) and an individual's needs (what the individual seeks in the environment to fulfill her/his goals). Two self-report instruments assessed variables of press and needs. The College Characteristics Index (measuring press) identified students' impressions of the college or university. The Activities Index (measuring needs) asked students about their involvement in activities (Hamrick et al., 2002). Environments with similar needs and press were determined to be growth-enhancing. Different needs and press within an environment contributed to unhappiness and slowed down personal development (Hamrick et al., 2002; Stern, 1970). These two indexes served as a foundation for today's College Student Experiences Questionnaire (CSEQ) and National Survey of Student Engagement (NSSE).

Moos's social climate model

Environmental personalities were the basis for Moos's (1976, 1979) social climate model. Every environment has three broad categories of dimensions, according to Moos, regardless of type: *relationship* (how people interact with each other), *personal development* (aspects of personal growth and self-development), and *system maintenance and change* (how an environment functions and the likelihood change will occur). The University Residence Environment Scale, one of many environmental assessment instruments developed by Moos (1976), focused on relationship (involvement and emotional support), personal development (independence, traditional social orientation, competition, academic achievement, and intellectuality), and system maintenance and change (order and organization, student influence, and innovation).

Campus culture

Kuh and his colleagues have explored campus culture, the factors that influence the development of campus culture, and the impact of campus culture (Kuh, 1993; Kuh & Hall, 1993; Kuh & Whitt, 1988; Kuh, Schuh, Whitt, & Associates, 1991). Campus culture is defined as the "confluence of institutional history, campus traditions, and the values and assumptions that shape the character of a given college or university" (Kuh & Hall, 1993, pp. 1–2). Strange (2003) identified four levels of culture found in campus environments: *artifacts, perspectives, values,* and *assumptions.*

Artifacts refer to *physical* (e.g., landmarks, buildings, and other physical aspects of the setting), *verbal* (e.g., history, stories, and unique language), and *behavioral* (e.g., special activities and events that occur on campus) aspects of environment that have agreed-upon meaning for members of that environment (Kuh & Hall, 1993). "The way things are done" on campus provide the *perspective* level of culture (Kuh & Hall, 1993, p. 6). Appropriate etiquette, student dress, and espoused values compose this aspect of campus culture. *Values* reproduce "what the members of a culture assert to be most important" (Kuh et al., 1991,

p. 96). Values underscore the way in which campus leaders make decisions and how they judge actions on campus. Many times mission statements formally affirm core values of the college and university (Strange, 2003). *Assumptions* are "tacit beliefs members use to define their role, their relationship to others, and the nature of the organization in which they live" (Kuh & Hall, 1993, p. 7). Assumptions are the least apparent level of culture, existing implicitly and rarely mentioned (Kuh et al., 1991).

Summary

Intentionally examining and designing campus environments are ways in which student affairs professionals can address students' growth and development and enhance student learning.

> The physical environment, the human aggregate, the organizational environment, and student perceptions all influence student satisfaction and success in college. The outcomes of higher education are shaped as much by the environment as they are by the characteristics of entering students. (Hamrick et al., 2002, p. 106)

Creating, sustaining, and enhancing a positive campus environment is critical to student success.

Applying theory to the student employment setting

Theory is useful in helping practitioners interpret what they are hearing from students (Evans, 2003). A framework for understanding students' concerns, attitudes, and thought processes arises from theoretical perspectives. Theory assists student affairs professionals in processing information and determining appropriate responses. Responses may include creating workshops, providing support and being present to students when they share, challenging student thinking and asking pertinent questions, advocating for changes in policy, and suggesting actions to students (Evans, 2003).

Authors of student affairs literature often discuss moving from theory to practice (Baxter Magolda, 1992; Braxton, 2003; Chickering, Dalton, & Stamm, 2006; Evans, 2003; Evans et al., 1998; Hamrick et al., 2002; King, 2003; Kuh, 2003; McEwen, 2003a, 2003b; Strange, 2003; Torres et al., 2003). DiCaprio (1974) offered four increasingly powerful uses of theory: (1) *description* – a portrayal of what is taking place; (2) *explanation* – depicting what causes the behavior; (3) *prediction* – envisioning an outcome; and (4) *control* – producing specific outcomes. Developmental theory focuses on the initial two uses, but few theories have moved into prediction or control. Perhaps this is why practitioners struggle with the regular use and application of theory. If prediction and control are not understood, many professionals may question the usefulness of developmental theories (Evans et al., 1998).

McEwen (2003a) stated: "A value both explicit and implicit in student affairs is that student affairs professionals should guide and inform their professional practice with appropriate theories" (p. 174). She went on to suggest professionals know and examine themselves prior to "learning, critiquing, and using theories" (p. 174). Theory connects closely to one's sense of self (McEwen, 2003a).

Thoughtful, insightful, and continuing introspection about oneself is a necessary part of student affairs professional's journey of learning, understanding, and using theory—about organizations, environments and their interactions with students, and, especially, college students and their development. (McEwen, 2003a, p. 175)

Taylor suggested it is "*not* a commitment to learning about *them*; instead, it is a commitment to learning about myself—and ultimately us" (p. 1).

Selecting appropriate theories and applying theories intentionally

Some student affairs professionals offer what McEwen (2003a) referred to as a "purist" approach; that is, when addressing a particular phenomenon only one theory should be selected and used. One theory provides needed assumptions, defines relationships, and describes how those relationships transpire under given conditions. These same individuals believe the use of more than one theory "may violate the assumptions of individual theories and thus may invalidate the relationships and beliefs prescribed within any theory" (McEwen, 2003a, p. 175). Professionals need to be cautions when selecting one theory to address a particular phenomenon, remembering the saying, "If the only tool you bring is a hammer, everything looks like a nail."

Another approach is the "eclectic" use of theory or drawing relevant and useful aspects of several theories and combining those aspects into a meaningful theoretical perspective (McEwen, 2003a). Practitioners using this approach believe it is stronger than using only one theory, allowing use of the best parts of many theories. Opponents raise concerns regarding violating individual theory assumptions or minimally not honoring them. Without one theory framing the process, consistency and replication will not be possible and common language is lost. On the other hand, a theory does not exist that is comprehensive enough to describe any given phenomenon (McEwen, 2003a).

McEwen (2003a) provided guidelines for selecting a theory. She suggested selecting something that makes sense to or is easily understandable for an individual administrator. If a theory is unclear, it can be very difficult to apply. She also said that "knowing yourself will help you decide which theories to choose and which ones to 'put back on the shelf'" (p. 175). If the theory seems to fit a specific individual, examine why it fits .(Does the theory describe experiences? If yes, whose experiences does it not describe?) (McEwen, 2003a) An assumption audit is an important step when using theory to identify explicit and implicit assumptions within the theory (McEwen, 2003a; Sue, Ivey, & Pederson, 1996). Think about how theories fit together when combining more than one aspect of a student's development (e.g., racial identity and cognitive development). Do they come into conflict? Can each contribute to understanding without upsetting their overall integrity? Evans (2003) recommended being thoughtful, intentional, and intelligent about using theory.

Troubleshooting the application of theory

Different concerns regarding theory application arise in response to various approaches. At the same time, each theoretical perspective provides a piece of the puzzle of student development (Evans, 2003). Student affairs professionals should view concerns from a "big picture" perspective and consider what each theoretical viewpoint offers to the student involved and particular issues at hand. Theories are not perfect. They do not exist in a vacuum. "Critical science offers a method by which we can examine how a theory has been socially constructed and how it may need to be deconstructed" (McEwen, 2003a, p. 176).

Psychosocial issues and identity development are complex and not always transparent without building extensive rapport and strong relationships with student employees. Professionals often feel ill-prepared to be effective facilitators of students' movement through stages. Descriptions of stages (behaviors, issues, and attitudes occurring within the stages) are just that—descriptions. Higher education and student affairs professionals may see signs of development occurring, yet practitioners need to plan intentional intervention or that development may be minimal or nonexistent.

Staff members must closely examine individual theories to see applicability in a setting with particular students. When working with individual students, student affairs professionals should build rapport with them before exploring their identity and psychosocial development. McEwen (2003b) challenged professionals to address the holistic development of the student at the same time as considering specific dimensions of development.

Many professionals view cognitive-structural theories as part of the intellectual arena and classroom. Yet these theories have strong implications for student employees, particularly when considering actions and decision-making. Awareness of the ways in which individuals process information and make meaning is important. Cognitive structural theories might offer insights into an individual's capability to learn position responsibilities and his or her work ethic. Additionally, keeping students' cognitive structural competencies in mind may assist in the design and implementation of workshops and training sessions.

Student affairs professionals often can visualize using typology theories in their work. Typologies theories are helpful for dealing with interpersonal interactions, working through conflicts, anticipating work styles, and assessing group strengths and limitations. Practitioners can analyze employee group interactions and formulate ways in which to tap into member strengths. Knowing learning styles or personality types can assist professionals in making work assignments.

Environmental theories provide a background for the employment area. Student affairs professionals can enhance any educational setting by taking advantage of physical, human aggregate, organizational, and constructed features.

> The potency of any educational environment, whether a classroom, a residence hall, a student organization, or an entire campus, is a function of its design (planned or not), what it encourages and expects students to do, and what end it serves. (Strange, 2003, p. 314)

Inclusive, involving, safe, and communal environments provide excellent space for practitioners to sustain and challenge students to learn, grown, and develop.

Using theory within the work setting

Which theory or theories are "attractive?" Which theories fit "best" in particular work settings? How can practitioners apply theory with student employees? One way to address these questions is to challenge the employment of theoretical premises by practitioners within particular work settings.

Practitioners can explore theory and expand personal knowledge in a number of ways. Staff meeting agendas might include a section for a presentation and discussion of a theory and the way it fits into a particular setting or with a particular student. Offer professional development sessions on theoretical topics. Establish professional reading groups to explore theory (challenge the group to read original theory). Create a theory bibliography and ask individuals to add to it each year. Recognize that theory allows the student affairs field to be a profession. Having a theoretical foundation provides professionalism and insights into working with students. Value this foundation and include it in daily practice and reflection.

References

Astin, A.W. (1984). Student involvement: A developmental theory for higher education. *Journal of College Student Personnel, 25*, 297–308.

Atkinson, D.R., Morten, G., & Sue, D.W. (1989). *Counseling American minorities* (Rev. ed.). Dubuque, IA: William C. Brown.

Atkinson, D.R., Morten, G., & Sue, D.W. (1993). *Counseling American minorities* (4th ed.). Madison, WI: Brown and Benchmark Publishers.

Baldwin, J.A., Duncan, J.A., & Bell, Y.R. (1992). Assessment of African self consciousness among black students from two college environments. In A.K.H. Burlew, W.C. Banks, H.P. McAdoo, & D.A. Azibo (Eds.), *African American psychology: Theory, research, and practice* (pp. 283–299). Newbury Park, CA: Sage.

Baxter Magolda, M.B. (1989). Gender differences in cognitive development: An analysis of cognitive complexity and learning styles. *Journal of College Student Development, 30*, 213–220.

Baxter Magolda, M.B. (1992). *Knowing and reasoning in college: Gender-related patterns in students' intellectual development*. San Francisco: Jossey-Bass.

Baxter Magolda, M.B., & King, P.M. (Eds.) (2004). *Learning partnerships: Theory and models of practice to educate for self-authorship*. Sterling, VA: Stylus Publishing.

Belenky, M.F., Clinchy, B.M., Goldberger, N.R., & Tarule, J.M. (1986). *Women's way of knowing: The development of self, voice, and mind*. New York: Basic Books.

Belenky, M.F., Clinchy, B.M., Goldberger, N.R., & Tarule, J.M. (1997). *Women's way of knowing: The development of self, voice, and mind* (2nd ed.). New York: Basic Books.

Braxton, J.M. (2003). Student success. In S.R. Komives, D.B. Woodard Jr., & Associates (Eds.), *Student services: A handbook for the profession* (4th ed., pp. 317–335). San Francisco: Jossey-Bass.

Caple, R.B., & Voss, C.H. (1983). Communication between consumers and producers of student affairs research. *Journal of College Student Personnel, 24,* 38–42.

Cass, V. (1979). Homosexual identity formation: Testing a theoretical model. *Journal of Sex Research, 20,* 143–167.

Chickering, A.W., Dalton, J.C., & Stamm, L. (2006). *Encouraging authenticity and spirituality in higher education.* San Francisco: Jossey-Bass.

Chickering, A.W., & Reisser, L. (1993). *Education and identity* (2nd ed.). San Francisco: Jossey-Bass.

Choney, S.K., Berryhill-Paapke, E., & Robbins, R.R. (1995). The acculturation of American Indians: Developing frameworks for research and practice. In J.G. Ponterotto, J.M. Casas, L.A. Suzuki, & C.M. Alexander (Eds.), *Handbook of multicultural counseling* (pp. 73–92). Thousand Oaks, CA: Sage.

Collins, P.H. (2002). Learning from the outsider within: The sociological significance of black feminist thought. In C.S. Turner, A.L. Antonio, M. Garcia, B.V. Laden, A. Nora, and C. Presley (Eds.), *Racial and ethnic diversity in higher education.* Boston: Pearson Custom Publishing.

Cross, W.E., Jr. (1971). The negro-to-black conversion experience. *Black World, 20,* 13–27.

Cross, W.E., Jr. (1991). *Shade of black: Diversity in African American identity.* Philadelphia: Temple University Press.

Cross, W.E., Jr. (1995). The psychology of nigrescence: Revising the Cross model. In J.G. Ponterotto, J.M. Casas, L.A. Suzuki, & C.M. Alexander (Eds.), *Handbook of multicultural counseling* (2nd ed., pp. 371–393). Thousand Oaks, CA: Sage.

D'Augelli, A.R. (1995). *Lesbian, gay, and bisexual identities over the lifespan: Psychological perspectives.* New York: Oxford University Press.

DiCaprio, N.S. (1974). *Personality theories: Guides to living.* Philadelphia: Saunders.

Erikson, E.H. (1950). *Childhood and society.* Gloucester, MA: Peter Smith Publisher.

Erikson, E.H. (1968). *Identity: Youth and crisis.* New York: W.W. Norton.

Evans, N.J. (2003). Psychosocial, cognitive, and typological perspectives on student development. In S.R. Komives, D.B. Woodard Jr., & Associates (Eds.), *Student services: A handbook for the profession* (4th ed., pp. 179–202). San Francisco: Jossey-Bass.

Evans, N.J., Forney, D.S., & Guido-DiBrito, F. (1998). *Student development in college: Theory, research, and practice.* San Francisco: Jossey-Bass.

Ferdman, B.M., & Gallegos, P.I. (2001). Racial identity development and Latinos in the United States. In C.L. Wijeyesinghe & B.W. Jackson III (Eds.), *New perspectives on racial identity development: A theoretical and practical anthology* (pp. 32–66). New York: New York University Press.

Gay, G. (1984). Implications of selected models of ethnic identity development for educators. *Journal of Negro Education, 54*(1), 43–52.

Gilligan, C. (1977). In a different voice: Women's conceptions of self and morality. *Harvard Educational Review, 47,* 481–517.

Gilligan, C. (1982/1993). *In a different voice: Psychological theory and women's development.* Cambridge, MA: Harvard University Press.

Hamrick, F.A., Evans, N.J., & Schuh, J.H. (2002). *Foundations of student affairs practice: How philosophy, theory, and research strengthen educational outcomes.* San Francisco: Jossey-Bass.

Hardiman, R. (2001). Reflections on white identity development theory. In C.L. Wijeyesinghe & B.W. Jackson III (Eds.), *New perspectives on racial identity development: A theoretical and practical anthology* (pp. 32–66). New York: New York University Press.

Helms, J.E. (1990). *Black and white racial identity: Theory, research, and practice.* Westport, CT: Praeger.

Helms, J.E. (1995). An update of Helm's white and people of color racial identity models. In J.G. Ponterotto, J.M. Casas, L.A. Suzuki, & C.M. Alexander (Eds.), *Handbook of multicultural counseling* (pp. 73–92). Thousand Oaks, CA: Sage.

Helms, J.E., & Cook, D.A. (1999). *Using race and culture in counseling and psychotherapy: Theory and process.* Needham Heights, MA: Allyn & Bacon.

Holland, J.L. (1958). A personality inventory employing occupational titles. *Journal of Applied Psychology, 42*, 336–342.

Holland, J.L. (1971). A theory-ridden, computerless, impersonal vocational guidance system. *Journal of Vocational Behavior, 1*, 167–176.

Holland, J.L. (1985/1992). *Making vocational choices: A theory of vocational personalities and work environments* (2nd ed.). Odessa, FL: Psychological Assessment Resources.

Horse, P.G. (2001). Reflections on American Indian identity. In C.L. Wijeyesinghe & B.W. Jackson III (Eds.), *New perspectives on racial identity development: A theoretical and practical anthology* (pp. 91–107). New York: New York University Press.

Ibrahim, F., Ohnishi, H., & Sandhu, D.S. (1997). Asian American identity development: A culture specific model for South Asian Americans. *Journal of Multicultural Counseling and Development, 25*, 34–50.

Jackson, B.W. (1976). Black identity development. In L.H. Golubchick & B. Persky (Eds.), *Urban social and educational issues* (pp. 158–164). Dubuque, IA: Kendall Hunt.

Jackson, B.W. (2001). Black identity development: Further analysis and elaboration. In C.L. Wijeyesinghe & B.W. Jackson III (Eds.), *New perspectives on racial identity development: A theoretical and practical anthology* (pp. 8–31). New York: New York University Press.

Josselson, R. (1987). *Finding herself: Pathways to identity development in women.* San Francisco: Jossey-Bass.

Jung, C.G. (1971). *Psychological types.* (R.F.C. Hull, Ed.; H.G. Baynes, Trans.). Volume 6 of *The collected works of C.G. Jung.* Princeton, NJ: Princeton University Press. (Original work published 1923).

Keefe, S.E., & Padilla, A.M. (1987). *Chicano ethnicity.* Albuquerque, NM: University of New Mexico Press.

Kim, J. (2001). Asian American identity development theory. In C.L. Wijeyesinghe & B.W. Jackson III (Eds.), *New perspectives on racial identity development: A theoretical and practical anthology* (pp. 67–90). New York: New York University Press.

King, P.M. (2003). Student learning in higher education. In S.R. Komives, D.B. Woodard Jr., & Associates (Eds.), *Student services: A handbook for the profession* (4th ed., pp. 234–268). San Francisco: Jossey-Bass.

King, P.M., & Kitchener, K.S. (1994). *Developing reflective judgment: Understanding and promoting intellectual growth and critical thinking in adolescents and adults.* San Francisco: Jossey-Bass.

Kitchener, K.S., & King, P.M. (1981). Reflective judgment: Concepts of justification and their relationship to age and education. *Journal of Applied Developmental Psychology, 2,* 89–116.

Kitchener, K.S., & King, P.M. (1990). The reflective judgment model: Ten years of research. In M.L. Commons et al. (Eds.), *Adult development: Models and methods in the study of adolescent and adult thought* (Vol. 2, pp. 63–78). New York: Oxford University Press.

Knefelkamp, L.L. (1982). Faculty and student development in the '80s: Renewing the community of scholars. In H.F. Owens, C.H. Witten, & W. R. Bailey (Eds.), *College student personnel administration: An anthology* (pp. 373–391). Springfield, IL: Thomas.

Knefelkamp, L.L., Widick, C., & Parker, C.A. (Eds.).(1978). *Applying new developmental findings, New directions for student services, No. 4.* San Francisco: Jossey-Bass.

Kohlberg, L. (1972). A cognitive-developmental approach to moral education. *Humanist, 7,* 13–16.

Kohlberg, L. (1976). Moral stages and moralization: The cognitive-developmental approach. In T. Lickona (Ed.), *Moral development and behavior: Theory, research, and social issues* (pp. 31–53). New York: Holt, Rinehart & Winston.

Kohlberg, L., & Hersh, R.H. (1977). Moral development: A review of the theory. *Theory into practice, 16,* 53–59.

Kolb, D.A. (1981). Learning styles and disciplinary differences. In A.W. Chickering & Associates (Eds.), *The modern American college: Responding to the new realities of diverse students and a changing society* (pp. 232–255). San Francisco: Jossey-Bass.

Kolb, D.A. (1984). *Experiential learning: Experience as the source of learning and development.* Englewood Cliffs, NJ: Prentice Hall.

Kolb, D.A. (1985). *The learning style inventory.* Boston: McBer.

Kuh, G.D. (Ed.). (1993). *Cultural perspectives in student affairs work.* Landham, MD: American College Personnel Association.

Kuh, G.D. (2003). Organizational theory. In S.R. Komives, D.B. Woodard Jr., & Associates (Eds.), *Student services: A handbook for the profession* (4th ed., pp. 269–296). San Francisco: Jossey-Bass.

Kuh, G.D., & Hall, J.E. (1993). Using cultural perspectives in student affairs. In G.D. Kuh (Ed.), *Cultural perspectives in student affairs work* (pp. 1–20). Landham, MD: American College Personnel Association.

Kuh, G.D., Schuh, J.H., Whitt, E.J., & Associates. (1991). *Involving colleges.* San Francisco: Jossey-Bass.

Kuh, G.D., & Whitt, E.J. (1988). *The invisible tapestry: Cultures in American colleges and universities* (ASHE-ERIC Report No.1). Washington, D.C.: Association for the Study of Higher Education.

LaFromboise, T.D., Trimble, J.E., & Mohatt, G.V. (1990). Counseling interventions and American Indian tradition: An integrative approach. *The Counseling Psychologist, 18*(4), 628–654.

Lewin, K. (1935). *A dynamic theory of personality.* New York: McGraw-Hill.

Lewin, K. (1936). *Principles of topological psychology.* New York: McGraw-Hill.

Linton, R. (1945). *The cultural background of personality.* New York: Century.

Maekawa Kodama, C., McEwen, M.K., Liang, C.T.H., & Lee, S. (2002). An Asian American perspective on psychosocial development theory. In M.K. McEwen, C. Maekawa Kodama, A.N. Alvarez, S. Lee, & C.T.H. Liang (Eds.), *Working with Asian American college students, New directions for student services, No. 97* (pp. 45–49). San Francisco: Jossey-Bass.

Marcia, J.E. (1966). Development and validation of ego-identity status. *Journal of Personality, 38,* 249–263.

McEwen, M.K. (2003a). The nature and uses of theory. In S.R. Komives, D.B. Woodard Jr., & Associates (Eds.), *Student services: A handbook for the profession* (4th ed., pp. 153–178). San Francisco: Jossey-Bass.

McEwen, M.K. (2003b). New perspectives on identity development. In S.R. Komives, D.B. Woodard Jr., & Associates (Eds.), *Student services: A handbook for the profession* (4th ed., pp. 203–233). San Francisco: Jossey-Bass.

Moos, R.H. (1976). *The human context: Environmental determinants of behavior.* New York: Wiley.

Moos, R.H. (1979). *Evaluating educational environments: Procedures, measures, findings, and policy implementations.* San Francisco: Jossey-Bass.

Myers, I.B. (1980). *Gifts differing.* Palo Alto, CA: Consulting Psychologists Press.

Myers, I.B., & McCaulley, M.H. (1985). *Manual: A guide to the development and use of the Myers-Briggs Type Indicator.* Palo Alto, CA: Consulting Psychologists Press.

Pace, C.R., & Stern, G.G. (1958). An approach to the measurement of psychological characteristics of college environments. *Journal of Educational Psychology, 49,* 269–277.

Parker, C.A. (1977). On modeling reality. *Journal of College Student Personnel, 18,* 419–425.

Perry, W.J., Jr. (1968). *Forms of intellectual and ethical development in the college years: A scheme.* New York: Holt, Rinehart and Winston.

Perry, W.J., Jr. (1981). Cognitive and ethical growth: The making of meaning. In A.W. Chickering & Associates (Eds.), *The modern American college: Responding to the new realities of diverse students and a changing society* (pp. 76–116). San Francisco: Jossey-Bass.

Piaget, J. (1952). *The origins of intelligence in children.* New York: International Universities Press.

Phinney, J.S. (1990). Ethnic identity in adolescents and adults: Review of the research. *Psychological Bulletin, 108,* 499–514.

Plato, K. (1978). The shift to student development: An analysis of the patterns of change. *NASPA Journal, 15*(4), 32–36.

Rest, J.R. (1979). *Development in judging moral issues.* Minneapolis: University of Minnesota Press.

Robinson, T.L., & Howard-Hamilton, M.F. (1994). An Afrocentric paradigm: Foundation for a healthy self-image and healthy interpersonal relationships. *Journal of Mental Health Counseling, 16*(3), 327–340.

Rodgers, R.F., & Widick, C. (1980). Theory to practice: Using concepts, logic, and creativity. In F.B. Newton & K.L. Ender (Eds.), *Student development practice: Strategies for making a difference* (pp. 5–25). Springfield, IL: Thomas.

Sanford, N. (1966). *Self and society.* New York: Atherton.

Schlossberg, N.K. (1989). *Overwhelmed: Coping with life's ups and downs.* San Francisco: Lexington.

Schlossberg, N.K., Waters, E.B., & Goodman, J. (1995). *Counseling adults in transition* (2nd ed.) New York: Springer.

Stage, F.K. (1994). Fine tuning the instrument: Using process models for work with student development theory. *College Student Affairs Journal, 13*(2), 21–28.

Stage, F.K., & Kuh, G.D. (1996). Student development in the college years. In B. Clark & G. Neave (Eds.), *The encyclopedia of higher education* [CD-ROM]. Oxford: Pergammon Press.

Stern, G. (1970). *People in context: Measuring person-environment congruence in education and industry.* New York: Wiley.

Strange, C.C. (1994). Student development: The evolution and status of an essential idea. *Journal of College Student Development, 35*(6), 399–412.

Strange, C.C. (2003). Dynamics of campus environments. In S.R. Komives, D.B. Woodard Jr. & Associates (Eds.), *Student services: A handbook for the profession* (4th ed., pp. 297–316). S,an Francisco: Jossey-Bass.

Strange, C.C., & King, P.M. (1990). The professional practice of student development. In D.G. Creamer & Associates (Eds.), *College student development: Theory and practice for the 1990s* (pp. 9–24). Alexandria, VA: American College Personnel Association.

Sue, D.W., Ivey, A.E., & Pedersen, P.B. (1996). *A theory of multicultural counseling and therapy.* Pacific Grove, CA: Brooks/Cole.

Tinto, V. (1975). Dropouts from higher education: A theoretical synthesis of recent research. *Review of Educational Research, 45,* 89–125.

Tinto, V. (1986). Theories of college student departure revisited. In J.C. Smart (Ed.), *Higher education: Handbook of theory and research* (Vol. 2, pp. 359–384). New York: Agathon Press.

Tinto, V. (1993). *Leaving college: Rethinking the causes and cures of student attrition* (2nd ed.). Chicago: University of Chicago Press.

Torres, V. (2004). Influences on the ethnic development of Latino college students in the first two years of college. *Journal of College Student Development, 44*(4), 532–547.

Torres, V., Howard-Hamilton, M.F., & Cooper, D.L. (2003). *Identity development of diverse populations: Implications for teaching and administration in higher education.* ASHE-ERIC Higher Education Report, *29*(6). San Francisco: Jossey Bass.

Upcraft, M.L. (1994). The dilemmas of translating theory to practice. *Journal of College Student Development, 35*(6), 438–443.

Upcraft, M.L. (1998). Do graduate preparation programs really prepare practitioners? In N.J. Evans & C.E. Phelps Tobin (Eds.), *State-of-the-art preparation and practice in student affairs: Another look* (pp. 225–227). Lanham, MD: University Press of America.

Wadsworth, B.J. (1979). *Piaget's theory of cognitive development* (2nd ed.). New York: Longman.

Zemke, R. (1992). Second thoughts about the MBTI. *Training, 29*(4), 43–47.

STUDENT DEVELOPMENT AND PERSONAL GROWTH IN EMPLOYMENT

by Ryan D. Padgett & David L. Grady

Student development through college is hardly one-dimensional; the collegiate experience is multifaceted, one that encompasses a myriad of interconnected relationships and interactions. The college experience is designed to emphasize development and personal growth through a student's maturation during college. When measuring student change through the progression of the undergraduate years, Sanford (1967) incorporated both growth and development when discussing the positive and negative effects change can exhibit. Given that time is finite in a day, today's college students have proven an uncanny ability to balance academics within a spectrum of cocurricular activities. Specifically, employed students face the additional complexity of balancing the rigors and demands of work and academics.

While colleges and universities provide students with opportunities to develop and promote personal interests, intellectual achievement and occupational preparation have historically been the primary outcomes upon which institutions have focused (Pascarella & Terenzini, 2005). Within this historical context, researchers tend to measure student outcomes in two different, yet synonymous, categories: intellectual growth and student development. Examining the research on student employment mirrors the historical focus colleges and universities placed on achievement and occupational preparation. A significant proportion of the literature examining the effects of student employment focuses primarily on academic achievement, retention, and financial implications during and after college as outcome measures. While these measures do provide insightful and practical evidence toward explaining the effects employment has on students during college, few studies have extended the effect of college employment toward specific student development and growth.

Using the general model for assessing change (Pascarella, 1985; Pascarella & Terenzini 2005) as a conceptual model, this chapter highlights studies investigating employed college students on two outcomes: (1) cognitive skills and intellectual growth and (2) student development. Pascarella and Terenzini's encyclopedic meta-analysis focusing on college impact and student development provides a framework for understanding the effects student employment has on these two outcomes. This chapter also examines the gaps in the literature and indicates implications for future research. The chapter concludes by providing practitioners with implications on how to apply these findings to their interactions and leadership with on-campus college student employees.

Pascarella's general model for assessing change

College impact models of student change attempt to explain college impact as it relates to environmental and institutional characteristics and student experiences (Astin, 1993; Pascarella & Terenzini, 2005). Considering both environmental and institutional characteristics, Pascarella created the general model for assessing change (Pascarella, 1985; Pascarella & Terenzini, 2005). Pascarella's five-set causal model is largely an extension of Astin's input-environment-outcome college impact model: the characteristics of a student upon entry into college are the *input*, the educational experiences of the college are the *environment*, and student characteristics upon completing college after exposure to the collegiate environment are the *outcome*. After examining the effects of student involvement, Astin (1993) summarized that a "student's academic and personal development can be enhanced by heavy involvement" (p. 382).

The general model for assessing change incorporates five key sets of variables that examine direct and indirect effects of student change (Pascarella, 1985; Pascarella & Terenzini, 2005). The first set, *student background/precollege traits*, features variables measuring background characteristics and traits that students exhibit before enrolling into college (e.g., achievement scores, aspirations, and ethnicity). The second set, *structural/organizational characteristics of institutions*, categorizes the structural and organizational identifiers (e.g., enrollment statistics, selectivity, and faculty-student ratio). Together these two sets establish the third set of variables examining the overall college environment through which a student interacts, labeled the *institutional environment*. It is important to distinguish that these three sets are the initial measurements of student change and college impact even before introducing any collegiate experiences.

The direct and indirect effects of these three sets influence the fourth variable set, *interactions with agents of socialization*. This variable set measures the primary socialization agents (e.g., faculty, peers, university staff, and supervisors) with whom a college student interacts on a daily basis. Interactions with agents of socialization, along with student background/precollege traits and institutional environment, correspond to the final variable set in the model, *quality of student effort*. Through the direct and indirect effects of each of these five variable sets, it is argued that student background/precollege traits, interactions with agents of socialization, and quality of student effort collectively measure student change as it relates to learning and cognitive development. Within the model, institutions' structural/organizational characteristics, mediated by the institutional environment, will indirectly effect student change (Pascarella, 1985; Pascarella & Terenzini, 2005). Pascarella (1985) emphasized that although the initial design of the model measured change pertinent to student learning and cognitive development, it is both relevant and appropriate to extend the model to other measures of student outcomes.

To this degree, this chapter examines where and how student employment can be incorporated within the general model for assessing change in evaluating various college outcome measurements. Coinciding with the framework for examining these effect measures, the model and the literature on student development and personal growth on employed students can together

FIGURE 2.1
ASSESSING THE EFFECTS OF DIFFERENTIAL ENVIRONMENTS ON STUDENT LEARNING & COGNITIVE DEVELOPMENT

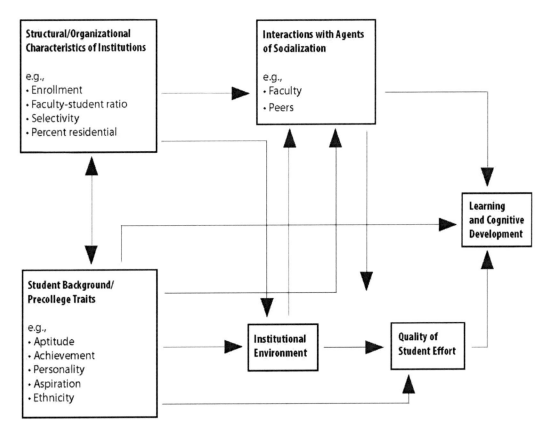

Pascarella, E.T. (1985). College environmental influences on learning and cognitive development: A critical review and synthesis. In J. C. Smart (Ed.), *Higher education: Handbook of theory and research* (Vol. 1, pp. 1–61). Reprinted with kind permission from Springer Science and Business Media.

provide useful and practical applications for practitioners who manage student employees. This chapter highlights the direct and indirect connections within this assessment model that practitioners may find most relevant.

Cognitive skills and intellectual growth

Researchers use interchangeable names when discussing cognitive skills, including "reasoning skills" and "critical thinking" (Pascarella & Terenzini, 1991, 2005). However, the phrase "cognitive skills" maintains a common theme and definition throughout the literature:

> Cognitive competencies and skills represent the general intellectual outcomes of college that permit individuals to process and utilize new information; communicate effectively; reason objectively and draw objective conclusions from various types of data; evaluate new ideas and techniques efficiently; become more objective about beliefs, attitudes, and values; evaluate arguments and claims critically; and make reasonable decisions in the face of imperfect information. (Pascarella & Terenzini, 1991, pp. 114–115)

Researchers also have argued that there is a motivational dimension to critical thinking: students must be open and willing to participate to enhance their cognitive competencies (Pascarella & Terenzini, 2005). Pascarella and Terenzini (2005) infer that the literature is consistent in indicating that students' peers play a significant and key role in their cognitive and intellectual growth. Further, meaningful faculty interactions about subject material in the classroom or issues of student development can positively support cognitive development. Thus, studies attempting to measure cognitive skills will examine students' gains in various college experiences, including agents of socialization and quality of student effort, as they proceed through the collegiate environment. A prior and comprehensive review of the literature indicated that students make statistically significant gains in critical thinking and reason throughout college (McMillan, 1987).

The literature examining college employment's impact on cognitive skills and intellectual growth through college is fairly inconsistent (Gellin, 2003; Pascarella & Terenzini, 2005). However, some of this inconsistency may be explained by the enrollment year of students in the studies. The general model for assessing change suggests that change can be observed only after a student participates in the college environment. In other words, the longer a student is enrolled in college and persists to a degree, the greater the likelihood of a visible change occurring in any student outcome. This timing may explain why the majority of studies found minimal to no significant gains during the first year of college. Terenzini, Yaeger, Pascarella, and Nora (1996) found students participating in a work-study program during their first year of college showed significant gains in reading and mathematics skills, but no significant gains in critical thinking skills. Examining the impact of on-campus versus off-campus employment on reading comprehension, mathematics, and critical thinking measures for first-year students, minimal or no significant differences were found to exist (Pascarella, Bohr, Nora, Desler, & Zusman, 1994; Pascarella, Bohr, Nora, & Terenzini, 1996; Pascarella, Edison, Nora, Hagedorn, & Terenzini, 1998). Similarly, the number of hours working on or off campus during the first year of college had a non-significant impact on reading comprehension, mathematics, and critical thinking (Pascarella et al., 1994). More surprisingly, employment on campus had the same minimal influence on these cognitive measures as working off campus. These trends were consistent in the second year of college (Pascarella et al., 1998). One study did find a slightly different outcome. Using the Collegiate Assessment of Academic Proficiency to measure cognitive outcomes on first-year students, Inman and Pascarella (1998) found that working students exhibit a negative influence on the development of critical thinking skills.

The research supports the causal representation of the change assessment model that as students progress through their undergraduate studies, a differential change does take place between employment and its effect on cognitive development. At the end of the third year of college, Pascarella et al. (1998) found similar non-significant composite measures for reading comprehension and critical thinking. However, the weighted sample of students employed part-time on and off campus had minimal positive impacts on cognitive development at the end of the third year. Working more hours than the typical part-time amount did significantly hinder cognitive development. This curvilinear effect does support prior research that working more than the typical part-time allotment (i.e., 10–15 hours per week) inhibits varying learning outcomes (Astin, 1993; Furr & Elling, 2000; Horn & Berktold, 1998; King & Bannon, 2002; Pinto, Parente, & Palmer, 2001). However, this curvilinear effect does reinforce that limited employment during the third year may support varying learning and cognitive development (Pascarella et al., 1998) and that employed students are equal across the three cognitive measures compared to non-employed students (Pascarella et al., 1994).

Astin (1993) found inconsistencies in the pattern of effects for students' employment on and off campus. Supporting Astin's assertion that working off campus has a negative association with intellectual growth, Furr and Elling (2000) found students employed off campus to be less integrated into the institution. These students also were less likely to participate in out-of-class activities associated with critical learning experiences. More specifically, students who are not employed were more likely to have meaningful discussions with faculty compared to students employed off campus. Utilizing the College Student Experiences Questionnaire with a large analytical sample (n = 3,774), Lundberg (2004) found similar, consistent results for off-campus employment. The more hours spent working off campus, the less likely that students would engage with peers and faculty for academic purposes and with peers for nonacademic purposes. These negative effects were especially prevalent for students who worked more than 20 hours per week off campus. Although these working students were less likely to be involved in meaningful learning experiences, work did not have a significantly negative effect on learning. This finding does contradict prior studies that found a negative association between working and academic achievement (Astin, 1993; Horn & Berktold, 1998; King & Bannon, 2002; Pinto, Parente, & Palmer, 2001).

Not all studies paint such a bleak picture, specifically when measuring the impact of work on participation in out-of-class experiences. Examining part-time employment during college, Kuh (1995) interviewed undergraduates from institutions known to provide enriching out-of-class experiences. Results suggest that employed students may benefit in personal development, but the effects are unrelated to intellectual growth. Terenzini et al. (1996) in their research on work-study programs found students participating in a work-study program, as compared to students who were not, were more likely to participate in campus organizations and have more positive peer interactions. Other researchers have found similar results: working students have identical or greater involvement in campus activities than their non-working peers (Fitch, 1991; Furr & Elling, 2000).

Previous researchers have identified inconsistencies prevalent throughout the literature (Gellin, 2003; Pascarella & Terenzini, 2005; Riggert, Boyle, Petrosko, Ash, & Rude-Parkins, 2006). However, the commonalities of the findings correspond both directly and indirectly with the general model for assessing change. As referenced previously, three component sets compose the learning and cognitive development outcomes. Important to the analysis of employment's effects on student development and personal growth, the findings from these studies help practitioners understand how the interactions with agents of socialization and quality of student effort affect a student's learning and cognitive development. A synthesis of this inconsistent empirical evidence leads researchers to conclude that employment in a part-time job on campus is found to have a positive association with cognitive and growth measures, yet employment in a part-time job off campus holds similar negative effects—including on students' interpersonal skills—associated with working full-time. In other words, on-campus employment strengthens student involvement and off-campus employment hinders it (Pascarella & Terenzini, 1991).

Astin (1993) attributed the likelihood of these patterns to the functionalities that on-campus employment can provide; students who work on campus are more likely to engage in conversations with peers and faculty. Even when employed students are less engaged with peers and faculty, they are able to compensate so that it does not hinder their overall learning experience (Lundberg, 2004). Thus, it appears employed students are learning valuable organization and time management skills (Pascarella et al., 1998).

Personal growth and development

In addition to students' cognitive growth during college, their ability to apply reason and intellect to their personal development also is enhanced (Pascarella & Terenzini, 2005). Unfortunately, few researchers have studied student employment relative to various personal growth and development measures. The literature that does exist falls into three categories that Pascarella and Terenzini (2005) identify as important developmental outcomes affected by college attendance: moral development, psychosocial change, and attitudes and values. This section will summarize the small body of literature on student employment as it pertains to these measures.

Moral development

Pascarella and Terenzini (2005) noted that moral development encompasses a broad array of themes: interpersonal, social, political, and ethical. The research on college employment and its impact on moral development is limited. Similar to that of cognitive skills and intellectual growth, the research on college employment and moral development is inconsistent and contradictory. Though the research is minimal, it supplements a practitioner's understanding of the quality of student effort as it relates to moral development.

The handful of college student employment studies in the moral development area focus on community service and volunteering. The intuitive assumption, as supported by the literature, is as the amount of working hours increases, the likelihood of volunteering decreases (Fitch, 1991; Marks & Jones, 2004). This is consistent with results discussed earlier for time allocated toward out-of-class activities (Furr & Elling, 2000; Terenzini et al., 1996). Using a large dataset comprised of 623 U.S. institutions, Cruce and Moore (2006) looked at first-year undergraduates who indicated a desire to volunteer or not volunteer, or who had already volunteered. Their results indicated that students who worked on campus up to 30 hours per week had a greater likelihood of volunteering. Students who worked off campus up to 15 hours per week during their first year indicated a minimal likelihood of volunteering. However, working more than 16 hours off campus substantially increased the likelihood of not planning to volunteer. Overall, Cruce and Moore (2006) concluded that working moderate levels either on or off campus may positively affect a student's desire to participate in community service activities.

Another valuable moral development measurement is academic dishonesty. Only two studies examined the employed student population, yet each study found different results. The first study found that students who work are less likely to cheat (Haines, Diekhoff, LaBeff, & Clark, 1986). However, caution should be taken given that the data for this study were obtained from 380 undergraduate students from only one institution. The second study (Pino & Smith, 2003) also conducted its analysis on one institution with a sample of 675 undergraduate students. Pino and Smith found that working has no significant effect on cheating. While the results of these two studies are inconsistent, when considered together, it is apparent and promising that students who are employed are less likely to cheat. Although these two studies limit the ability to discuss student employment's affects on cheating between colleges, it can be presumed that the socialization with faculty and peers and the quality of student effort may attribute to the student's moral decisions. This presumption is similar to Cruce and Moore's (2006) findings that working a moderate amount positively affects a student's desire to volunteer. In other words, a student who is more involved and engrossed in the college environment may be more morally supportive of themselves and their surroundings.

Psychosocial change and attitudes and values

Conceptually defining psychosocial change can be confusing and encompass a myriad of different interpersonal and self-identity definitions (Pascarella & Terenzini, 1991, 2005; Robbins, Lauver, Le, Davis, Langley, & Carlstrom, 2004). In their meta-analysis, Pascarella and Terenzini (1991, 2005) summarized the research by the following categories: identity development, self-concept, self-esteem, autonomy, independence, locus of control, self-efficacy, interpersonal relations, and leadership skills. Similarly, researchers have found measuring the attitudes and values of college students to be a challenging endeavor (Pascarella & Terenzini, 2005). This difficulty is in part due to the similarities between an attitude and a value. Further, measuring the changes of a student's attitude during college is complicated because it is difficult to distinguish if a college experience contributed to a behavioral change or if a student's maturation through college effected the change (Pascarella & Terenzini, 2005). While psychosocial change and attitudes and values are conceptually different, the limited research on these measures for student employment combines the two outcomes when measuring self-worth.

Locus of control, defined as the extent to which students consider themselves to be in control and responsible for the decisions in their life (Luzzo & Ward, 1995), is a valuable psychosocial measurement when examining the working student population. Among other factors, practitioners and faculty alike would hope that students are enrolling in majors consistent with their future employment interests. The same expectation can be attributed to a student's employment during college in that a student should be choosing a job that provides insight and interest to future career endeavors. Two studies in particular examined students' self-selection into college employment and their congruency to post-college aspirations. Students with an internal career locus of control have a minimal likelihood, when compared to those who do not, to find part-time employment consistent with their career ambitions (Luzzo & Ward, 1995). The magnitude of this finding may be marginal, but the minimal direction implies a desire among students to work in a field related to their interests while enrolled in college. Further evidence found students employed in engineering, science labs, health care, computer science, and teaching reported working in jobs that aligned with their career ambitions (Kane, Healy, & Henson, 1992).

Whereas a student's self-selection and locus of control for one's life can affect a student's career ambitions, self-esteem also can directly influence a student's work achievement and career attitudes (Crook, Healy, & O'Shea, 1984). This finding implies that a student's self-esteem is integral in the work environment as it relates to career ambitions. The more confident a student employee feels, the greater the production and overall attitude toward the job. Crook and associates found further evidence indicating career attitudes can directly influence a student's academic and work achievement in college. Moreover, career attitudes are positively related to the occupational level of a student's college job and the length of college employment (Healy, O'Shea, & Crook, 1985). In other words, entry into a college employment position with predetermined career attitudes does influence production, job type for which a student applies, and how long he or she will remain employed.

Psychosocial change and attitudes and values, along with moral development, are embedded in a student's background characteristics and traits. Students are predisposed with these traits upon entry into college. As the change assessment model highlights, these traits play an integral part in shaping student development through agents of socialization and the quality of student effort (Pascarella & Terenzini, 2005). The research on working students indicates that the quality of effort that students exhibit is in part influenced by their psychosocial and moral traits and attitudes and values. The results of these outcome measures are generally encouraging; working students who have positive self-attitudes and motivation appear to be developing in a positive way toward post-college ambitions.

Future research

The research on student employment is narrowly tailored to examining student achievement and retention measures as outcome variables. As summarized throughout the chapter, few studies have examined student employment as it relates to development and student growth. Those studies that do examine development and growth typically had inconsistent results from similar studies' findings. Moreover, a significant amount of studies that did examine working students tended to control for these students in the models rather than target them as an analytic sample. This approach has in effect limited the ability of researchers and practitioners to understand the relationship between student employment and higher education (Riggert et al., 2006).

A significant amount of studies have explored out-of-class experience and its influence on numerous higher education outcomes. However, while many researchers and practitioners classify student employment as an out-of-class experience, they do not take into consideration the unique population of students opting to work during college. For example, a student working part-time in a chemistry laboratory will likely have different measures across various student development outcomes compared to a student working part-time as a cashier in residential food services. To account for these differences, future research on college employment needs to examine specific on- and off-campus job types and their influence on student development and growth measures.

Prior research examining working students in relation to development and growth outcomes have tended to focus on cognitive measures. This research provides valuable results in understanding student traits and abilities imperative to success in the workplace that may not be entirely captured by academic achievement measures. However, there is still a substantial gap in the research on development and growth measures of working students, especially for psychosocial and moral development and attitudes and values. Theoretically, these outcomes are just as valuable as cognitive skills or academic achievement when examining satisfaction and job performance in any type of employment. Employers would ideally want employees who are not only capable of the work but also who are highly motivated, ethical, and positive. Future research on student employment needs to emphasize how working students' precollege traits and their quality of effort relate to student development. In particular, while prior research examined attitudes and values exhibited in employment after college, more research needs to focus on looking at these and other developmental outcomes during college.

Practitioner focus

Research can provide practitioners with evidence of varying outcomes, but incorporating these findings into practice can support student development and growth. It is important to note that practitioners and administrators ultimately shape the environment in which students interact and work. While there is some level of control over these factors, one cannot shape a student's traits or effort. Rather, practitioners can focus on supporting and creating key aspects that the research indicates as providing students with an environment in which to grow. The research outlined through this chapter provides practitioners with many insights and opportunities to strengthen this growth. One major opportunity that prior research found, on which the practitioner focus is based, is encouraging students to choose an employment opportunity on campus rather than off campus. The positive implications that immersion into the college campus has on student growth are simply not as great for off-campus employment (Astin, 1993).

Specifically, practitioners can incorporate these research findings to structure the on-campus job opportunities in ways that positively affect cognitive skills and intellectual growth. Supervisors play an important role as agents of socialization. To assume that role, supervisors must view themselves as educators rather than just a "boss." This function can be accomplished with meaningful and intentional interaction and reflection with student employees by making efforts to relate their employment responsibilities to their coursework. By incorporating problem-solving situations that align with a student's coursework, practitioners would be creating a real-world situation that the student is likely to encounter in a future career.

Other strategies that practitioners can apply include limiting the number of hours worked each week to less than 15 hours. The research, while inconsistent, did highlight that those students who worked more hours tended to have more negative impacts on various college outcomes. Further, encourage students to be involved with their peer co-workers in extracurricular activities outside of work. Strengthening the bond between socialization outside work may provide for more meaningful interactions at work. Another strategy is aggressively and effectively marketing the educational benefits of working on campus to students and parents. Campuses are quick to highlight the importance of becoming involved with campus activities on college tours, yet tend to neglect the usefulness of part-time college employment. Bringing to light the value of campus employment and its effect on development and growth provides another practical way students can become involved on campus in a positive way.

Part-time employment is also a way to develop student leaders. Working part-time on campus increases the likelihood of being elected and holding a student leadership position (Astin, 1993). In many campus employment settings, students are given a great deal of responsibility. In college unions, for example, students are often in charge of the facilities at night and weekend events without any direct supervision from full-time staff. In addition, university entities with retail operations place students in positions of responsibility with money and inventory that can exceed hundreds of thousands of dollars. This level of responsibility contributes to the development of a student's self-esteem and independence. Moreover, students typically choose the employment opportunities in which they wish to participate. Therefore, by providing an environment that supports their attitudes and values, practitioners can ultimately influence job performance and satisfaction at work. The work habits that students develop during their college employment do affect career attitude. Therefore, it is important that students are given suitable responsibility, appropriate feedback on job performance, and the opportunity for promotion when available.

Conclusion

Anecdotal evidence from student employees indicates that working during college can build self-confidence that carries forward in their future professions (Scannell & Simpson, 1996). If students recognize the impact employment can have on their growth into future careers, it is imperative that practitioners and administrators encourage more research for dissemination to incoming and enrolled students and to inform their practice as employers. Prior research on development and growth for student employees, though inconsistent, does provide a context through which practitioners can incorporate practical and meaningful applications to aid in student growth. The research also indicates major gaps that need to be explored. Student employees play a vital role in the functioning of higher education institutions through their on-campus employment by providing important services and programs, working in research laboratories, and teaching in the classroom. As such, the number of and the reliance upon student employees is not likely to decrease anytime soon. More attention needs to be placed on student employees and the ways in which practitioners and administrators can support their academic and personal development and growth.

References

Astin, A.W. (1993). *What matters in college? Four critical years revisited.* San Francisco: Jossey-Bass.

Crook, R.H., Healy, C.C., & O'Shea, D.W. (1984). The linkage of work achievement to self-esteem, career maturity, and college achievement. *Journal of Vocational Behavior, 25,* 70–79.

Cruce, T.M., & Moore, J.V., III (2006, May). *First-year students' plans to volunteer: An examination of the predictors of community service participation.* Paper presented at the annual forum for the Association for Institutional Research, Chicago, IL.

Fitch, R.T. (1991). Differences among community service volunteers, extracurricular volunteers, and nonvolunteers on the college campus. *Journal of College Student Development, 32,* 534–540.

Furr, S.R., & Elling, T.W. (2000). The influence of work on college student development. *NASPA Journal, 37*(2), 454–470.

Gellin, A. (2003). The effect of undergraduate student involvement on critical thinking: A meta-analysis of the literature 1991–2000. *Journal of College Student Development, 44*(6), 746–762.

Haines, V.J., Diekhoff, G.M., LaBeff, E.E., & Clark, R.E. (1986). College cheating: Immaturity, lack of commitment, and the neutralizing attitude. *Research in Higher Education, 25*(4), 342–354.

Healy, C.C., O'Shea, D., & Crook, R.H. (1985). Relation of career attitudes to age and career progress during college. *Journal of Counseling Psychology, 32*(2), 239–244.

Horn, L.J., & Berktold, J. (1998). *Profile of undergraduates in U.S. postsecondary education institutions: 1995–96.* National Center for Education Statistics, Washington, DC.

Inman, P., & Pascarella, E.T. (1998). The impact of college residence on the development of critical thinking skills in college freshmen. *Journal of College Student Development, 39*(6), 557–568.

Kane, S.T., Healy, C.C., & Henson, J. (1992). College students and their part-time jobs: Job congruency, satisfaction, and quality. *Journal of Employment Counseling, 29*, 138–144.

King, T., & Bannon, E. (2002). *At what cost? The price that working students pay for a college education.* United States Public Interest Research Group, Washington, DC.

Kuh, G.D. (1995). The other curriculum: Out-of-class experiences associated with student learning and personal development. *Journal of Higher Education, 66*(2), 123–155.

Lundberg, C.A. (2004). Working and learning: The role of involvement for employed students. *NASPA Journal, 41*(2), 201–215.

Luzzo, D.A., & Ward, B.E. (1995). The relative contributions of self-efficacy and locus of control to the prediction of vocational congruence. *Journal of Career Development, 21*(4), 307–317.

Marks, H.M., & Jones, S.R. (2004). Community service in the transition: Shifts and continuities in participation from high school to college. *Journal of Higher Education, 73*(3), 307–339.

McMillan, J.H. (1987). Enhancing college students' critical thinking: A review of studies. *Research in Higher Education, 26*(1), 3–29.

Pascarella, E.T. (1985). College environmental influences on learning and cognitive development: A critical review and synthesis. In J. C. Smart (Ed.), *Higher education: Handbook of theory and research* (Vol. 1, pp. 1–61). New York: Agathon Press, Inc.

Pascarella, E.T., Bohr, L., Nora, A., Desler, M., & Zusman, B. (1994). Impacts of on-campus and off-campus work on first year cognitive outcomes. *Journal of College Student Development, 35*, 364–370.

Pascarella, E.T., Bohr, L., Nora, A., & Terenzini, P.T. (1996). Is differential exposure to college linked to the development of critical thinking? *Research in Higher Education, 37*(2), 159–174.

Pascarella, E.T., Edison, M.I., Nora, A., Hagedorn, L.S., & Terenzini, P.T. (1998). Does work inhibit cognitive development during college? *Educational Evaluation and Policy Analysis, 20*(2), 75–93.

Pascarella, E.T., & Terenzini, P.T. (1991). *How college affects students.* San Francisco: Jossey-Bass.

Pascarella, E.T., & Terenzini, P.T. (2005). *How college affects students: A third decade of research* (Vol. 2). San Francisco: Jossey-Bass.

Pino, N.W., & Smith, W.L. (2003). College students and academic dishonesty. *College Student Journal, 37*(4), 490–500.

Pinto, M.B., Parente, D.H., & Palmer, T.S. (2001). College student performance and credit card usage. *Journal of College Student Development, 42*(1), 49–58.

Riggert, S.C., Boyle, M., Petrosko, J.M., Ash, D., & Rude-Parkins, C. (2006). Student employment and higher education: Empiricism and contradiction. *Review of Educational Research, 76*(1), 63–92.

Robbins, S.B., Lauver, K., Le, H., Davis, D., Langley, R., & Carlstrom, A. (2004). Do psychosocial and study skill factors predict college outcomes? A meta-analysis. *Psychological Bulletin, 130*(2), 261–288.

Sanford, N. (1967). *Where colleges fail: A study of the student as a person.* San Francisco: Jossey-Bass.

Scannell, J., & Simpson, K. (1996). *Shaping the college experience outside the classroom.* Rochester, NY: University of Rochester Press.

Terenzini, P.T., Yaeger, P.M., Pascarella, E.T., & Nora, A. (1996, May). *Work-study program influences on college students' cognitive development.* Paper presented at the meeting of the Association for Institutional Research, Albuquerque, NM.

STUDENT LEARNING OUTCOMES: EMPIRICAL RESEARCH AS THE BRIDGE BETWEEN THEORY AND PRACTICE

by Jonathan S. Lewis & Sebastian Contreras Jr.

It's a vexing problem: How can higher education administrators translate learning outcomes from literature to lived experience while ensuring that they reflect the specific intricacies, values, and realities of their institution, division, or unit? Empirical research provides an excellent means for administrators to select and implement those theoretical principles that can best inform their work. In addition to contributing to the growing literature on student learning outcomes, conducting empirical research produces data-driven practical applications of theory that are tailored for each unique educational setting (Lewis & Contreras, 2008).

In this chapter, one such study is presented that focuses on student learning in employment and the transformative changes that followed from its results. Readers will examine these changes at one particular institution's college union in areas such as student employment program philosophy, learning outcome development, job description focus, student employee performance evaluation, and recognition. In doing so, an argument will be made that administrators, zeroing in on their primary role as educators, can utilize empirical research as the most effective method to enliven broad theories on their way to becoming meaningful practice.

Learning and student employment

Much of the research on learning has concluded that, to acquire new forms of knowledge successfully, the delivery of information should take place in the context where it will be applied. While many educators know this instinctively, it is important to identify a few researchers who laid the foundation for what has become a well-known principle. Vygotsky (1978) developed a theory of zones of proximal development, where an instructor inspires learning in students by presenting them with increasingly difficult (yet no less authentic) tasks; he called this method of instruction "scaffolding." Similarly, Kolb (1984) described a cycle of concrete experience, observation, reflection, and abstraction that anchored his theory of experiential learning. Brown, Collins, and Duguid (1989) presented a framework they called "situated cognition"—a combination of authentic activity, context, and the surrounding culture—which at its most practical level utilized a traditional apprenticeship model to spark learning. Wenger (2004) focused on the learning that emerges organically from within a social or working group in writings on communities of practice. According to Wenger, individuals who work in similar content areas share common challenges, voluntarily form a cohesive community through their interactions, and often come together to learn and grow from one another. This practice can occur in settings as diverse as the workplace, the classroom, government, or even youth gang culture.

The primary concepts these theorists put forward translate directly to student employment and complement much of the current literature on student development (American Association for Higher Education, American College Personnel Association, & National Association of Student Personnel Administrators, 1998; Keeling, 2004). The principles of learning that provided much of the foundation for the present study are:

- Challenges should be presented to a learner in increments of increasing difficulty.
- Learning is most effective when information is embedded within the context where it will be applied.
- Learning occurs as part of a cycle of observation, experience, and reflection.
- Self-selecting groups who share a common purpose produce meaningful learning.

To learn meaningfully, student employees must be challenged by activities, tasks, and projects that are authentic to their position and involve a certain amount of reflection. However, student employee supervisors have a responsibility to purposefully select challenges that call upon the specific concepts, skills, and values that are recognized as meaningful or important to higher education institutions. Only through this practice will two equally important goals be achieved: students will meaningfully gain, remember, and utilize new knowledge in future situations, and this knowledge will fulfill the stated learning outcomes our institutions have claimed to advance (AAHE et al., 1998).

Methods

Research tenets

In 2007, a study of student employment and learning outcomes was conducted at Northwestern University's college union, the Norris University Center (Lewis, 2007). The Norris Center is a 160,000 square-foot facility that includes the campus bookstore, student newspaper, meeting rooms, and food court, among other services. This study attempted to understand the learning that was taking place across student employment positions to better catalyze future student development. The study's goals were both theoretical and practical:

- To assess the extent to which student employees and their supervisors believed learning was taking place on the job.

- To understand what specific workplace experiences produced greater reported levels of learning.
- To identify relationships between these workplace experiences and student learning in established domain areas.
- To integrate these findings into every aspect of the student employee's experience, from application to graduation.

To construct an empirical study that would have clear practical relevance to this particular organization, the first task was to select those specific workplace experiences that were both grounded in theory and that were likely to occur in this setting. A list of theoretically informed practices was narrowed to include: formal training, informal training, observation of one's co-workers engaging in similar tasks, collaboration and teamwork, feedback from one's peers, feedback from one's supervisor, informal interactions with one's supervisor, task repetition, problem solving, experimenting with new ideas, reflecting about one's job, intuitive decision making, and congruence between job tasks and coursework or career interests. Examples of how each workplace experience could translate from theory to student employment practice are listed in Table 3.1.

After identifying specific, measurable workplace experiences—ones that could reasonably exist in this particular student employment program and were grounded in the learning literature—the next step involved choosing which learning domains to study. Research was drawn from the relevant literature on student development, with particular emphasis given to the arguments put forward in "Learning Reconsidered" (Keeling, 2004). It was decided that the domains singled out for inclusion in the study should be chosen from a list compiled by Northwestern's Division of Student Affairs because the division recognized these domains as most relevant to the specific institutional setting. Within that list, the five selected learning domains also had been lauded as important according to "Learning Reconsidered," the Council for the Advancement of Standards in Higher Education (CAS), or both. The five selected domains were career development, civic and community engagement, leadership, ethics and values, and responsible independence. These domains are listed in Table 3.2, along with others considered, from all three aforementioned sources.

Having collected 13 workplace experiences and five learning domains to study—primarily from organic sources and perspectives within the university and the specific department, but also from literature on learning and student development—the following two-part hypothesis was developed:

- Both students and their professional staff supervisors would report that learning was taking place in the key domain areas due to the student employment program.
- The workplace experiences would have a significant relationship with learning in one or more of those domains.

The next step was to analyze the data within this construct of an investigation based on theory.

TABLE 3.1 WORKPLACE EXPERIENCES

Experiences	Theoretical Foundation	Sample Practices
Formal training	Eraut (2000)	New employee orientation; tutorial in job tasks; retreat
Informal training	Eraut (2000)	Quick reminders; rapid feedback
Observation of co-workers	Collins, Brown, & Newman (1990); Eraut (2000)	Shadowing experienced peers in job tasks
Collaboration and teamwork	Brown, Collins & Duguid (1980); Eraut (2000); Gardner (1993); Resnick (1987); Wenger (2004)	Collective problem solving; practicing multiple roles within a group; "communities of practice"
Feedback from peers	AAHE, ACPA, & NASPA (1998); Chickering & Reisser (1993); Eraut (2000); Wenger (2004)	"360-degree" performance reviews; round-table discussion at meetings
Feedback from supervisor	AAHE et al. (1998); Chickering & Reisser (1993); Eraut (2000); Wenger (2004)	Performance reviews; one-on-one meetings; e-mail, phone, or other communications about work
Informal interactions with supervisor	AAHE et al. (1998)	Mentoring relationships; office reception or party; working group outing
Task repetition	Eraut (2000)	Answering the phone; providing consistent information to clients; processing paperwork; complying with human resource policies or regulations
Problem solving	AAHE et al. (1998); Resnick (1987); Wenger (2004)	Supervisory-level decisions; managing peers; greater authority when interacting with clients; work after standard business hours
Idea experimentation	AAHE et al. (1998); ACPA (1996)	Different interaction styles for managing co-workers; creating an innovative solution to a client problem
Reflection	Eraut (2000); Little & Chin (1993)	Analyzing aspects of the job they like or dislike; discovering what parameters enable them to be productive; assessing fit with supervisor's style

Intuitive decision-making	Eraut (2000); Vygotsky (1978)	Departing from routine procedures when the situation warrants; accepting more difficult or complex situations on one's own; "scaffolding"
Congruence between job & coursework or career path	AAHE et al. (1998); Braskamp, Trautvetter, & Ward, (2006); Keeling (2004); Luzzo (1993); Pascarella & Terenzini (2005)	Leadership roles; research projects; opportunities to present in front of a group; using discipline-specific knowledge, such as a student who studies marketing designing a promotional campaign

TABLE 3.2 LEARNING DOMAINS

Northwestern University	CAS	Learning Reconsidered
Career development	Intellectual growth	Cognitive complexity
Civic & community engagement	Effective communication	Knowledge acquisition, integration, & application
Intrapersonal & interpersonal competence	Enhanced self-esteem	Humanitarianism
Ethics & values	Realistic self-appraisal	Civic engagement
Healthy living	Clarified values	Interpersonal & intrapersonal competence
Intercultural competence/maturity	Career choices	Practical competence
Leadership	Leadership development	Persistence & academic achievement
Responsible independence	Healthy behavior	
	Meaningful interpersonal relationships	
	Independence	
	Collaboration	
	Social responsibility	
	Satisfying & productive lifestyle	
	Appreciating diversity	
	Spiritual awareness	
	Personal & educational goals	

Data sources and samples

Data were gathered from three different sources—a process known as triangulation—in hopes that added perspectives would more closely refine the results. The three data sources were artifact analyses of student employee job descriptions, quantitative and qualitative surveys of student employees, and a quantitative survey of supervisors.

Position descriptions for all student employee positions were collected (n = 30) and coded for language that identified opportunities for learning on the job. More specifically, these position descriptions were analyzed for explicit or implicit mention of the five learning domains or 13 workplace experiences chosen to be part of this study.

Next, two surveys were compiled for electronic distribution to student employees (n = 164) via an Internet-based survey tool. The student employee population was recruited from all units within the Norris Center, including the information desk, games room, building managers, campus bookstore, marketing, and maintenance. The first survey focused on gathering quantitative data and consisted of six major sections:

- A prompt asking students to rate the frequency with which they engaged with each of the 13 workplace experiences while on the job.
- A two-sentence description of each of the five learning domains, followed by a prompt asking students to rate themselves on how much they believed that they embodied the principles outlined. For example, one such prompt read: "Civic and community engagement involves active participation in campus life and the broader society. It includes your connectedness to others, involvement in groups, and commitment to socially responsible action." The language for these prompts was based upon principles the Division of Student Affairs outlined (Lewis & Contreras, 2005).
- A prompt asking students to identify the extent to which each of the 13 workplace experiences may have had an impact on their self-rating in each learning domain.
- A prompt asking students to identify the extent to which each of six control experiences— employment elsewhere; extracurricular activities, such as student organizations or sports team participation; living in a residence hall; participation in a fraternity or sorority; classroom experiences; and experiences prior to attending college—may have had an impact on their self-rating in each learning domain. This section was included to account for the fact that student learning in the domains of interest may have occurred in non-employment settings.
- A job satisfaction questionnaire, to identify whether a relationship existed between learning and self-reported levels of job satisfaction.
- Demographic questions.

The second survey focused on gathering qualitative data and was distributed only to those students who completed the initial survey (n = 97). Students were asked to respond in two or three paragraphs to two open-ended questions:

- "Beyond the specific duties of your job(s), what do you feel that you have learned from working at the Norris Center?"

- "What specific experiences/components of your job(s) contributed to the learning you outlined above?"

A third survey was compiled for electronic distribution via an Internet-based survey tool to full-time, professional staff at the Norris Center who directly supervised student employees (n = 15), as well as two student employees who supervised large numbers of their peers. These staff members represented a wide range of both young and experienced administrators and worked in offices across the union, including cash operations, technical services, and information technology. This survey focused on gathering quantitative data and consisted of three major sections:

- A prompt asking staff to rate the frequency with which they believed each student they supervised engaged with the 13 workplace experiences.
- A two-sentence description of each of the five learning domains, followed by a prompt asking staff to rate their student employees on how much they believe that each embodied the principles outlined.
- Demographic information.

Staff supervisors were asked to complete this survey in its entirety for each student they supervised. This structure allowed the researcher to gather two data points for each student employee—a self-rating and an outsider rating—which further strengthened the triangulation of data points and thereby strengthened the results as well.

Two concerns arose in the planning and execution of this survey that required attention. First, as a consequence of the researcher's position as a professional staff member of the organization during the course of this study, approximately 75 of the 164 student employees eligible to complete this survey reported to the researcher as their primary supervisor. This situation posed a problem with respect to confidentiality (survey responses should not be traceable to individual respondents) and data collection (the researcher would have to complete the professional staff survey for many students, rendering the data potentially unreliable).

To neutralize the concern over confidentiality, a research assistant was recruited from another department to download and compile the data. Before forwarding the data to the researcher for analysis, the assistant—who did not know any of the student participants—substituted the respondent names with random study participant numbers. Therefore, at no time did the researcher—or any other staff member or student employee—have access to identifiable data from any of the study participants.

To minimize the concern over data collection, the researcher asked two student employees—as "area supervisors," they technically were the immediate supervisors of students in "attendant" or "assistant" positions—to complete the staff survey on behalf of 31 students under their charge. In the end, the researcher had to complete the staff survey on behalf of 12 student employees (12 percent of the total student sample).

Analysis

The purpose of analyzing position descriptions was to identify to what extent the proverbial "stage" is set for learning well before a student actually begins in the position. Are students made aware of what they will learn if they are offered and accept a position with the organization? Do the job descriptions mention or effectively describe any of the workplace experiences that—according to the literature—should lead to growth and student development? Coding was completed on 30 different position descriptions. The wording was analyzed to ascertain whether the descriptions referenced the learning that would occur in the work setting.

Correlation analyses were run using the data from the initial student survey and from the staff survey. Adopting the perspective that neither the student employees nor their professional staff supervisors would be entirely accurate reporters, the two sets of data drawn from each sample were averaged to create a composite measure of each workplace experience and a composite of each learning domain. In other words, students' responses about their own workplace experiences and learning were averaged with those of their staff supervisors. For example, students' self-ratings on the frequency of their engagement in problem solving and in their amount of learning in the domain of career development were combined with their supervisor's assessment of their performance in each of those areas. These composites were then used in further analyses to identify relationships between reported levels of workplace experiences and learning in the key domain areas. Additionally, partial-correlation analyses were used to isolate any impact on learning from the control experiences identified.

Results

Ninety-seven students (57 women and 40 men) responded to the initial (quantitative) survey, a 59 percent response rate. The sample was generally representative of the university student body with respect to gender, race, and academic affiliation (the majority of students at Northwestern are enrolled in the Weinberg College of Arts & Sciences). Additionally, the sample represented approximately 6 percent of all undergraduate students working part-time while enrolled full-time at the university, as of January 2007 (Northwestern University, 2007). Fifteen staff members and two student supervisors (nine men and eight women) completed their survey, a 100 percent response rate. Some had to take the survey multiple times, completing it once for each student they supervised. Thirty-six students completed the follow-up survey, a 37 percent response rate.

The analyses of these results indicated four primary findings:

- Student employees were learning in each of the five domain areas included in this study. Students rated the extent to which they embodied the ideal of each of five learning domains on a scale from one to seven, with one indicating no learning whatsoever and seven indicating a complete identification with the domain competencies. Staff supervisors were asked to make their own judgment about each of their students on the same scale. Average scores from

TABLE 3.3 DESCRIPTIVE STATISTICS:
Learning composite & five learning domain composites

Composite	Mean	SD	Range
Learning	4.76	0.77	2.60–6.60
Career development	4.40	1.09	1.50–6.50
Civic & community engagement	4.43	1.00	2.00–7.00
Leadership	4.72	0.87	2.00–7.00
Ethics & values	5.20	0.87	2.50–7.00
Responsible independence	5.11	0.91	2.50–7.00

students and staff in each domain were well above the mid-point on the seven-point scale, indicating that each group believed that students were learning in key areas (see Table 3.3).

- Each of the 13 measured workplace experiences are occurring on the job. Since the literature indicated that these experiences could produce meaningful growth and development, this finding validated the Norris Center as a place where student employees can learn. Average scores for 11 of the 13 experiences were above the mid-point on a seven-point scale (see Table 3.4).
- Twelve of 13 workplace experiences correlated significantly and positively with a composite measure of learning. Therefore, both student employees and their staff supervisors reported a connection between engaging with these concrete experiences while working and making gains in the more abstract learning domains. Statistically significant relationships are shown in Table 3.5.
- The relationships between engagement with specific workplace experiences and learning in the domains of interest remained significant even after controlling for the potential impact of learning that may have come from activities unrelated to employment with the organization of study. While five of the six control variables—all but residence hall living—correlated significantly and positively with learning, they had a non-significant impact on the statistical relationships between workplace experiences with the organization and domains in which students learn. In other words, students confirmed what student development theorists (e.g., Braskamp, Trautvetter, & Ward, 2006) had previously written: they learn from many varied places on campus, but student employment is a separate and equally valid context, imparting knowledge that is both important and unique within the undergraduate journey. Additionally, there was no statistically significant relationship between job satisfaction and student learning.

TABLE 3.4 DESCRIPTIVE STATISTICS OF COMPOSITE WORKPLACE EXPERIENCES

	Mean	SD	Range
Formal training	3.21	0.90	1.00–6.00
Informal training	4.37	1.05	1.50–6.50
Observation	4.14	1.35	2.00–7.00
Collaboration	5.07	1.25	2.50–7.00
Feedback from peers	3.89	1.18	1.50–7.00
Feedback from supervisor	4.59	1.12	1.50–7.00
Informal interaction with supervisor	4.66	1.23	2.00–7.00
Task repetition	5.40	1.01	3.00–7.00
Problem solving	4.84	1.16	2.00–7.00
Idea experimentation	4.37	1.27	1.50–7.00
Reflection	4.05	1.18	1.50–6.50
Intuition	4.45	1.28	2.00–7.00
Congruence	2.98	1.08	1.00–5.50

In summary, high levels of learning were identified by both student employees and their staff supervisors. This learning appeared in five domain areas identified as important by Northwestern University's Division of Student Affairs and remained significant even after factoring in control variables. Student learning is catalyzed through engagement with 12 concrete experiences, tasks, or activities as part of their positions at the Norris Center. These experiences are authentic to the employment context and are reinforced in the literature as means to spark meaningful growth and development in the learner.

TABLE 3.5 CORRELATIONS BETWEEN LEARNING & DOMAIN COMPOSITES & WORKPLACE EXPERIENCES

	Learning	Career Development	Civic & Community Engagement	Leadership	Ethics & Values	Responsible Independence
Formal Training	0.09	0.05	0.00	0.16	0.06	0.05
Informal Training	0.26*	0.33**	0.16	0.27*	0.14	0.08
Observation	0.25*	0.15	0.06	0.28**	0.13	0.20
Collaboration	0.46**	0.45**	0.32**	0.37**	0.23*	0.38**
Feedback from Peers	0.38**	0.41**	0.22*	0.33**	0.19	0.15
Feedback from Supervisor	0.42**	0.36**	0.25*	0.35**	0.32**	0.27**
Informal Interaction with Supervisor	0.27*	0.26*	0.27**	0.15	0.18	0.20
Task Repetition	0.23*	0.20	0.23*	0.12	0.17	0.24*
Problem Solving	0.68**	0.53**	0.43**	0.51**	0.51**	0.46**
Idea Experimentation	0.48**	0.45**	0.34**	0.44**	0.36**	0.06
Reflection	0.41**	0.26*	0.30**	0.32**	0.33**	0.24*
Intuition	0.61**	0.39**	0.46**	0.51**	0.40**	0.51**
Congruence	0.44**	0.45**	0.32**	0.42**	0.18	0.16

$* \ p<0.05, ** \ p<0.01$

Data from the follow-up student survey supported the findings of the initial surveys and also provided insight into student employees' perspectives on where their jobs intersect with learning. Many students referred to growth in "people skills," teamwork, leadership, customer service, and problem solving through their positions. The most revealing statements were often the ones where students explicitly connected concrete workplace experiences with gains in one or more of the five measured learning domains. For example, one student wrote about how practicing varied interpersonal skills while working directly contributed to gains in career development:

> My workplace included a lot of people-to-people interaction, not only within the staff, but with a number of students as well. I feel that this has greatly helped me to develop and hone certain aspects of my social skills. I've also come to learn more about myself as working at Norris has helped me to realize what is important for me or what really matters for me in a work setting

Another student wrote succinctly about how collaboration and problem solving in a work setting led to a personal growth in leadership skills and career development:

> I have learned to work in a team environment, doing things such as planning and problem solving. Doing so has also given me leadership experience and made me realize how much I enjoy working in a team.

Yet another student wrote about the experience of being a supervisor, and how it has contributed to growth in competencies that would fall under the domain of responsible independence:

> I also feel that I have gained useful organizational skills from my employment. Managing a staff of employees, keeping communication with outside contacts, and having a working relationship with my supervisor while juggling a class schedule, has forced me to carefully keep track of time and activities in an orderly manner.

These and other statements from the follow-up survey indicated that student employees at the Norris Center could effectively articulate specific experiences where they learned something new through their job, but more importantly that the workplace experiences and the learning they generate are tightly interwoven. To analyze them separately is to lose the complex meaning, and therefore the students' writings echoed much of the literature on learning as discussed here. Thus, the findings from the qualitative data strongly supported the findings drawn from the quantitative data: that engaging in specific workplace experiences uniquely produces learning in domains of interest.

After coding descriptions for 30 different positions, on the whole it was clear that they did not make much reference—explicit or implicit—to learning that might occur while working. While every job description did mention some form of task repetition, and a fair number indicated that the job would include some sort of formal training as well as feedback from a supervisor, explicit mention of opportunities for problem solving or leadership appeared only in a few of the higher-level, supervisory positions. Another interesting finding was that skills and competencies that could reasonably be classified as "responsible independence"—organizational skills, good attendance record, following unit protocols, etc.—were listed most often in prerequisite qualifications for attaining the job, as opposed to knowledge that could be learned from the job itself. Thus, it appeared that these position descriptions did not reasonably set the stage for student employees to learn while working, nor did they communicate to potential applicants the knowledge or skills they might obtain through certain positions throughout the organization.

Discussion

This study identified several areas where administrators who work with student employees could make positive changes to enhance student learning. A primary focus for improvement is communication between supervisors and students. Understanding where opinions differed has enabled administrators to develop plans to bridge those gaps, bringing expectations into greater alignment.

For example, in two key areas—the relative frequency of supervisor feedback and opportunities for congruence between a student's employment position and his or her curriculum—the students' perspectives differed sharply from those of their professional staff supervisors. Students reported a much higher level of supervisor feedback, and supervisors reported a much lower level of curricular congruence. This gap in expectations demonstrated a pressing need for administrators to better understand their employees' workplace experiences. This study suggests that these concrete experiences may affect meaningful learning outcomes in student employees.

Additionally, supervisors can audit and possibly rewrite student employee job descriptions, ensuring that each focuses on specific, concrete experiences that students may engage with through their employment and describes how each experience may translate into measurable growth and development. If learning is to be the core around which a successful student employment program operates (Keeling, 2004), then students and staff ought to be in agreement about what the job will entail from Day 1. A learning-centered job description also would communicate to the broader community and general public that staff members expect student employees' work to produce more than just a paycheck.

Administrators also should revisit their recognition and evaluation protocols to ensure they pair well with the revised job descriptions. Ideally, student employees are assessed, rewarded, and disciplined according to the expectations laid out for them when they accept the position. To that end, administrators will need to determine whether students are formally evaluated on learning outcomes or other job-related domains alongside traditional performance measures. (See Chapter 12 for more information.)

This section highlights how the organization being studied translated results identified through the study into a practical application with intentional and significant programmatic changes. Figure 3.1 offers a step-by-step approach to creating a student employment program based on learning outcomes. It also compares the previous student employment program to the new, comprehensive, and coherent student employment program.

FIGURE 3.1
A COMPREHENSIVE STUDENT EMPLOYMENT PROGRAM:
Norris University Center

Employment Program Categories	Old Program	New Program
Learning outcomes	N/A	Six identified outcomes & indicators
Student employment program philosophy	N/A	Theory- & learning-based philosophy
Performance evaluation	End-of-year management form	Learning assessment & management tool
		Assessment & management plan
Job descriptions	Task- & payroll-based	Learning- & functions-based
Recognition program	Customer service & action-focused	Six-dimensional & learning-focused

Organizational implications

Identified learning outcomes

From a basic analysis of the results, one could confidently assert that learning was occurring during the student employment experience. After careful consideration of the multitude of learning domains outlined by the CAS College Union Standard, the Division of Student Affairs learning domains, and the results of this study—and understanding the importance for congruence between all sets of information—the organization identified six learning outcomes expected of all student staff members: customer service, teamwork, autonomy, responsibility, leadership, and management. The last of these learning outcomes (management) was assessed only for student supervisors and managers. This more complex, postformal reasoning skill (Pascarella & Terenzini, 2005) includes resolving issues around multidimensional problems "for which there is likely to be conflicting or incomplete information, unspecified problem parameters, and a number of plausible solutions, none of which may be verifiably correct" (p. 160). Specific learning objectives for student supervisors and managers included reflective thinking, personal and peer management, and operations reporting.

Within each learning domain, a set of achievement indicators is explicitly outlined to provide students and staff with a more in-depth understanding of how mastery of an indicator might look. For example, the learning domain "leadership" is defined by five achievement indicators: risk-taking, goal orientation, collaboration, clarification of values, and empowerment. The achievement of "risk-taking" is defined by the following: "Demonstrates willingness to think creatively in order to improve quality. Takes risks and encourages evaluation of processes." The achievement of "clarification of values" is defined by the following: "Can articulate personal and professional values and belief systems. Sets the example for team and peers. Acts as a role model." These performance indicators or definitions would prove to be essential to various aspects of the new student employment program.

Student employment program philosophy

It has long been espoused that no institutional factor is more influential in directing identity, affiliation, tone, community characteristics, and purpose than an institution's mission and philosophy (Barr, 2000). Toward this end, "creating institutional conditions that encourage students to take advantage of learning and personal development opportunities must begin with clarifying institutional aims and translating these aims into appropriate expectations for student behavior" (Kuh, 2000, p. 53). Most, if not all, university departments have mission statements that clarify their role in providing student services and enhancing student development and learning. Similarly, university administrators leading student employment programs can follow this higher education protocol to guide day-to-day practices and make clear what employment experiences are attempting to accomplish.

With Astin's (1999) involvement theory as a theoretical framework, the following statement was used to guide the student employment philosophy toward a coherent, purposeful, and learning-centered end: "The extent to which students can achieve particular developmental goals is a direct function of the time and effort they devote to activities designed to produce these gains" (p. 522). In an attempt to find congruence between the uniquely academic focus of the university's mission and the Division of Student Affairs' priorities centering on complementing students' academic experiences, the organizational philosophy emphasizes how the six learning outcomes enhance the college experience for each student. Moreover, the organization commits to creating an integrated community of support and challenge (for student staff members) that helps foster a certain level of competence in the identified learning outcomes.

Learning assessment and management tool

To critically analyze the student employment program's effectiveness in helping students learn the six identified learning outcomes, a tool and method of measuring this effectiveness were needed.

More importantly, administrators wanted to quantify outcomes data by showing a relationship between a learning outcome (e.g., leadership, autonomy, and teamwork) and the various components of the employment program (e.g., formal and informal training, on-the-job experience, instructive feedback sessions, and performance reviews). It is important to note that within this paradigm the difference between research and assessment is clear: this measurement tool does not intend to demonstrate a research-based causation, correlation, or statistical significance (research); it is simply an effort to collect feedback from program participants/student staff members (assessment). Feedback collected from students, in turn, is used to guide changes in formal and informal training programs and to influence changes to the definitions of the achievement indicators, and could be used to add, remove, or edit the learning outcomes identified as specific to the organization.

It was determined that the best manner to assess a student's level of learning within the six outcomes would be to create a measurement tool that gathers both summative and formative information and quantitative and qualitative data. Explicit instructions for students are detailed on the measurement tool: students are asked, "To what extent have you learned each of these competencies/skills on the job?" On a five-point Likert scale (strongly agree, agree, neutral, disagree, strongly disagree), students assess their level of learning for each of the performance indicators followed by an overall rating of their level of learning for each of the learning outcomes. Furthermore, students are given an opportunity to provide qualitative comments (related directly to each learning outcome and related generally to their overall learning) that can add texture and levels of insight into each student's unique job experience—an aspect of the learning process that can be missed when only looking at quantitative data.

The organization recognized the importance not only assessing student learning but also of leadership in managing a large number of student employees. As a learning-centered department, administrators wanted "to provide students with the opportunity to reflect on their efforts to achieve success/learning and inspire them to construct meaning out of their work experience" (Lewis & Contreras, 2008, p. 33). Toward that end, the aforementioned learning assessment tool was intentionally designed to also act as a performance management tool for student staff and their supervisors.

The addition of a statement, directly under the student instructions, that directs supervisors to assess "to what extent has your student employee learned each of these competencies/skills on the job?" transformed this measurement tool from a single-purpose form (assessing student learning) into a dual-purpose learning assessment and management form. Utilizing this tool as the foundation for formal, performance-based evaluation sessions, the organization created a process by which (1) students reflected upon their learning and job performance, (2) supervisors reflected upon their students' progress toward accomplishing the learning outcomes and job performance components, and (3) student and supervisor came together to talk about their individual assessments, discuss discrepancies and/or consistencies, and set future goals for increased learning and performance. This dual-purpose learning and management tool has allowed students and supervisors to recognize that the learning outcomes identified in the student staff employment program philosophy (as outlined previously) are inherently the same performance measures by which students will be measured against throughout their employment.

Assessment and management plan

Both CAS (2003) and "Learning Reconsidered" (Keeling, 2004) describe university programs and services and cocurricular involvement—including participation in comprehensive student employment programs—as having the potential to develop and influence key student learning outcomes. Yet, without a clear and effective plan or process by which to collect assessment and performance management information, a student employment program would certainly fall short of living up to this potential. To create a comprehensive student employment program, an assessment and management plan or process needs to be established and could include the following:

- Established and agreed-upon learning outcomes or performance expectations.
- An understanding of what learning outcome or performance measure is being evaluated.
- An opportunity for self-evaluation and supervisor review.
- Regular and formal opportunities for communication between employee and supervisor.
- A climate that allows for developmentally supportive and challenging dialogue throughout the assessment or management process.

Following these guidelines, the organization was able to develop a year-long assessment and management plan and process that complemented the overall intent of the learning-centered student employment program.

- The newly established learning outcomes became the syllabus/employment program outline for students and staff managers.
- The newly defined achievement indicators clearly explain the performance measures to be evaluated. Additionally, these learning outcomes and achievement indicators were given to student staff supervisors and managers at the orientation training program.
- The dual-purpose measurement tool provided students the opportunity to self-evaluate and receive an evaluation review from their supervisor.
- The dual-purpose measurement was delivered on a pre-year, mid-year, and end-of-year basis for learning assessment purposes and delivered on a mid-year and end-of-year basis for performance management purposes.
- Thoughtful, safe, and ability-building conversations were established.

Put simply, "assessment should be used as a feedback loop to tell students how they are doing and where they need to continue to improve" (Fried, 2006, p. 7). Without this type of formal process, the learning opportunities for student employees and their supervisors to assess, reflect, and construct meaning out of their employment experiences do not exist.

Learning-focused job descriptions

Data analysis demonstrated a deficit in staff job descriptions, so the organization began writing learning-centered job descriptions that summarized general duties and essential functions, explained departmental organizational structure, and explained how specific job functions and skill sets translated into the six identified learning outcomes. Additionally, each job description begins with the student staff employment program philosophy so that students can connect the specific student employment experience to the larger context of learning. With these format changes, the departmental stakeholders (i.e., future and current student employees, clients, departmental professional staff, and student affairs partners) and students applying for positions are clear about how employment experiences translate into measurable growth and development, what the roles and expectations of students are, and what the job entails.

Learning-focused recognition program

While administrators envision a fully staffed, hard-working, and intrinsically motivated student workforce, it is understood that this may not be the case for exceptionally busy, highly stressed, and consistently tired students. To help combat some of this lack of motivation, a student employment program can include a recognition program that is fair, highly visible, and consistent. A purposeful student staff recognition program will explicitly outline what type of behavior/performance is expected, provide opportunities for students to attain a certain/higher level of performance, provide opportunities for staff and student peers to recognize behavior/performance, ensure that increased effort will result in private and public recognition (resulting in an increased occurrence of that effort/behavior), and administer rewards that are valued within the community.

To motivate, enhance, and reinforce learning, Northwestern's student staff recognition program was redesigned so that students being "caught in the act" for exemplary service were also being "caught in the act" for learning. The recognition program identifies six key areas for which students can be recognized or nominated: customer service, teamwork, autonomy, responsibility, leadership, and management. Upon witnessing actions, behaviors, or indicators of excellence in service or learning, customers, peers, supervisors, and administrators are asked to fill out a nomination form that lists the nominee, describes the act being recognized, and identifies of which six learning outcomes the act was an example. The nominee receives a "goodie bag" full of treats, a copy of the nomination form for his or her records, a physical representation of the achievement near the student employee time clock, and all students recognized in each of the six learning outcome areas are qualified to be nominated for the Employee of the Year award.

A recognition program centered on learning outcomes allows an organization's student employees to practice, observe, and recognize the highest level of service and the development of learning in others and, consequently, themselves. This minor adaptation in the recognition program has elevated the community into an organization that creates a work environment of shared success, commitment, and cooperative learning (Lewis & Contreras, 2008).

General implications

There is no question that the past decade in higher education and student affairs specifically has been shaped by greater accountability standards for explaining what students are learning while at college. Boards of trustees, regents, legislative and accreditation bodies, institutional presidents, professional associations, and the larger national conversation are providing no exemptions from this challenge (Keeling, 2004; Komives & Schoper, 2006). University administrators have historically demonstrated an active commitment to providing programs where students can explore, practice, and integrate classroom knowledge with real-life and out-of-class experiences—the primary tenet of cocurricular involvement (Braskamp et al., 2006). Likewise, administrators responsible for managing student employees have demonstrated an active commitment to personal and leadership development, interpersonal relations, and career skill building. A research component can become a focus to solidify and corroborate what administrators have always known: learning, indeed, takes places within higher education programs and services. As demonstrated in the current study, who better to tell the stories of learning than those who focus daily on the lives of undergraduate students?

The next call for action is for administrators to think, lead, and create in a transformative manner—transforming thought and person and transforming how student employment programs are led. By advancing the definition of leadership, a seamless learning environment can be created that supports the integration of curricular, extracurricular, and cocurricular experiences for students (Astin & Astin, 2000). The following implications and considerations align accordingly to this call for action:

1. To create seamless learning environments that integrate curricular and cocurricular realms of learning, administrators must define and identify themselves as educators. For some, being an educator means incorporating a new frame of reference, a new way of thinking, and a new way of working that involves a philosophical change in the interaction with and leadership of students, staff, peers, and faculty. This transformational change in mindset means purposefully identifying the knowledge and skill acquisition that occurs in student employment programs and engaging in and modeling the learning outcomes to be developed in students.

2. As educators, university administrators can utilize empirical research as the primary method by which to identify the learning embedded in student employment experiences. Workplace experiences for students who share a common purpose and the learning sparked from those experiences are tightly interwoven. As demonstrated in the study, student employees are able to identify specific experiences that contribute to knowledge acquisition. Within the framework of a controlled and empirical study, university educators can transform summative and formative data into meaningful practice and programs unique to their organizations.

3. Empirical studies such as this could be replicated and expanded upon to validate, enhance, or challenge the results of this study. Administrators might measure student learning in pre- and post-assessments, giving their students identical surveys at the beginning of the year and

again at the end. Collecting data points before student employees begin work and after they complete a full year could demonstrate concrete gains in learning. Similarly, it would be interesting to investigate student employees' learning in domains outside the bounds of this project, such as intra-/interpersonal competence, healthy living, and humanitarianism.

4. Transformative educators and empirical researchers should focus on the following strategic and appreciative approach when evaluating current student employment programs: appreciate and value the best of "what is" and "what works," envision "what might be," dialogue "what should be," and innovate "what will be" (Hammond, 1998). Initial stages of research development could focus on those aspects of our student employment programs that work, centering our empirical research to substantiate those practices, and transforming training programs, employment mission statements, recognition programs, and assessment and management plans to create organizational communities and cultures that support student learning. Administrators do not have to create a new paradigm of learning with research; rather they can simply validate their work by adding empirical evidence.

Conclusion

In many cases, student employment programs have been allowed to stagnate, which does not allow for the enhancement of student learning nor the opportunities for meaningful growth and development. Given present realities and pressures from key stakeholders, administrators who oversee student employee programs must ensure that they are focused on improving student learning.

Too often, assessment is done piecemeal, without any real direction as to why it is being conducted or plans to translate raw data into everyday practice (Upcraft & Schuh, 2000). Administrators may lack the knowledge, confidence, or experience to know how to begin an assessment project. Furthermore, even if they possess the skills needed, they may not have the large amounts of quiet and uninterrupted time to accomplish the task. However, university administrators are, indeed, in the best position to influence, impact, or effect change. The ideal is:

> … that theory, research on students, and their learning and assessment results will be used in immediate and direct action involving policies, programs, or practices. Translating theory, research, and assessment results directly to practice is easiest when the focus of the "action" is in an area for which the student affairs administrator has direct responsibility. (Desler, 2000, pp. 298–299)

Who better to assess student learning in cocurricular and work-related experiences than the administrators (entry-, mid-, or upper-level) responsible for the countless number of students working daily in higher education organizations?

In this study, research was used to determine the extent to which students and staff believe learning is taking place through student employment; understand workplace experiences' impact on reports of student learning; identify relationships between workplace experiences and student learning in established learning outcome areas; and integrate these findings into every aspect of student employees' experience, from application to graduation.

There are many tools available to help administrators in the beginning stages of research. For example, higher education researchers Pascarella and Terenzini (2005) have identified methods by which student employment programs can have a critical impact on student development (see Chapter 2 for more detail), and professional organizations have coalesced around key learning outcomes. Supplemented with a review of the relevant literature, a collection of student and staff experiences and reflections, and a reference to values-laden artifacts such as mission and vision statements, administrators can design and recommend program improvements that would effectively speak to the specific needs of their unit or institution.

Improvements that flow from this sort of effective research will serve both the learning needs of student employees and the performance objectives of unit managers. In the end, a workplace that is rigorous both in gathering data and in helping students learn will find before long it has fostered the seamless learning environment toward which faculty and administrators aspire.

References

American Association for Higher Education, American College Personnel Association, & National Association of Student Personnel Administrators. (1998, June). *Powerful partnerships: A shared responsibility for learning.* Washington, DC: Authors.

Astin, A. (1999). Student involvement: A developmental theory for higher education. *Journal of College Student Development, 40*(5), 518–529.

Astin, A., & Astin, H. (2000). *Learning reconsidered: Engaging higher education in social change.* Battle Creek, MI: W.K. Kellogg Foundation.

Barr, M.J. (2000). The importance of the institutional mission. In M. Barr & M. Desler (Eds.), *The handbook of student affairs administration* (pp. 25–49). San Francisco: Jossey-Bass.

Braskamp, L.A., Trautvetter, L.C. & Ward, K. (2006). *Putting students first: How colleges develop students purposefully.* Bolton, MA: Anker Publishing.

Brown, J.S., Collins, A., & Duguid, P. (1989, January-February). Situated cognition and the culture of learning. *Educational Researcher, 18*(1), 32–42.

Council for the Advancement of Standards in Higher Education. (2003). *The book of professional standards for higher education 2003.* Washington, DC: Authors.

Desler, M. (2000). Translating theory and assessment results to practice. In M. Barr & M. Desler (Eds.), *The handbook of student affairs administration* (pp. 285–310). San Francisco: Jossey-Bass.

Hammond, S.A. (1998). The thin book of appreciative inquiry. Plano, TX: Thin Book Publishing.

Fried, J. (2006). Rethinking learning. In R.P. Keeling (Ed.), *Learning reconsidered 2: A practical guide to implementing a campus-wide focus on the student experiences* (pp. 3–9). Washington, DC: ACPA, ACUHO-I, ACUI, NACA, NACADA, NASPA, NIRSA.

Keeling, R.P. (Ed). (2004). *Learning reconsidered: A campus-wide focus on the student experience.* Washington, DC: ACPA, NASPA.

Kolb, D.A. (1984). *Experiential learning: Experience as the source of learning and development.* Englewood Cliffs, NJ: Prentice-Hall.

Komives, S.R., & Schoper, S. (2006). Developing learning outcomes. In R.P. Keeling (Ed.), *Learning reconsidered 2: A practical guide to implementing a campus-wide focus on the student experiences* (pp. 17–41). Washington, DC: ACPA, ACUHO-I, ACUI, NACA, NACADA, NASPA, NIRSA.

Kuh, G. (2000). Understanding campus environments. In M. Barr & M. Desler (Eds.), *The handbook of student affairs administration* (pp. 50–72). San Francisco: Jossey-Bass.

Lewis, J. (2007). *Student employment and learning.* Unpublished master's thesis. Northwestern University.

Lewis, J., & Contreras, S., Jr. (2005). *Student learning outcomes project.* Evanston, IL: Northwestern University.

Lewis, J.S., & Contreras, S. (2008, January). Research and practice: Connecting student employment and learning. *The Bulletin of the Association of College Unions International, 76*(1), 30–38.

Northwestern University. (2007). Northwestern facts. Retrieved April 15, 2007 from http://www.northwestern.edu/about/facts

Pascarella, E.T., & Terenzini, P.T. (2005). *How college affects students: A third decade of research* (Vol. 2). San Francisco: Jossey-Bass.

Upcraft, M.L. & Schuh, J.H. (2000). Assessment in student affairs. In M. Barr & M. Desler (Eds.), *The handbook of student affairs administration* (pp. 249–264). San Francisco: Jossey-Bass.

Vygotsky, L.S. (1978). *Mind in society: The development of higher psychological processes.* Cambridge, MA: Harvard University Press.

Wenger, E. (2004, January). Communities of practice: A brief introduction. *Ivey Business Journal,* 1–7.

LEARNING OUTCOMES AND STUDENT EMPLOYMENT PROGRAMS

by Brett Perozzi, Janelle Kappes, & Deborah Santucci

A climate of budget restrictions, increased accountability demands by legislators, and heightened accreditation standards in higher education has created the need for quality assessment initiatives, particularly in the form of student learning outcomes. Student learning outcomes are defined as outcomes that exemplify learning (Bresciani, 2003). Outcomes assessment helps determine how well organizations have met their goals; it is central to organizational development and effectiveness (Wagenaar, 2002). One of the primary purposes of assessing student learning outcomes is to provide institutions with feedback that they can use to improve educational quality.

Student employment composes a growing sector of the educational experience. Although approximately 80 percent of all college students are employed while completing their baccalaureate degree, there is considerable inconsistency in the literature regarding the impact of work on the overall college experience (Riggert, Boyle, Petrosko, Ash, & Rude-Parkins, 2006). Given the complexities of student employment, a learning outcomes approach can provide a better understanding of this experience and its impact on student learning. Learning outcomes are particularly relevant in evaluating the effectiveness of student employment because they allow the evaluator to align program goals with outcomes.

For outcomes to be achieved, whether in the student employment context or at the institutional level, there must be a clear definition of the skill or competency to be acquired, assessment tools to measure the attainment of the skill, and measurement or documentation that reports the extent to which the skill has been acquired (Friedlander & Serban, 2004). An example of a learning outcome in the student employment context might be that "students will increase their critical thinking skills as a result of working as a resident advisor as measured by a pre- and post-test instrument administered at the beginning and end of their employment." Another example could be that "students will enhance their interpersonal communication skills through working as a fitness instructor at the recreation center as demonstrated by periodic peer evaluations."

This chapter addresses how learning outcomes can be developed and implemented into student employment contexts. It reviews commonly recognized sources for student learning outcomes, including accrediting associations, higher education institutions, professional associations, and scholarly research and literature. This chapter also discusses the process of identifying learning outcomes and ensuring the outcomes are appropriate for a particular context. Once learning outcomes are successfully identified, they must be "taught" and subsequently evaluated; therefore, the final section of this chapter is comprised of a brief methodology for potentially teaching and measuring learning outcomes.

Deriving student learning outcomes

Deriving student learning outcomes can be a challenging and tedious process. However, there are a variety of institutions, agencies, and resources available to assist institutions in the creation of these outcomes. Accreditation agencies, professional associations, individual higher education institutions, and scholarly literature and research are four recognized and accessible resources for institutions and individuals seeking guidance in developing and implementing learning outcomes.

Accrediting agencies

Accrediting associations are responsible for holding institutions accountable not only to students in higher education but also to the public and increasingly the federal government. Accrediting agencies have recast the meaning of institutional effectiveness to require that institutions' assessment efforts include the measurement of student learning outcomes (Beno, 2004). In 2001, the eight regional accrediting associations conducted a collaborative research study on the use of learning outcomes in accreditation, which furthered each accrediting association's commitment to using outcomes in the accreditation process (Beno, 2004).

Given that the majority of the regional accrediting agencies have recently altered their standards to incorporate student learning outcomes, these agencies hold a wealth of samples for interested institutions. In addition, these agencies frequently host workshops and institutes concerning outcomes assessment in higher education. For example, the Middle States Commission on Higher Education hosts a range of workshops related to assessment for both institutions just embarking on assessment initiatives and those institutions that are advanced in evaluation and assessment. Similarly, the North Central Association of Colleges and Schools offers two-day workshops that focus on building shared responsibility and an institutional culture for a student-learning assessment model.

Professional associations

Professional associations and external partners in higher education also provide resources for divisions, colleges, and departments that are implementing student learning outcomes. For the past several years, the American Association for Higher Education has offered workshops that pair experienced practitioners with institutional teams that are just beginning the development and design of learning outcomes. External partners such as American College Testing, Noel-Levitz, the National Survey of Student Engagement, and the Higher Education Research Institute are available to assist institutions with the assessment process as a whole—such as choosing a sample population, administering surveys, conducting analyses, and providing a results summary (Bresciani, 2003). Additionally, the Council for the Advancement of Standards has numerous presentations, consultants, and resources available to assist campuses; it also offers its Frameworks for Assessing Learning and Development Outcomes.

Individual institutions

In addition to accrediting agencies and professional associations, individual colleges and universities have an abundance of information on student learning outcomes. The learning outcomes movement is occurring in institutions across North America, and several institutions have spent years exploring, documenting, and publishing articles concerning outcomes on their campus. Alverno College in Wisconsin, for example, is perhaps the most well-known institution for its commitment to student learning outcomes. The Alverno College Educational Research and Evaluation Office has been conducting ongoing research on learning outcomes since 1976. In addition to its numerous studies on this topic, Alverno College has published its findings, most notably in the award-winning publication "Learning that Lasts: Integrating Learning, Development, and Performance in College and Beyond" (Jossey-Bass, 2000).

Another example of a higher education institution committed to quality assessment and student learning outcomes is California State University, Monterey Bay. "California State University, Monterey Bay, a relatively new institution, was designed to provide institutional processes that ensure adequate feedback from assessment of student learning outcomes to institutional processes for decision making" (Beno, 2004, p. 70). The learning outcomes are thoroughly integrated into each academic unit. For instance, the Division of Social, Behavioral, and Global Studies created a set of learning outcomes that students must demonstrate to graduate. Further, the institution has integrated learning outcomes into the overall graduation structure, requiring each student to demonstrate mastery though a set of "graduation learning outcomes."

Two-year institutions are engaged in learning outcomes assessment as well. The staff at Mesa Community College in Mesa, Ariz., designed an approach to assess outcomes and utilized this research to improve curriculum, instruction, and learning (Beno, 2004). In fact, Mesa Community College was awarded the Council for Higher Education Accreditation Award for Progress in Student Learning Outcomes.

As institutions move through the learning outcomes process, the development of an assessment tool to measure the learning outcomes will undoubtedly arise. Rose-Hulman Institute of Technology in Indiana developed such a tool to determine whether a specific learning outcome is covered within a course and the degree to which the outcome is covered (Beno, 2004). This institution also has been awarded the Council for Higher Education Accreditation Award for Progress in Student Learning Outcomes.

Individual institutions are excellent resources for not only sample student learning outcomes but also sample measurement and grading tools. Reviewing or visiting other institutions can provide information about the committee or structure in which the learning outcomes were derived and measured, as well as the strategies for garnering buy-in for student learning outcomes from key stakeholders. When reviewing learning outcomes at various institutions, it will be useful to consider the type of institution that is most appropriate and the "best fit" for the need. Size, mission, geographic location, history, and the age of the institution will likely affect the institution's learning outcomes to some extent. Learning outcomes can generally be found in institutional missions or visions or through the institution's assessment office. Many single institution examples are included throughout the chapters in this book, which can serve as a point of identification for various applications.

Literature and research

Current scholarly literature on student learning outcomes can provide further insight as well. Arguably the most well-known sources on this subject are "Learning Reconsidered: A Campus-Wide Focus on the Student Experience" (Keeling, 2004) and "Learning Reconsidered 2: Implementing a Campus-Wide Focus on the Student Experience" (Keeling, 2006). "Learning Reconsidered 2," in particular, provides powerful insights regarding the creation of dialogue around institution-wide assessment and learning outcomes, as well as how to implement a learning outcomes model. The "Learning Reconsidered" movement has generated numerous workshops, learning institutes, conference sessions, and even its own website, *http://www.learningreconsidered.org*.

In addition to "Learning Reconsidered," there are peer-reviewed, refereed journals that frequently contain research articles related to assessment and learning outcomes. In addition to some that are fairly common and/or mainstream, such as *The NASPA Journal, Journal of College Student Development*, and *About Campus*, there are a number of other regularly published journals. *Assessment and Evaluation in Higher Education* is an international journal that publishes on all aspects of assessment and evaluation within higher education. *Studies in Educational Evaluation* publishes original reports concerning evaluation and assessment in educational systems around the world. Finally, the *Review of Higher Education* journal publishes a broad spectrum of articles and research findings related to critical issues affecting higher education. These six publications—in addition to others often affiliated with professional associations—offer accessible, up-to-date information about a variety of issues facing higher education, including assessment, and provide a vehicle for sharing new and innovative practices.

Finalizing outcomes

Student affairs professionals are increasingly required to supply direct and indirect evidence that their programmatic initiatives are having an effect on student learning. Given the abundance of resources, how does an institution identify and select learning outcomes appropriate for its student employment context? Undergoing an evaluation of the organization using a few criteria as guides is a good way to begin. Looking critically at an organization and evaluating or making initial determinations about a variety of organizational characteristics is a solid first step toward an outcomes-focused approach.

There are four primary areas for self-reflection when beginning the process of developing learning outcomes for student employees or a student employment program. First, it is essential to go into the identification process understanding the learning outcomes' intended use within the unit or organization. This concept is tied to the basic assessment notion of measuring outcomes or capturing data that are meaningful to the organization, not what is convenient or readily lends itself to measurement. Second, the organization must determine the scope or breadth of use of the student learning outcomes. For example, development of learning outcomes for one or two student employees will be far more specific than learning outcomes that are construed to encompass an entire college or large department. Additionally, the organization may want to consider the overall timeline as well as potential milestones to reach along the way. Third, decisions need to be made about how the organization will embrace or implement a final selection of outcomes. If the employment program spans one large department, will the department use the college's or division's outcomes or will it develop its own set? If so, will those locally developed learning outcomes be aligned with the college/division and the overall educational institution? Fourth, the organization will want to map out a process for outcomes development that keeps in mind the key stakeholders and constituents who need to be involved in the process.

What's next?

The final two areas to be embraced prior to implementation are how the selected learning outcomes will be taught to student employees and how the outcomes will ultimately be measured. Having these questions satisfied before the process is underway will provide a solid roadmap and set of criteria to guide the implementation process.

Intended use of student learning outcomes

Why is the organization beginning a process to develop student learning outcomes? Is the organization interested in providing more succinct position descriptions, or attempting to align student jobs across position types or across an organization? Is it desirable to provide sequencing within positions or units so that students have a progression for which to strive? Is this an effort to demonstrate the centrality of the organization to the core of the institution by making student learning outcomes more evident in the employment arena? These and many other questions can be relevant to the self-evaluation process about the intended use of learning outcomes in a specific employment situation.

Faculty, student affairs staff, and central administrators are all working toward the same goals of student learning around basic concepts highlighted in other chapters of this book, such as critical thinking, problem solving, and communication skills. The creation of overt student learning outcomes within the employment setting enables an organization to demonstrate common goals among various facets of the academy. Is the organization hoping to improve alignment with the institution's academic mission by creating and implementing learning outcomes in the student work environment? Is the organization interested in providing students with a solid work experience that will assist them into the future by teaching specific skills, imparting valuable knowledge, or offering specific post-graduation training? Learning outcomes that are in concert with students' desired or current majors can assist in the exploration of potential career paths and may pay dividends for them if the program architects are attuned with the current realities of career skills and knowledge in specific fields. Student learning outcomes are an end product around which all members of the academy can rally, be they biology, business, or bursar. Employment crosses many higher education sectors, and having a solid understanding of how the learning outcomes will be used in a particular setting can help guide the implementation and, more importantly, sustain the effort over time.

The development of learning outcomes for student employees also can create a research- and theory-based approach to growth and progression for students. Intentionally identifying outcomes that are derived from or directly relate to student development theory can provide a context for development that can be shared with students and their supervisors. (See Chapter 1 for more information.)

Finally, are learning outcomes being implemented to demonstrate the employment program's value? Does the organization desire to be seen as essential in the learning process and is there a need to show that? Or, is this a way to reveal student employment's value by codifying what has been observed over time? Indeed, both research and anecdotal information has shown for many years that student employment affects student development during college (Perozzi, Rainey, & Wahlquist, 2003).

Scope

Another major step in the development of a learning outcomes model for employment is determining the project's scope. Be cautious to begin at an appropriate level for the organization. Schuh (2009) warns that when assessment projects attempt to accomplish a number of objectives, including "measuring the student learning outcomes of all the experiences and activities in a single year, it is likely that the process will not get off the ground" (p. 10). Characteristics of student employees will vary significantly based on a number of institutional variables, such as enrollment, on-campus population, and organizational structure. For example, an office of multicultural student services at a small, residential college may have just one front desk or office assistant, whereas the health and wellness operation at that same college may have 12 peer educators. Similarly, large universities may employ hundreds of students in the college union, dining services, residential life, etc., and determinations about inclusion in the program can be critical. In addition, departments that fall within the division of student affairs (or business affairs or auxiliary services) often employ large numbers of students (for example, those mentioned previously and campus recreation, orientation, and bookstores). These areas are ripe for review when assessing the intended project's scope. Some organizations may have fewer student employees given the nature of their work and/or the sensitivity of the information available, such as counseling centers, dean of students offices, and academic departments, which typically have lean administrative structures.

So, what is the "unit of analysis?" Is the organization defined as the institution, division, college, department, unit, or program? And, which student employees are most logical for inclusion? Situations will vary and may depend on existing programs or portions of programs currently in place in the primary organization or elsewhere on the campus.

The entity initiating the project will likely dictate the scope to a large extent. For example, if the chemistry department is interested in developing and implementing a student learning outcomes program, it may consider its own student employees before considering whether students in a related subject area could benefit from participation. The scope does not need to be discipline- or department-specific, as synergies may exist given location, existing partnerships, employment experience, etc. However, one should consider which key individuals are needed to ensure the program's success and continuation.

Student participation

A major step in the planning process is actually determining which student employees will be included in the program. While this seems like a simple concept, it can actually be quite confounding. For example, many students in leadership roles, such as president of the nursing club or president of the student government, receive paid stipends for the work they perform and the time they dedicate to their leadership roles. Does this deem them student employees? The construction of "student employment" will vary from organization to organization. In a unit that deals primarily with "paid student volunteers," such as a college union program board, it might make sense to include all paid student leaders as student employees. In other situations, such as a student government unit, there are likely to be both paid volunteers as well as students who earn an hourly wage for their work. There can be further complications when those in traditional volunteer positions are paid an hourly wage, which may or may not accurately reflect the number of hours they spend working (as opposed to an annual, semester, monthly, or weekly stipend). Such situations can potentially cloud distinctions between student employee classifications. A clear set of criteria may be necessary to differentiate between various employee types. An organization may decide that all students receiving any type of university compensation will be included, yet in some circumstances—for example, if an organization has dozens or hundreds of student employees—some distinction may need to be made. A new program, for instance, may desire to begin with a smaller number of employees before expanding to include additional student employment types, other units, and various departments.

Arizona State University (ASU) provides an example of managing scope and collaboration. The learning outcomes-based student employment program began in the Student Development and Memorial Union department. The ASU union already had a collaborative training program with the campus recreation department. The union began developing the learning outcome component of the employment program and determined which student employees would be initially included. The inclusion of all paid students would have been more than 200 employees; therefore, decisions were made to pilot the program with only students who reported to a supervisor as opposed to those who "reported to" an advisor. The goal of this decision was to keep the program manageable initially and to provide a solid model for future scalability. As a result of the decision, student government and program board leaders who received university stipends were eliminated from the outcomes-focused cohort. The training programs continued as they had, although they were modified to better address the student learning outcomes. The campus recreation department continued to partner with the training program and waited until implementation had taken place before deciding whether to join in the full learning outcome effort.

One final aspect regarding the scope of an outcomes-based student employment program is to determine the current state of any existing program(s). If a program for student employees already exists, augmenting the program to include learning outcomes may require fewer organizational resources than a situation in which a somewhat comprehensive program has not yet been established. An established program would already have training in place for students (see Chapter 11), assessment measures being used (see Chapter 12), and pay and equity balances in check (see Chapter 10). These factors should be contemplated and will determine whether an existing program will be augmented or if the organization is essentially creating a new employment program. These factors also will influence the timeframe used to accomplish the program's implementation.

An agreed-upon timeline for implementation can be helpful for all involved in the employment program, yet this can present challenges in itself. An outcomes-based program is front-loaded with critical determinations and evaluation that must occur prior to implementation as well as research, staff training, development of measurement tools, student training design, etc. A careful consideration of the essential elements and consistent reviews of timeline drafts can help ensure a smooth process from planning to assessment.

Distribution

After the scope is determined, an organization will want to work through how the learning outcomes will be adopted and used with the intended population of student employees. For example, to what areas of the program will the learning outcomes be applied and from where will they be derived? Will each individual student employee have his or her own set of learning outcomes? Will each position or position type embrace one or more learning outcomes? Or is there a set of learning outcomes from which supervisors and managers can choose? While the development process (discussed next) may seem straightforward enough, the actual use and implementation of specific outcomes can pose philosophical challenges for the organization.

If student learning outcomes are identified for an entire institution, will those be specific enough to address the needs and responsibilities of student employees in one unit? Has the college or division identified learning outcomes, and are those sufficiently explicit for the intended use? It may make sense for an organization undertaking the task of outcomes implementation in the employment area to carefully review the outcomes available from the sources presented at the beginning of this chapter and determine how those outcomes will be modified/adapted or used directly for the intended purpose. They must be written at the appropriate level for their intended use (Maki, 2004).

Further, determinations should be made prior to implementation about the number of learning outcomes to be embraced. For example, a division or college may choose to implement or focus on just one primary learning outcome across all departments. Yet, employment opportunities often allow students the ability to develop more than one high-level skill through both the normal course of their work as well as through the intentional training programs (discussed later). Another option would be for a college, division, or department to develop a meaningful and appropriate set of learning outcomes from which departments or units within the entity can choose. For example, if a student affairs division has created a set of eight learning outcomes, it could be possible for a department within the division to embrace one, several, or all of those outcomes.

If the employment program effort is driven divisionally or at the college level, the possibilities and permutations are many. Departments could be allowed to choose from the full array, asked to incorporate all outcomes across various employment categories and types, or asked to embrace different outcomes (in an attempt to cover all of them within the division/college). Alternatively, they could be assigned learning outcomes. The most germane student learning outcomes to that employment area can be allowed to emerge from the students or those working most closely with the positions' daily operations or functions.

Five Strategies for Writing Learning Outcomes:

1. **Use existing mission statements to extract meaningful organizational information and core concepts and values.**

2. **Review and adapt outcomes presented by professional organizations.**

3. **Examine student work and use an iterative process to build and challenge consensus.**

4. **Richly describe outcomes through the use of an epistemological and ethnographic process.**

5. **Explore the full continuum of learning from surface to deep learning approaches.**

Adapted from Maki (2004)

Sample Employment Teams

Keep them as small as possible while representing all key areas.

Career Services
Career Services assistant director*
Supervisor (staff)*
Supervisor (staff)
Student employee*
Employer (partner company)

College Union
Union director*
Graduate assistant for assessment*
Student employee
Operations supervisor (staff)*
Programs supervisor (staff)
Faculty member

* Core team members

Processes for determining student learning outcomes

Actually creating or determining learning outcomes for the organization may come after a group of individuals becomes familiar with learning outcomes in general, reviews the literature and resources available, and gains a solid understanding of their context within higher education and the employment arena. This same group may work through the outcomes' intended use, scope, and distribution. Next, it would be time to actually select the learning outcomes for the unit.

The selection or appointment of a team to guide the process will vary significantly by institution type, level of analysis (e.g., university-wide, college/division, program), and other factors. The most important aspect of the team is to involve critical stakeholders in the process, especially those who may be working with students and front-line supervisors to modify position descriptions, implement training, and evaluate progress. An inherent conundrum in this process is reminiscent of the classic "chicken or egg" dilemma. Many of the decisions that need to be made prior to the program's implementation should be embraced by the committee, yet the decisions themselves dictate who should be on the committee. It could be helpful for a smaller core group to make some preliminary decisions prior to expanding the group.

Two primary methodologies can be employed for the development of student learning outcomes: a literature- and research-based identification process or an organic, emergent process. In the former process, literature, research, accrediting agencies, and other legitimate and credible sources are sought to seek alignment with the organization and these resources. For example, many student affairs divisions have a natural alignment and affinity with "Learning Reconsidered" (Keeling, 2004) and "Learning Reconsidered 2" (Keeling, 2006). This is certainly appropriate and can work well in terms of administrative needs and the ability to tie the process to existing literature. And, associating college employment with existing research can help raise the awareness and legitimacy of the process as it relates to student development and learning during college.

The second methodological approach is to go to units within the identified organization and seek the learning that is taught or required by students in their various positions. This might mean attending staff meetings, talking with students and staff in that department, reviewing position descriptions, and learning about any training that is currently offered. While not specifically targeted at student employment, this approach was implemented at Weber State University, where student affairs staff members were asked to write technical learning outcomes based on their work with students. The emergent student learning outcomes were categorized and codified through an extensive and iterative process and eventually became the backbone of the divisional learning outcomes.

It also is possible to blend these two methodologies. This was the process several departments at Arizona State University utilized. The process began in a similar manner as the Weber State example, but the learning outcomes were being identified across a few departments rather than an entire division. Information was gathered from directors, supervisors, and students through a process that included focus groups, one-on-one meetings, staff meeting attendance, and e-mail solicitations. The data were gathered centrally and codified into color-coded spreadsheets and "themeatized." The resulting matrix was then provided to the employees, supervisors, and managers to more specifically hone in on the learning outcomes most closely aligned with their employment opportunities. Upon that process's completion, the most salient student learning outcomes were selected as the primary or core outcomes that were applied across all areas. Each individual employment area also retained a few learning outcomes unique to its unit. The team working on the process then returned to the literature after these emergent outcomes were identified to ascertain whether the organically identified student learning outcomes corresponded with those presented in the literature. Ultimately, macro categories were developed that aligned with those from "Learning Reconsidered 2" (Keeling, 2006) and subcategories retained the specific concepts that emerged from the departments participating in the process.

Often the development of learning outcomes happens in an uncoordinated manner. There are well-meaning faculty and staff who are working with learning outcomes, students, and programs, and the concepts either evolve naturally or are intentionally embraced. These naturally occurring instances can be capitalized on and synergy sought among the units. Rather than competing, units can learn from one another and gain collective experience and wisdom based on the work completed to that point. Because student learning outcomes are becoming mainstream throughout the academy, this will be happening more and more, where various entities throughout the college or university will be working on their own process or program. The unique aspect of this book is the focus on student employment. How can existing or developing student learning outcome concepts be adapted and implemented into the college student work environment? It is possible to capitalize on the positive work already taking place, modify current thinking and/or conceptions, and embrace appropriate learning outcomes for the benefit of student employees.

"Teaching" student learning outcomes

There may be an expectation in student work roles that the employees will gain skills and knowledge as a result of their everyday work. While that may be the case to some extent, educational institutions are obligated to ensure employees are appropriately trained and have access to the resources to acquire the knowledge expected (see Chapter 11). Just as faculty members would not expect students to learn just by attending class, employment roles and learning outcomes need to be presented and available to student employees. Therefore, it is incumbent upon all educators to provide training that is specific to the targeted student learning outcomes within each employment environment, as enhancing student success is a central tenet of all educational institutions (Manning, Kinzie, & Schuh, 2006).

Tying to the previous example, Arizona State University used a preexisting student training program in which staff across several departments agreed to modify the content so that learning outcomes could be specifically addressed during each training session. Learning outcomes can be incorporated into the employment landscape in multiple ways. Job descriptions for student employees can be rewritten to enhance interaction with student learning outcomes (Lewis & Contreras, 2008). For example, a tour guide or student ambassador may align a public speaking role with a public speaking learning outcome embedded in the position description.

The primary method of teaching learning outcomes to student employees is through consistent and required professional development programs. The programs will ideally be designed using an experiential learning pedagogy. Tailoring the content to the learning outcomes streamlines the programs yet can create some difficulty in finding appropriate persons to deliver the content in its relatively specific format. Manning, Kinzie, and Schuh's (2006) literature review concluded that several institutional conditions support student success, three of which are ongoing application of learned skills, learning-centered pedagogy, and active learning.

At Arizona State University, an existing student employee professional development program, Student Employees Learning, Experiencing, and Communicating Together (SELECT), was reinvented. The program emphasizes employee training based on three student learning outcomes developed through an extensive process that ultimately aligned with combined outcome categories included in "Learning Reconsidered 2" (Keeling, 2006): practical competence, interpersonal and intrapersonal competence, and civic engagement and humanitarianism. This program has three-and-one-half hour training programs each semester provided for student employees, each focusing on one of the learning outcomes. The program outlines for each of three SELECT trainings are briefly explained in the following section.

SELECT I: Practical competence

Student employees will be able to enhance their practical competence skills through a series of interactive, experiential learning-based activities. First, university professionals present briefly on the following subjects: budgeting, time management, ethical decision making, campus resources, and career exploration. Presenters also distribute resources that students can use to increase their knowledge of the respective skill. For example, students will be given links to track their personal spending and career guides to help them write cover letters and resumes.

After the presentations, student employees are divided into groups and charged with the task of solving a case study. Students in the budgeting group are given a scenario in which a student has a $512 monthly budget. The students then prepare a budget including rent, transportation, insurance, food, and other expenses. The second scenario outlines a fictional student's weekly schedule. The students are given a list of fictional commitments such as a class schedule, student organizations, internships, study time, meals, socializing, and physical fitness. The group is charged with the task of creating a weekly schedule for the fictional student. The third case study allows students to practice ethical decision making. The group is given a list of various scenarios, and they are to review the scenarios, decide their course of action, and provide justification for their decisions. The fourth case study exposes students to campus resources through a fictional story of a distressed student. The fictional student is experiencing trouble adjusting to college life, has trouble finding friends, and is not maintaining a healthy lifestyle. The group is charged with the task of developing a plan to point the student to campus resources that may assist the distressed student. The final case study focuses on career exploration. The group is provided with the beginning of a resume. The resume lists a student's degree, previous jobs, and awards. The group is charged with the task of creating a resume for the fictional student. Also, the group is asked to brainstorm and list ideas for the types of internships that the fictional student may qualify for or desire. Once all groups are done working through their case studies, they present their findings to the entire group, allowing them to practice their public speaking skills.

SELECT II: Interpersonal and intrapersonal competence

The second SELECT program focuses on activities aimed to improve student employees' leadership and teamwork skills. For this training program, the committee partners with the university's recreation center to deliver the content. The recreation center creates team workshops fostering healthy communication. Students are divided into two groups and charged with the task of building a bridge with limited materials. Throughout the session, students encounter roadblocks and have to work as a team to overcome the challenges. Once these activities are complete, a staff member leads a group discussion about how the student employees learned to overcome these challenges. The staff member then asks the student employees to reflect on how this activity relates to their current position, to their coursework, and to their career development. Student employees learn about their own leadership styles, how to improve their communication, and how to work effectively as a team.

SELECT III: Civic engagement and humanitarianism

The final SELECT program aims to allow students to gain leadership experiences and give back to the community. This program is designed to provide students with a general outline for completing a community service project rather than actually completing one during the session. The community service plan was to create entertainment packages for the troops overseas. The committee set certain guidelines that student employees had to follow, but it was up to the student employees to decide how the project would be implemented. The student employees were asked to decide where to collect donation items, how to advertise the project, when to end the project, and how to collect and send the items. This project ensured that students had the opportunity to engage in a leadership role, work as a team, and become engaged in a community service project.

Measuring student learning outcomes

The measurement of learning outcomes can be among a student employment program's most difficult aspects. Chapter 12 provides a full accounting of available methodologies and specific methods, so here the focus is on the process's organization, particularly in regard to staff responsibilities. Direct supervisors of students, and in some organizations the staff responsible for the full program, have a significant role in ensuring that the program moves forward with student development at both the core and leading edge of the effort.

An effective and proven method for measuring value added is to employ a pre- and post-test of student workers (Suskie, 2004). Significant staff effort is needed to create the tool, administer the pre-test, and especially have students complete a post-test when they leave employment. Subtle issues come into play particularly in terms of how to administer the test and when to conduct the testing. An ideal implementation method is to develop a web-based interface that can both administer and archive the results based on a student identification number. If the testing is computer-based, students can take the pre-test as part of their normal training process. The pre-test can be administered at the initial intake meeting with new students, at the first staff meeting, or during some sort of an orientation/training program. A more difficult situation is ensuring students complete a post-test when they leave employment. Since part of a high-quality student employment program provides a "ladder" for students to climb as they gain skills and responsibility, the question arises about when students should take the post-test. Is it at the end of their employment with the organization or when they complete their employment in that specific job or job category? This question is up to each organization; however, it may be preferable to decide this on the front end so that all testing is completed in the same manner.

Self-reported data are frequently not as reliable as other forms of data. Therefore, a pre- and post-test method can employ general questions about knowledge and skills in particular areas as they relate to the chosen learning outcomes and also present students with case studies or scenarios that are designed to elicit responses related to the learning outcomes. For example, at Arizona State University, the second half of the pre- and post-tests consist of several work-related scenarios that are designed to draw out a level of performance around one of the three primary learning outcome areas. The pre- and post-test scenarios are different scenarios, but crafted to measure the same outcome.

This two-part pre- and post-test gets back to staff involvement. Not only do staff members have to be sure the tests are administered in a logical and practical way to match the results, they must also be involved with evaluating the responses. Developing and employing a rubric to help determine the quality and/or extent of the progress or development will necessitate trained staff involvement. Making judgments about quality and success take significant amounts of staff time in discussion and education. And actually scoring responses requires considerable coordination and time, especially to attain a high level of inter-rater reliability.

Results of student employees' pre- and post-tests can only be used as a thumbnail sketch, unless they are administered and analyzed in a scientific way so that variables can be statistically controlled to provide a more accurate accounting of how and to what degree certain skills and/or knowledge was acquired. In other words, were these skills/knowledge acquired as a result of the employment situation or through natural maturation and development? A control group of students can be sampled to help provide greater accuracy and accountability along these lines.

Utilizing the regular review or evaluation process can be an important way to obtain another measure of student growth along the outcomes the organization selected. There is significant discussion about the measurement of student learning outcomes in the work environment alongside the measurement of more traditional factors of employment such as promptness, customer service, presentability, etc. The question remains whether it is the student's responsibility to learn, know, or value the content of the learning outcome or the organization's responsibility to teach or ensure that the employee acquires the desired outcome. In either case, staff must be integrally involved with the development or modification of regular evaluations and must have input on how often they are conducted and in what manner.

An implementation plan

It is virtually a universal concept for higher education institutions to employ students. Most colleges and universities are not inventing a set of employment opportunities. However, they may be taking what currently exists and forming a program or set of concepts and values that work together to define or provide boundaries, direction, etc., for an organization or collection of student employees. Given this, it is likely that faculty and staff will be augmenting or modifying concepts, policies, or practices already in place at the institution. With this context as a backdrop, this section offers brief suggestions about moving through the development and implementation of an employment program focused on learning outcomes.

It is best to gather a core group of students, staff, and others who directly affect employment positions (see also the previous discussion about an initial, core group with the eventual expansion of the group). Be selective so that the group is not too unwieldy, yet represents the cross-section necessary for inclusive involvement. Ideally the team will have a champion, preferably someone empowered organizationally to make decisions and direct resources to the program. This person's ability to influence top officials in terms of assessment will be helpful, especially if the program is to be broad-based (Suskie, 2004). Incorporating at least one student employee and one staff member who works directly with student employees can keep the group grounded and provide feedback on the realities of implementation, etc. It also can be beneficial to include one person who has a solid understanding of organizational assessment, methodological concepts, and data analysis. Finally, selecting one person who is an "outsider" to some extent that can provide an unbiased review of the group's work and look in on the process from the outside as the implementation progresses can pay dividends in the long run. For example, this person could be a faculty member if the unit of analysis is a non-academic area. Alternatively, when analyzing a service-learning program the outsider might be a community member or an involved alumnus. The most important aspect of launching the program is taking time once the team is assembled to educate the group about learning outcomes by availing them of the myriad resources and literature available and presented in the first section of this chapter.

If a student employment program already exists, how will the learning outcomes be incorporated? The team will need to work through the intended use of the outcomes and understand why the organization is moving in this direction. Why develop and implement learning outcomes? What advantages does this approach provide to the organization and the institution? Initial intentions, decisions, and results will help drive the process forward and will root it in the values clarified on the front end.

The scope of each student employment program will vary by institution. Who is driving the process, and who or what entity has created the initial team? From what "level" is the process emanating? Is the project's scope one student in the financial aid office, does it span all departments of a single college, or are two units collaborating to create a solitary program? The answers to these questions will be instructive in creating the program's initial boundaries. Institutional characteristics also must be carefully considered at this stage. For example, what percentage of students live on campus, work off campus, live in the surrounding community, are upper-division or graduate students, etc.?

This is an appropriate time to discuss team goals, staff's commitment, and organizational buy-in over the long term. To do that, discussions must occur around staff involvement and resources as well as a timeline for the project based on the program's scope. Both long- and short-term timeframes should be embraced, with predetermined milestones along the way. For example, if the team hopes to have measureable results in one year, what steps need to be executed to achieve that goal?

As the organization continues through the process, other variables will emerge. For example, are there existing student learning outcomes that will be adapted from a university-wide, divisional, college, or departmental perspective? If the outcomes are being derived at the local/unit level it is obvious which ones will be embraced in the program; however, their alignment with existing outcomes will be important. If the program embraces larger student learning outcomes or those presented at a different level of the organization, the team must discuss how those outcomes will be broken down for implementation at the localized level. The process of working through the outcomes' distribution will inevitably lead to the actual selection of the organization's learning outcomes. Whether they are emerging from the students and supervisors, being imposed from another level of the organization, being borrowed from the literature, or any combination of these, ultimately the team will need to decide which learning outcomes are most appropriate for their students and employment opportunities.

How students are taught or exposed to the concepts embedded in the learning outcomes is a critical phase of implementation. Bresciani's (2006) research on program review indicated that "Eighty-seven percent of the institutions … reported that it is somewhat to very important for students to understand the outcomes articulated for each program" (p. 66). Due to the myriad issues associated with training and broad, accurate communication, this phase can necessitate enormous organizational resources and should be considered fully. The methods and pedagogy available to deliver the content vary broadly, and each organization will have access to different types of resources to offer the training. Are there natural or pre-existing opportunities to deliver training focused on the learning outcomes—for example, orientations, year-end programs, etc.? Does the organization have access to faculty or others who specialize in areas the outcomes address—for example, communications professors?

The measurement and analysis of students' potential growth and development is paramount. This phase of the planning and implementation will require a great deal of research and adaptation to the localized setting. Choosing an appropriate methodology and assessment tools for the unique setting is important and may vary widely. The concept of triangulating the data assists with increased data integrity on the one hand, yet on the other hand it infuses additional complexity and ultimately staff and student time and resources into the system. Gathering reliable data that can be checked throughout the process so that results can be fed back into the system for improvement is a difficult task that can be simplified by spending time in the planning stages deciding on the best methods for the organization.

Conclusion

Infusing learning outcomes into the student employment process is not easy, yet it adds significantly to students' experiences. Given all that is known about student learning while in college, it is logical to embrace these concepts in the employment setting. When describing the "student-driven model," Manning, Kinzie, and Schuh (2006) state that through "meaningful campus work experiences, students become vested members of the campus community. They take the initiative and responsibility to positively contribute to campus and community life as well as assume greater responsibility for the quality of the undergraduate program" (p. 105).

As the landscape continues to shift in global higher education toward outputs as opposed to inputs, college employment is a viable and desirable way to help educate students in vital areas such as problem solving, cultural competence, and critical thinking. Colleges and universities that implement outcomes-based employment programs help the overall institution in meeting accreditation goals and attaining general education ideals. An often-overlooked aspect of students' lives is their college work experience. Employment roles are central to their overall college experience and are significant factors in student socialization to the academic environment. Structuring meaningful and intentional work environments will assist students in their growth and development in college.

References

Beno, B. (2004). The role of student learning outcomes in accreditation quality review. In A.M. Serban & J. Friedlander (Eds.), *Developing and implementing assessment of student learning outcomes, New directions for community colleges, No. 126* (pp. 65–72). San Francisco: Jossey-Bass.

Bresciani, M.J. (2003). External partners in assessment of student development and learning. In M.B. Snyder (Ed.), *Student affairs and external relations, New directions for student services, No. 100* (pp. 97–110). San Francisco: Jossey-Bass.

Bresciani, M.J. (2006). *Outcomes-based academic and co-curricular program review: A compilation of institutional good practices.* Sterling, VA: Stylus Publishing.

Friedlander, J., & Serban, A. (2004). Meeting the challenges of assessing student learning outcomes. In A.M. Serban & J. Friedlander (Eds.), *Developing and implementing assessment of student learning outcomes, New directions for community colleges, No.126* (pp. 101–109). San Francisco: Jossey-Bass.

Keeling, R.P. (Ed.).(2004). *Learning reconsidered: A campus-wide focus on the student experience.* Washington, DC: ACPA, NASPA.

Keeling, R.P. (Ed.).(2006). *Learning reconsidered 2: A practical guide to implementing a campus-wide focus on the student experiences.* Washington, DC: ACPA, ACUHO-I, ACUI, NACA, NACADA, NASPA, NIRSA

Lewis, J.S., & Contreras, S., Jr. (2008, January). Research and practice: Connecting student employment and learning. *The Bulletin of the Association of College Unions International, 76*(1), 30–38.

Maki, P.L. (2004). *Assessing for learning: Building a sustainable commitment across the institution.* Sterling, VA: Stylus Publishing, LLC.

Manning, K., Kinzie, J., & Schuh, J. (2006). *One size does not fit all: Traditional and innovative models of student affairs practice.* New York: Routledge.

Perozzi, B., Rainey, A., & Wahlquist, Z. (2003). A review of the effects of student employment on academic achievement. *The Bulletin of the Association of College Unions International, 71*(5), 15–20.

Riggert, S.C., Boyle, M., Petrosko, J.M., Ash, D., & Rude-Parkins, C. (2006). Student employment and higher education: Empiricism and contradiction. *Review of Educational Research, 76,* 63–92.

Schuh, J.H. (2009). *Assessment methods for student affairs.* San Francisco: Jossey-Bass.

Suskie, L. (2004). *Assessing student learning: A common sense guide.* Bolton, MA: Anker Publishing Company.

Wagenaar, T. (2002). Outcomes assessment in sociology: Prevalence and impact. *Teaching Sociology, 30,* 403–413.

SECTION II

DEMOGRAPHICS AND SPECIAL POPULATIONS

THE IMPACT OF EMPLOYMENT ON STUDENT ENGAGEMENT: RESULTS FROM NSSE

by John V. Moore & Melanie Rago

Colleges have been assisting students who need financial support since the early 1900s, when many smaller colleges tried to boost enrollment by creating work-study programs for lower-income or first-generation students (Lucas, 1994; Rudolph, 1977). Although these programs were not necessarily successful in recruiting or retaining students, their existence shows an early acknowledgement by higher education institutions that not all students have the finances to attend college and that students may, at times, need to seek employment to afford university attendance. More recently, an increasing number of students have been working while attending college. The count of working college students had increased from 29 percent in 1959 to 43 percent in 1986 (Stern & Nakata, 1991). In the 1999–2000 academic year, King (2003) reported that 80 percent of college students were working. This represented an 8 percent increase from the previous decade when Cuccaro-Alamin and Choy (1998) found that 72 percent of students were both working and attending college. Although many researchers have examined the effects of working while in college, the outcomes of these projects have been varied and contradictory, and have often been limited to a single or a small number of institutions. This chapter presents a study that, by examining the effects of employment on students' engagement with their university, addresses the issue broadly and also explores differential impacts of students' demographic factors and motivation for working as predictive factors.

Literature review

Research on the impact of working on students

The amount of time students spend working has become an increasing concern for the educators who serve them and, in growing instances, the policy-makers who study what impact working has on persistence rates and time to graduation (Tuttle, McKinney, & Rago, 2005). This concern also has led to a greater interest in research on the effects of working on the college experience—which has resulted in diverse findings (Riggert, Boyle, Petrosko, Ash, & Rude-Parkins, 2006). Many of these studies view work through a lens that reinforces the ideas of Tinto (1975) and Bean and Metzner (1985) who theorized that students need to make significant connections to their university and that tasks or activities that interrupt these connections decrease their chances of remaining at the institution. Subsequent researchers of student employment have assumed that work, generally, is a nonacademic venture that serves to take time away from students' ability to bind themselves to campus. Hodgson and Spours (2001), for example, found that students working off campus end up splitting their attention between their two commitments and fail to make significant connections to either one. The link between a student's integration into collegiate life and off-campus employment has been further explored by researchers Fjortoft (1995) and Lundberg (2004) who found that working students, unsurprisingly, devote less time to academic or social activities. And Hey, Calderon, and Seabert (2003) found that working students are more likely to struggle with higher levels of academic stress from trying to meet the demands of work and school.

The research findings on the impact of these disconnections from college life have been mixed and contradictory, however. In investigating the results of working on student outcomes, Hunt, Lincoln, and Walker (2004) found that compared to their nonworking peers, employed students have lower grade point averages. Canabal (1998), however, reported the opposite effect on GPA. DesJardins, Ahlburg, and McCall (2002) found that working had a positive influence on timely graduation while not affecting graduation rate. Beeson and Wessel (2002), also, found that working students had both higher retention and graduation rates than nonworking students.

Others have posited that the link between working and academic integration is not as straightforward as portrayed in the simple working/not-working dichotomy. Several studies (Harding & Harmon, 1999; King, 2002; Pascarella & Terenzini, 1991; Perna, Cooper, & Li, 2006; Stinebrickner & Stinebrickner, 2003) have found the negative effects of working begin to appear only as the number of hours worked increases (to more than 15 hours per week, for example). This resonates with evidence that students believe that working a large number of hours is detrimental to their academic commitments (Curtis & Shani, 2002; Hunt et al., 2004; Long & Hayden, 2001). For employed students whose time at work is at or under a certain amount (again, usually 15–20 hours a week), the impact of working has been found by some researchers to be positively associated with academic outcomes (Choy & Berker, 2003; Dundes & Marx, 2006–2007; Hood, Craig, & Ferguson, 1992; Moore & Rago, 2007; Rago, Moore, & Herreid, 2005), yet other researchers have found no relationship between any amount of work and academic outcomes (Bradley, 2006; Furr & Elling, 2000, Harding & Harmon, 1999; High, 1999; Nonis & Hudson, 2006; Pascarella & Terenzini, 2005).

A broader examination of students' working patterns and the impact of work may be helpful and clarifying in this debate. For example, a large number of these studies are of a single institution or small regional group of schools. This, in itself, is an implicit critique of the literature that points to the need for more studies that examine student employment as a broader phenomenon. Because of the sample size mandated by these smaller studies, students are not able to be examined by differing demographic group. Older and younger students, for example, are considered together; the working behaviors at urban and rural schools are not able to be compared; differences in the impact of working by gender or race are not explored; on- and off- campus employment is often conflated. This also points to the need for a larger sample of students to be included in the analysis. Additionally, the amount of students working and the volume at which they are working is increasing. These higher employment trends have implications for student employees' academic lives and warrant continued study. For those who work with students, understanding these patterns is critical in crafting appropriate support and advice for working students.

The student engagement framework for research

A relatively recent and important addition to the literature on student success in college is the research of Kuh and others on the links between student engagement and student success. Kuh (2003) defines student engagement as "the time and energy students devote to educationally purposeful activities" and as "the single best predictor of [student] learning and personal development" (p. 24). Conceptually, student engagement grows out of the research and theory of several prominent scholars in higher education: Astin (1993), Pace (19080), Pascarella and Terenzini (1991). Higher levels of engagement among students have been positively linked to gains in critical thinking (Kuh, Hu, & Vesper, 2000; Kuh & Vesper, 1997; Pike, 1999, 2000; Pike, Kuh, & Gonyea, 2003; Terenzini, Pascarella, & Blimling, 1996), in grades (Astin, 1977, 1993), and in persistence (Astin, 1985; Pike, Schroeder, & Berry, 1997).

The student engagement framework also fits well into traditional theories of retention, such as those of Tinto (1975) and Bean and Metzner (1985) in which students' connection to the university plays a vital role in persistence. This connection develops through a student's engagement on campus. This type of engagement has been operationalized in surveys such as the National Survey of Student Engagement (NSSE) in the United States, which was developed to investigate the extent to which students participate in activities that are signifiers of student-campus relationships (e.g., interacting with faculty and peers, contributing to interactive classroom behaviors, interfacing with people of different backgrounds and beliefs, preparing well for academics, and partaking in educational activities outside the confines of the traditional classroom) as well as to investigate the relationships between these types of interactions and the school environment (Carini, Kuh, & Klein, 2006; Kuh, 2001, 2003; Zhao, Kuh, & Carini, 2005).

NSSE has been used with a wide variety of populations including blacks and Hispanics (Nelson Laird, Bridges, Salinas Holmes, Morelon, & Williams, 2007), gays and lesbians (Gonyea & Moore, 2007), commuter students (Kuh, Gonyea, & Palmer, 2001), first-generation students (Filkins & Doyle, 2002), members of fraternities and sororities (Hayek, Carini, O'Day, & Kuh, 2002), women (Umbach, Kinzie, Thomas, Palmer, & Kuh, 2007), and athletes (Umbach, Palmer, Kuh, & Hannah, 2004). NSSE scores have been linked to higher education outcomes measures such as GPA and student persistence in college (Kuh, Cruce, Shoup, Kinzie, & Gonyea, 2007; Kuh, Kinzie, Cruce, Shoup, & Gonyea, 2006). Although several of these NSSE studies include working students in their models, none specifically examines the differences between working and nonworking students or the differences between on-campus and off-campus employment.

Student motivation and employment

Some researchers have suggested that students' motivations for working may have an important effect on their studies. Perna, Cooper, and Li (2006) examine students' motivations for working through four lenses, each focusing primarily on the necessity of paying or defraying college costs. This view is reflected in the findings of some researchers (Curtis & Williams, 2002; Ferguson & Cerinus, 1996; Ford, Bosworth, & Wilson, 1995). Others, however, have found that working students are largely using their income for spending money (Dundes & Marx, 2006–2007), car expenses (Rago et al., 2005), or nonessentials like vacations, clothes, and social events (Lee, Mawdsley, & Rangeley, 1999). While interesting, these results are not without their challenges. Lee et al., for example, note that differentiating essential and nonessential expenses is problematic without knowing the details of a student's life. Cars, for example, may be a necessity for some students and an option for others. These and other important details of students' lives (such as cost or type of vehicle) are missing in these examinations.

In most of these studies, only a small number of students are motivated to work by interest or alignment with future career goals (e.g., Curtis & Williams, 2002; Ferguson & Cerinus, 1996; Ford et al., 1995). Luzzo, McWhirter, and Hutcheson (1997) found important developmental benefits of this congruence between students' career goals and their college experiences. Further, Loizou (2000), Gleason (1993), and Curtis and Williams (2002) note there can be longer-term employment benefits for working students, although others discuss contrary findings (Hotz, Xu, Tienda, & Ahituv, 2002). This study will build on these earlier studies by examining further the issues of motivation and engagement in the college experiences of working students.

Methods

Research questions

This study examines several aspects of the working student experience, specifically addressing the following questions:
1. What are the patterns of working across various institutional and student demographics?
2. What is the impact of working (both on and off campus) on these groups on grade point average on different student types?
3. What are the differences among working students between working on campus and working off campus in the impact on student engagement?
4. Do working students' motivations for working affect the engagement of these students on campus?

These questions were intentionally developed to fill perceived gaps in the literature. Answers to these questions have the potential to aid practitioners to better assist students in making more informed decisions about working and to point to practices that would further engage students in their educational environments.

Data sources and samples

NSSE was designed by a team of higher education researchers under the auspices of the Indiana University Center for Postsecondary Research. The survey consists of approximately 98 items (including demographic questions) that assess students' educational experiences, interactions with university officers and peers, and perceptions of campus culture. The items were developed based on research into good practices in higher education. The benchmarks are five groups of NSSE questions that are used to assist institutions in understanding areas in which they can improve practice on their campus (National Survey of Student Engagement, 2003a).

The data for this study originated in the 2005 administration of NSSE. NSSE was developed to explore student participation in educationally purposeful activities while in college and is administered each spring to first-year students and seniors at four-year colleges across the United States. In 2005, 529 institutions participated in the survey with more than 230,000 students responding to the employment-related questions. These numbers reflect the broader, national picture of both four-year colleges in the United States and the students who attend them.

As a set of experimental items, the questions about students' motivations for working were distributed to a subset of 30 institutions participating in the larger NSSE project. These schools represent a range of sizes, locations, research orientations, and selectivity. Schools that were midsized (n = 10), in the mid-Atlantic (n = 8) or the Midwest (n = 8) regions, baccalaureate (n = 14), and very competitive (n = 14) were most common. There were more than 6,000 usable student cases and, of these, 64 percent were female, 13 percent were of nontraditional age (over 24 years old), 11 percent were students of color, and 58 percent were seniors.

Variables

The variables of interest for the first research question come from single items on the NSSE survey: "About how many hours do you spend in a typical seven-day week doing each of the following: Working for pay on campus?" and "About how many hours do you spend in a typical seven-day week doing each of the following: Working for pay off campus?" Responses were on an eight-point Likert scale that ranged from "0 hours per week" to "30 or more hours per week" in five-hour increments. Student demographics included gender (male or female), race/ethnicity (African American or black; non-Hispanic white; Asian or Pacific Islander; Hispanic, Latino, Mexican, and Puerto Rican; and other, including Native American and multiracial due to small sample sizes for these groups), enrollment status (full-time, part-time), class year (first year, senior), and age (19 or younger, 20–23, 24–29, 30–39, 40–55, over 55). Institutional variables included Carnegie classification, competitiveness (as designated by Barron's), urbanicity (a 1–7 scale of "rural" to "large city"), and control (public or private).

For the second question, GPA came from a question on the NSSE survey that asks for self-reported GPA from a Likert scale. The question asked: "What have most of your grades been up to now at this institution?" and the responses ranged from "A" to "C- or lower." The demographics used were the same as for the previous question.

The five dependent variables for the third research question were drawn from the NSSE benchmarks for educational practice. Definitions of these benchmark variables are as follows:

- Academic Challenge: The extent to which a student feels challenged by in- and out-of-class coursework
- Active and Collaborative Learning: The amount of participation a student reports having with other students in and out of the classroom to complete academic work
- Student-Faculty Interaction: The amount and quality of a student's reported contact with faculty on academic and career issues
- Enriching Educational Experiences: The level of a student's involvement in beneficial educational and cocurricular activities such as an internship, community service, or a learning community
- Supportive Campus Environment: The student's rating of the school climate in terms of its support for the student and the quality of the student's relationships with peers, faculty, and staff
  (NSSE, 2003b)

To answer the final question regarding students' motivations for working, variables with specific reasons for working were used: to pay for tuition, to pay for books and supplies, to pay back education-related debt, to pay for living expenses (rent, utilities, food), to pay for transportation expenses (loans, gas, repair, bus, or train costs), to gain experience, to meet an academic requirement, to support family members, to comply with parent/family demand, to pay for entertainment/social expenses (clothes, music, dining out), to continue a job held prior to college, to pay back noneducation debt, and to increase savings. Responses for the motivation items were scored on a six-point Likert scale, ranging from 1 (not at all important) to 6 (very important).

Analysis

To answer the first question (about differences in working patterns among student and institutional demographics), regression analyses were run for gender, race, age, enrollment status, and class year for students employed both on and off campus. Additionally, regressions were run for the institutional characteristics (Carnegie classification, competitiveness, urbanicity, control, and geographic region). Crosstabs on employment and each of the demographic variables also were run. The results will inform as to whether different types of students have different working patterns.

For the second question, a regression was run with GPA as the dependent variable for students who work either on or off campus. The regression included, and therefore statistically controlled for, a number of other potential predictors of GPA such as SAT/ACT score, gender, race, major, and enrollment status. These additional variables were included to parse out the individual impact of working on or off campus.

The third research question, regarding the differences in the impact on student engagement between working on campus and working off campus, was addressed through a series of parallel regressions: one set for students working on campus and one set for students working off campus. A pair of regressions was run for each of the five benchmark variables. Predictor variables in the model included the individual and institutional characteristics listed previously as well as the information about number of hours worked as well as some additional controls such as major and athletic and greek life participation. These have been found in past research to be related to student engagement. The parallel regressions allowed for a contrast between effects of on-campus versus off-campus employment on student engagement; thus, students who worked both on and off campus were not included in the models.

To address the final research question, regarding how students' motivations for working affect their engagement, parallel regressions were again run for on-campus and off-campus employment. In addition to all the predictors listed previously, the variables related to students' motivations for working were added to the models. For both analyses, the students' time spent working was added as a series of dummy variables to capture potential changes by the number of hours at work, with 16 to 20 hours per week as the reference group (the group to which all others are compared). This group was chosen as the reference in acknowledgement of a number of studies that suggest working 15 to 20 hours per week as a turning point in the impact of working on students (see Perna et al., 2006, for a review of these studies).

Results

General patterns of student employment

Among the total sample, almost two-thirds (62.1 percent) of the responding students worked either on or off campus. Just under one in five students (19.4 percent) worked exclusively on campus, and more than one-third (34.5 percent) worked exclusively off campus. The remaining 8.2 percent had some combination of on- and off-campus employment. Because of the large sample of working students contained in the study, each of the regressions were significant, meaning that there were different patterns of on-campus employment between and among these various groups. Although statistically significant, however, the practical differences in many of the groups were not large. When examining differences at the institutional level, however, there were some important, and significant, differences worthy of note.

Student demographics

Differences by gender

Men and women worked in quite similar proportions. On campus, women worked more than men. Females were slightly more likely to work a minimal number of hours (10 percent worked 6–10 hours a week on campus compared to 8 percent of males), but worked slightly more at the higher levels of employment. Off campus, men were more likely to not work at all (61 percent of men did not work off campus versus 56 percent of women). However, when they did work off campus, men worked more hours than women.

Differences by race/ethnicity

Each of the studied minority groups worked more than white students on campus. Asian students were the most likely to work on campus (30 percent worked on campus at some level) while Hispanics and Native Americans were the least likely to hold a job on campus (26 percent of these students were employed by their schools). Native American students also were more likely to be highly employed by their schools (30 or more hours per week). Just over 3 percent worked at this high level compared to 1 to 2 percent of other ethnic groups. Students who work at this high level are likely to be full-time employees of the institution who also are enrolled in classes. Given that, this last result is from the inclusion of several tribal colleges in the sample.

Off campus, the results were somewhat similar to those of working on campus; however, Asians were less likely to work off campus than white students (62 percent had no off-campus work). Hispanic and black students worked more than white students. They were the most likely to have off-campus employment—just under half of each group reported some level of work outside of their college. Asians and white students worked at high levels (more than 30 hours per week off campus) at a much lower rate (6 percent and 9 percent, respectively) than other minority groups (16 percent of Native Americans and blacks and 15 percent of Hispanics). Students whose race was "other, multiracial, or unknown" also were less likely to work at all than white students.

Differences by age

As would be expected, older students worked more hours off campus and fewer hours on campus. Non-traditionally aged students not only worked fewer hours than younger students but also were less likely to work at all on campus. Among the non-traditionally aged students (those 24 and older) fewer than 20 percent were employed on campus. For students ages 20 to 23, 35 percent were employed on campus.

Off-campus employment followed an opposite pattern: every age group was more likely to work than those 19 and under. While just over 25 percent of students younger than 19 worked off campus, almost 70 percent of students in their 30s and 40s reported working off campus. The percent of students with jobs away from school increased in each age group until the final category (those aged 55 and up), where it decreased to just over half of students working (53 percent) off campus. Among older students who worked, that employment also was much more likely to be approaching full time. Forty percent of students in their 30s and 47 percent of those in their 40s worked more than 30 hours per week.

Differences by class year and enrollment status

Again, as might be expected, more advanced students were more likely to work both on and off campus. One quarter of first-year students worked on campus while 31 percent of seniors did so. Off campus, again just over 25 percent of first-year students worked while over half of seniors did so.

Part-time students (75 percent) also were much more likely to have off-campus employment than full-time students (39 percent). They also were less likely (13 percent) to have on-campus employment than their full-time peers (30 percent).

Institutional demographics

Like the differences by student characteristics, many of these characteristics were significant. On-campus and off-campus employment most often seem to work in tandem; as the likelihood of working on campus increases, the likelihood of working off campus decreases at specific types of institutions. This suggests that the colleges may be responding to students' needs as well as the availability of jobs in the community. Specific differences among groups are presented in this section.

Differences by urbanicity

Students at colleges in large cities or their urban fringe were less likely to work on campus. This might be due to the greater number of opportunities available to them off campus. The less populated the area around the school, the more likely the students were to work on campus. While 24 percent of students in large cities worked on campus, 34 percent of those in small towns or rural areas did.

Students at schools in urban areas were more likely to work off campus than those at rural institutions. Half (50 percent) of these students held off-campus employment while about a third of students at small-town (33 percent) or rural (35 percent) institutions did so. Students at these urban schools also were the most likely to have near full-time employment; 12 percent of those students worked more than 30 hours a week while attending school.

Differences by competitiveness

Students attending more competitive schools were more likely to work more hours on campus. As compared to students at schools rated by Barron's as competitive, those at less competitive or non-competitive schools were less likely to work on campus. Those at very competitive, highly competitive, or most competitive schools were more likely to do so. More than a third (35 percent) of students at the most competitive schools worked on campus while less than half that percent (17 percent) of those at noncompetitive schools had employment there. This trend carried through to the highest levels of employment as well. More than 5 percent of students at the most competitive schools were employed by their college more than 30 hours a week, while about 1 percent of those at most other types of schools worked at near full-time status.

The case was reversed for working off campus; almost two-thirds (64 percent) of students at the least competitive schools worked away from school, while only 15 to 17 percent of those at the most competitive schools did so. In the largest difference in the study, students at noncompetitive schools were about 26 times more likely to have near full-time employment than those at the most competitive institutions.

Differences by control

Students at private schools were more likely to work more hours on campus. While employment rates above 15 hours a week were almost identical, in categories of fewer hours, students at private schools worked on campus at a rate almost three times that of public school students. (Fifteen percent, for example, worked 6–10 hours a week on campus while only 6 percent of their public school peers worked at that level on campus.)

Public school students, however, were more likely to hold some form of off-campus employment (45 percent) than those at private schools (38 percent). They also were slightly more likely to work at the highest level (11 percent) than those at other institutions (8 percent).

Differences by Carnegie classification

As compared to students at master's level institutions, those at doctoral and baccalaureate levels were less likely to work on campus. The students at master's level schools, however, were more likely to work off campus than students at other types of schools.

Impact of employment on GPA

Working on campus

The relationship between working on campus and academic achievement is not a simple linear correlation. In other words, it is not necessarily true that as students work more hours they have significantly lower GPAs, nor that those who do not work on campus, those who work 16 to 20 hours a week, and those who work more than 30 hours a week on campus report lower grades. Those who work moderate amounts (1–5 and 10–15 hours per week) have slightly (although statistically significant) higher grades. Students who work in other amounts do not have significantly different self-reported grades. Among the control variables, women students, minority students, first-year students, part-time students, and younger students all had higher reported grades. Students at less selective, more urban, private, and doctoral (as compared to master's level) schools reported higher grades.

Working off campus

Off-campus employment seemed to have a more straightforward relationship with grades. Compared to those who work 16 to 20 hours a week, students who work 10 or fewer hours (0 hours, 1–5 hours, and 6–10 hours a week) reported higher grades. Those who worked more than 25 hours a week (26–30 hours, more than 30 hours a week) reported lower grades. Among the control variables, women students, minority students, younger students, first-year students, and part-time students reported lower grades. Students at more rural, more selective, public, and baccalaureate schools also reported lower grades.

Impact of employment on student engagement

The models of students who worked on campus and of those who worked off campus produced similar results and indicated that working had only a marginal impact on students' engagement in college. The five benchmarks, as in other studies of engagement, were found to be highly related to the institutional factors and the factors regarding students' backgrounds, characteristics, and behaviors. Once these factors were controlled for, hours spent working were only influential in the extreme positions on two of the benchmarks. Students not working on campus at all (as compared to students working 16–20 hours per week on campus) were significantly less involved in active and collaborative learning activities. Students who worked on campus one to five hours per week perceived the campus environment as significantly more supportive than those who worked on campus 16 to 20 hours a week. Students' perception of the campus environment's supportiveness also was affected by the extreme values for those working off campus. Compared to students working 16 to 20 hours a week off campus, students not working at all off campus rated the campus significantly more supportive, and those working more than 31 hours a week off campus saw the campus environment as significantly less supportive.

In terms of other characteristics, students at smaller, private, and more selective schools were generally more engaged. Full-time students, those involved in greek life, seniors, and minority students also were more engaged. Student major also was an important factor in student engagement. However, there was no consistent pattern to the impact of major on engagement. Compared to arts and humanities majors, students majoring in pre-professional fields had higher scores on supportive campus environment and lower scores on enriching educational experiences. Those studying education saw the campus as more supportive and were more likely to engage in active and collaborative learning activities when compared to arts and science majors. The one consistent predictor was being undecided about major. Students in this group scored lower on all five of the benchmarks.

Working students' motivation and engagement

There were some noteworthy, although not entirely unexpected, differences between the mean level of importance that respondents placed on motivations for working based on whether they worked on or off campus. Off-campus workers ranked transportation needs, living expenses, and savings as their three top motivations for working. On-campus workers, meanwhile, listed books and supplies, living expenses, and entertainment as most important. As motivations for working for both on-campus and off-campus workers, educationally related expenses were all similarly important, as reflected in the mean scores on these items: tuition (3.77 on-campus, 3.80 off-campus), books and supplies (4.20 on-campus, 4.14 off-campus), and education debt (3.63 on-campus, 3.70 off-campus). The greatest differences between on-campus and off-campus workers in motivations for working were in transportation expenses (3.72 on-campus, 4.80 off-campus), continuing in a job held prior to college (1.63 on-campus, 2.77 off-campus), and non-education debt (2.48 on-campus, 3.26 off-campus), with off-campus workers ranking each of these as more important. Those employed off campus, in fact, rated each motivation—with the exception of books and supplies—as more important than the on-campus workers did.

When entered into the regression equation, student motivations for working affected several of the benchmark scores. For example, students who worked off campus and who were more motivated to work to pay for books and supplies reported experiencing higher levels of academic challenge and saw the campus as more supportive. Those who worked on campus reported higher levels of active and collaborative learning. Many of the motivations, however, had no impact on engagement. The one striking exception was students motivated to work to gain experience in their field. Whether working on or off campus, these students reported higher levels of engagement in all five benchmarks.

Discussion

This study examines the relationships among institutional and student characteristics, working patterns, self-reported grade, motivations for work, and engagement across a random sample of more than 200,00 college students around the United States. The study's findings generally support the growing body of multi-institutional research suggesting that a moderate level of work does not necessarily have a negative affect on student success in college. In fact, in most cases it appears that even working many hours each week does not impact a student's engagement on campus and only minimally impacts self-reported GPA. Although this finding does not speak directly to a working student's retention or success, the close relationship between self-reported GPA and actual GPA as well as that between engagement and these other measures points to an association between the two that would suggest similar findings would be uncovered if such a study were undertaken.

Regarding GPA, working on campus in moderate amounts clearly provides a small positive impact on student performance while working off campus has a negative impact on grades, particularly at higher levels of employment. By teasing apart the separate impacts of on-and off-campus employment, it becomes clear that they work in different ways.

Overall, this study's results regarding student engagement echo those of Kuh and associates, finding that institutional characteristics (e.g., size, selectivity, and control) and student characteristics (e.g., gender, age, enrollment status, and greek life membership) have more influence on a student's engagement than working (Kuh et al., 2006). When students' motivations were added to the model, however, a new strong predictor emerged. Students motivated to work by a desire to gain experience in a field were more likely to have higher levels of engagement in each of NSSE's five benchmarks— even when significant school and personal attributes were controlled for.

This study may also shed light on findings from previous research that working students may have better employment prospects after college (Curtis & Williams, 2002; Gleason, 1993; Luzzo et al., 1997). Students who are not only gaining employment experience but also actively making connections between work and school would understandably be more attractive to prospective employers. Perhaps such fostered connections can be productively examined within the context of the linkages between motivation and engagement among working students.

Given the results of the study, it would seem that encouraging students to engage in some sort of work while in school would benefit them. And if one had to choose, it would appear that work on campus provides some additional advantages over off-campus work. This provides a unique opportunity for on-campus employers to maximize learning and growth opportunities. It is important that these experiences continue to provide the best environment for student development. Indeed, this study follows many others that indicate the question is no longer whether students should work or not; they are. Now it is imperative to develop and research practices that support them in their decision to work and devise strategies for them to receive the most benefit from their working experiences.

Implications

For those who work with student employees, the findings presented in this chapter have important ramifications for ensuring that students get the most out of their working experiences. First, there are students who are less likely to work on campus, where the greatest benefits of working seem to be realized. How can practitioners reach out to these students to offer them the same advantages that other students are reaping from working on campus? Second, if we know that students who connect their employment to future goals are more engaged in their college experiences, then how can we help students make those connections to ensure they get the most out of their working experiences? Finally, what future areas of research can be identified that would cultivate a better understanding of working students' experiences?

Reaching new students

First-year students show an important differential between working on and off campus. On-campus work benefits their GPA, for example, while off-campus work harms it. For first-year students who need to work, it would be important to encourage them to try and find that employment on campus. This could be done through orientation or a first-year experience program, where potential on-campus employers could reach out to students and inform them of the benefits of and opportunities for working at their college.

Similar outreach programs would likely benefit other groups who are both less likely to work on campus and who could benefit more from such employment. For example, advisors might encourage part-time students, who are less likely, given their reduced time on the physical campus, to develop the types of close relationships that have been documented to be important to student success (Chickering & Gamson, 1987; Gerdes & Mallinckrodt, 1994; Light, 2001), to work some hours on campus. This may prove to be a challenge for those who are working full-time at an off-campus job, but the potential for growth among those who can work on campus could make a difference in their persistence. Their additional out-of-classroom experiences also could be valuable for offices on campus.

Cultural centers could encourage Hispanic and Native American students (the groups least likely to have on-campus employment) to engage in work at their schools—a great boon to groups of students with some of the highest college dropout rates (Fox, Lowe, & McClellan, 2005; Fry, 2002; Reddy, 1993). While Hurtado and Carter (1997) found that work did not contribute to Hispanic students' sense of belonging on campus, Nora (1990) did find that college work-study was positively related to college persistence. Among Native American student populations, it has been noted that these students face large barriers in the career development process (Hoffmann, Jackson, & Smith, 2005) and that mentoring surrounding career or vocational aspiration is critical to their long-term success (Jackson & Smith, 2001; Jackson, Smith, & Hill, 2003). Similarly, making college officials aware of on-campus employment's benefits and informing them as to which groups could gain from working on campus might promote greater outreach to those groups.

Reaching out to students may be particularly difficult at more urban institutions. As mentioned previously, students at these schools are less likely to work on campus and more likely to work off campus. This is likely due to the greater availability of part-time work in an urban setting. Cruce and Moore (2007) found similarly lower patterns of participation in volunteer and community service activities, hypothesizing that students are simply choosing to participate in a wider range of available activities outside those structured by their campuses. Schools in urban areas may need to work even harder to sell the benefits of on-campus employment to their students. Rago, Moore, and Herried (2005) presented, in part, a case of an urban university that was able to increase on-campus student employment through work-study programs; the institution was able to pay students at rates competitive with area employers and touted the benefits of working and going to school at the same place.

Helping students connect with their employment

If students who see connections to their future interests perform better in school, then university administrators need to develop techniques that assist them in seeing these connections in their employment. This would clearly be easiest (and most beneficial, given other findings) if it could be done with on-campus jobs. With this in mind, how can administrators be more intentional in structuring campus employment opportunities to help students develop skills that will assist them in their future careers? Allen (2006) describes a way for employers to connect their student employee positions to Chickering's (1969) vectors by defining the skills that each position would develop. This could be done at all phases of student employment: hiring, training, supervision, and evaluation.

In the hiring process supervisors can structure their advertisements for student employees around the skills it will both require and cultivate. Interviews for positions can be constructed not only about the qualities that a student currently possesses, but also those they wish to acquire and how they see their work connecting with their major and their future career options. This early framing of employment will help students begin to think of their work in terms of how it can contribute to their later goals. This long-term perspective also has been observed by Sedlacek (2004) and Tracey and Sedlacek (1987, 1988, 1989) as important predictors when examining student GPA and persistence. Given that body of research, these types of conversations may be doubly beneficial. After students are hired, there are more opportunities to assist students in linking their employment to future job skills. Continued reinforcement of skill development in the training, supervision, and performance evaluation processes can be used to create a habit of thinking in a future-oriented way. (See Chapters 9–12 for more detail.)

Directions for future research

This chapter leads to some important directions for investigation. While the case is becoming clear that moderate levels of working, particularly on campus, are beneficial to students while they are in college, less is known about the specific impact types of work have on students. Do different types of jobs on or off campus affect students differently? This information might help us explore the mechanisms by which students benefit from work. Also, an interesting area for exploration would be a deeper look into the ways in which student development occurs for working and nonworking students. For example, do students in particular types of work develop higher levels of self-efficacy or a more advanced level of self-authorship? Additionally, few have investigated the longer-term effects of working. An investigation into the future career paths of students employed while in college could prove interesting and valuable for researchers and practitioners alike. Also of potential interest to colleges is the opportunity for a return on investments in student workers; do students who work on campus give more as alumni? These are important questions and issues for both institutions and students. Continued inquiry can lead to better understanding that ultimately translates to policy and action.

Conclusion

Employment is now a reality of college life for most students, and a growing body of literature demonstrates the positive affect of moderate amounts of work on the college experience. Therefore, it is important that those who work with students as advisors, mentors, or supervisors do not lose sight of the developmental opportunities embedded in students' work lives. These individuals should be aware of employment's benefits and understand the importance of helping students connect their future goals to their current work scenarios. Practitioners should be as comfortable talking with students about their working experiences as they are discussing their academic or social development. In the same way that faculty and staff might refer students to academic support services if they see them struggling with coursework, university personnel also should be at ease in referring students to career services if they are not benefiting from their employment. Those who work with student employees must be well versed in the literature if they are to help individuals grow by engaging in these types of deep conversations.

References

Allen, K.E. (2006). Student development: Applying theory to student employees. Retrieved February 3, 2009, from http://www.kathleenallen.net/modules.php?op=modload&name =Articles&file=index

Astin, A.W. (1977). *Four critical years*. San Francisco: Jossey-Bass.

Astin, A.W. (1985). The changing American college student. *Review of Higher Education, 21*(2), 115–135.

Astin, A.W. (1993). *What matters in college? Four critical years revisited.* San Francisco: Jossey-Bass.

Baum, S. (2005). *Financial barriers to college access and persistence: The current status of student reliance on grants, loans, and work.* Paper prepared for the Advisory Committee on Student Financial Assistance, Washington, DC.

Bean, J.P., & Metzner, B.S. (1985). A conceptual model of nontraditional undergraduate student attrition. *Review of Educational Research, 55*(4), 485–540.

Beeson, M.J., & Wessel, R.D. (2002). The impact of working on campus on the academic persistence of freshmen. *NASFAA Journal of Student Financial Aid, 32*(2), 37–45.

Bradley, G. (2006). Work participation and academic performance: A test of alternative propositions. *Journal of Education and Work, 19*(5), 481–501.

Canabal, M.E. (1998). College student degree of participation in the labor force: Determinants and relationship to school performance. *College Student Journal, 32*(4), 597–605.

Carini, R.M., Kuh, G.D., & Klein, S.P. (2006). Student engagement and student learning: Testing the linkages. *Research in Higher Education, 47*(1), 1–32.

Chickering, A.W. (1969). *Education and identity.* San Francisco: Jossey-Bass.

Chickering, A.W., & Gamson, Z.F. (1987). *Seven principles for good practice in undergraduate education.* Racine, WI: Johnson Foundation.

Choy, S., & Berker, A. (2003). *How families of low- and middle-income undergraduates pay for college: Full-time dependent students in 1999–2000* (NCES 2003-162). Washington, DC: U.S. Department of Education, National Center for Education Statistics.

Cruce, T. & Moore, J.V., III. (2007). First-year students' plans to volunteer: An examination of the predictors of community service participation. *Journal of College Student Development, 48*(6), 655–673.

Cuccaro-Alamin, S., & Choy, S.P. (1998). *Postsecondary financing strategies: How undergraduates combine work, borrowing, and attendance* (NCES 98088). Washington, DC: U.S. Department of Education, National Center for Education Statistics.

Curtis, S., & Shani, N. (2002). The effect of taking paid employment during term-time on students' academic studies. *Journal of Further and Higher Education, 26*(2), 129–138.

Curtis, S., & Williams, J. (2002). The reluctant workforce: Undergraduates' part-time employment. *Education + Training, 44*(1), 5–10.

DesJardins, S.L., Ahlberg, D.A., & McCall, B.P. (2002). A temporal investigation of factors related to timely degree completion. *Journal of Higher Education, 73*(5), 555–581.

Dundes, L., & Marx, J. (2006-2007). Balancing work and academics in college: Why do students working 10 to 19 hours excel? *Journal of College Student Retention, 8*(1), 107–120.

Ferguson, C., & Cerinus, M. (1996). Students in employment: Learning and working. *Nurse Education Today, 16*, 373–375.

Filkins, J.W., & Doyle, S.K. (2002, June). *First generation and low income students: Using the NSSE data to study effective educational practices and students' self-reported gains.* Paper presented at the annual forum of the Association for Institutional Research, Toronto, Canada.

Fjortoft, N.F. (1995, April). *College student employment: Opportunity or deterrent?* Paper presented at the annual meeting of the American Education Research Association, San Francisco.

Ford, J., Bosworth, D., & Wilson, R. (1995). Part-time work and full-time higher education. *Studies in Higher Education, 20*(2), 187–202.

Fox, M.J.T., Lowe, S.C., & McClellan, G.S. (Eds.) (2005). *Serving Native American students: New directions for student services, No. 109.* San Francisco: Jossey-Bass.

Fry, R. (2002). *Latinos in higher education: Many enroll, too few graduate.* Philadelphia, PA: Pew Hispanic Center.

Furr, S.R., & Elling, T.W. (2000). The influence of work on college student development. *NASPA Journal, 37*(2), 454–470.

Gerdes, H., & Mallinckrodt, B. (1994). Emotional, social, and academic adjustment of college students: A longitudinal study of retention. *Journal of Counseling and Development, 72*(3), 281–288.

Gleason, P.M. (1993). College student employment, academic progress, and postcollege labor market success. *The Journal of Student Financial Aid, 23*(2), 5–14.

Gonyea, R., & Moore, J., III. (2007, November-December). *Gay, lesbian, bisexual, and transgender students and their engagement in educationally purposeful activities in college.* Paper presented at the annual meeting of the Association for the Study of Higher Education, Louisville, KY.

Harding, E., & Harmon, L. (1999). *Higher education students' off-campus work patterns.* Olympia, WA: Washington State Institute for Public Policy.

Hayek, J.C., Carini, R.M., O'Day, P.T., & Kuh, G.D. (2002). Triumph or tragedy: Comparing student engagement levels of members of greek-letter organizations and other students. *Journal of College Student Development, 43*(5), 643–663.

Hey, W., Calderon, K.S., & Seabert, D. (2003). Student work issues: Implications for college transition and retention. *The Journal of College Orientation and Transition, 10*(2), 35–41.

High, R.V. (1999). *Employment of college students.* Rockville Center, NY: Molloy College, Department of Mathematics.

Hodgson, A., & Spours, K. (2001). Part-time work and full-time education in the UK: The emergence of a curriculum and policy issue. *Journal of Education and Work, 14,* 373–388.

Hoffmann, L.L., Jackson, A.P., Smith, S.A. (2005). Career barriers among Native American students living on reservations. *Journal of Career Development, 32*(1), 31–45.

Hood, A.G., Craig, A.R., & Ferguson, B.W. (1992). The impact of athletics, part-time employment, and other activities on academic achievement. *Journal of College Student Development, 35,* 364–370.

Hotz, V.J., Xu, L.C., Tienda, M., & Ahituv, A. (2002). Are there returns to the wages of young men from working while in school? *The Review of Economics and Statistics, 84*(2), 221–236.

Hunt, A., Lincoln, I., & Walker, A. (2004). Term-time employment and academic attainment: Evidence from a large-scale survey of undergraduates at Northumbria University. *Journal of Further and Higher Education, 28*(1), 3–18.

Hurtado, S., & Carter, D.F. (1997). Effects of college transition and perceptions of the campus racial climate on Latino college students. *Sociology of Education, 70*(4), 324–345.

Jackson, A.P., & Smith, S.A. (2001). Postsecondary transitions among Navajo Indians. *Journal of American Indian Education, 40*(2), 28–47.

Jackson, A.P., Smith, S.A., & Hill, C.L. (2003). Academic persistence among Native American college students. *Journal of College Student Development, 44*(4), 548–565.

King, J.E. (2002). *Crucial choices: How students' financial decisions affect their academic success.* Washington, DC: American Council on Education, Center for Policy Analysis.

King, J.E. (2003). Nontraditional attendance and persistence: The cost of students' choices. In J.E. King, E.L. Anderson, & M.E. Corrigan (Eds.), *Changing student attendance patterns: Challenges for policy and practice, New directions for higher education, No. 121* (pp. 69–83). San Francisco: Jossey-Bass.

Kuh, G.D. (2001). *The National Survey of Student Engagement: Conceptual framework and overview of psychometric properties.* Bloomington, IN: Indiana University, Center for Postsecondary Research.

Kuh, G.D. (2003). What we're learning about student engagement from NSSE. *Change, 35*(2), 24–32.

Kuh, G.D., Cruce, T., Shoup, R., Kinzie, J., & Gonyea, R.M. (2007, April). *Unmasking the effects of student engagement on college grades and persistence.* Paper presented at the annual meeting of the American Educational Research Association, Chicago.

Kuh, G.D., Gonyea, R.M., & Palmer, M. (2001). The disengaged commuter student: Fact or fiction? *Commuter Perspectives, 27*(1), 2–5.

Kuh, G.D., Hu, S., & Vesper, N. (2000). "They shall be known by what they do": An activities-based typology of college students. *Journal of College Student Development, 41(2)*, 228–244.

Kuh, G.D., Kinzie, J., Cruce, T., Shoup, R., & Gonyea, R.M. (2006). *Connecting the dots: Multi-faceted analyses of the relationships between student engagement results from the NSSE, and the institutional practices and conditions that foster student success: Final report prepared for Lumina Foundation for Education.* Bloomington, IN: Indiana University, Center for Postsecondary Research.

Kuh, G.D., & Vesper, N. (1997). A comparison of student experiences with good practices in undergraduate education between 1990 and 1994. *Review of Higher Education, 21*(1), 43–61.

Light, R.J. (2001). *Making the most of college: Students speak their minds.* Cambridge, MA: Harvard University Press.

Lee, T., Mawdsley, J.M., & Rangeley, H. (1999). Students' part-time work: Towards an understanding of the implications for nurse education. *Nurse Education Today, 19,* 443–451.

Loizou, N. (2000, April 8). Propping up the student bar could help you find a good job: Even working as a bouncer can be useful in your future career. *The Guardian.* Retrieved November 27, 2007, from http://www.guardian.co.uk/money/2000/apr/08/jobsadvice.careers9

Long, M., & Hayden, M. (2001). *Paying their way: A survey of Australian undergraduate university student finances, 2000.* Canberra, Australia: Australian Vice Chancellor's Committee.

Lucas, C.J. (1994). *American higher education: A history.* New York: St. Martin's Griffin.

Lundberg, C.A. (2004). Working and learning: The role of involvement for employed students. *NASPA Journal, 41*(2), 201–215.

Luzzo, D.A., McWhirter, E.H., & Hutcheson, K.G. (1997). Evaluating career decision-making factors associated with employment among first-year college students. *Journal of College Student Development, 38*(2), 166–172.

Moore, J.V., III, & Rago, M.A. (2007, May). *The working student's experience: The hidden costs of working on college student success and engagement.* Paper presented at the annual meeting of the Association for Institutional Research, Kansas City, MO.

National Survey of Student Engagement. (2003a). Construction of the 2000–2003 NSSE benchmarks. Retrieved March 20, 2008, from http://www.iub.edu/~nsse/2003_annual_report/html/benchmarks_construction.htm

National Survey of Student Engagement. (2003b). 2003 annual report. Retrieved March 20, 2008, from http://www.iub.edu/ percent7Ensse/2003_annual_report

Nelson Laird, T.F., Bridges, B.K., Salinas Holmes, M., Morelon, C.L., & Williams, J.M. (2007). African American and Hispanic student engagement at minority serving and predominantly white institutions. *Journal of College Student Development, 48*(1), 39–56.

Nonis, S.A., & Hudson, G.I. (2006). Academic performance on college students: Influence of time spent studying and working. *Journal of Education for Business, 81*(3), 151–159.

Nora, A. (1990). Campus-based aid programs as determinants of retention among Hispanic community college students. *Journal of Higher Education, 61*(3), 312–331.

Pace, C. (1980). Measuring the quality of student effort. *Current Issues in Higher Education, 2*, 10–16.

Pascarella, E.T., & Terenzini, P.T. (1991). *How college affects students*. San Francisco: Jossey-Bass.

Pascarella, E.T., & Terenzini, P.T. (2005). *How college affects students: A third decade of research* (Vol. 2). San Francisco: Jossey-Bass.

Perna, L., Cooper, M.A., & Li, C. (2006). *Improving educational opportunities for students who work*. Paper prepared for the Indiana Project on Academic Success, Bloomington, IN.

Pike, G. (1999). The effects of residential learning communities and traditional residential living arrangements on educational gains during the first year of college. *Journal of College Student Development, 38*, 609–621.

Pike, G. (2000). The influence of fraternity or sorority membership on students' college experiences and cognitive development. *Research Higher Education, 41*, 117–139.

Pike, G.R., Kuh, G.D., & Gonyea, R.M. (2003). The relationship between institutional mission and students' involvement and educational outcomes. *Research in Higher Education, 44*(2), 241–261.

Pike, G.R., Schroeder, C.C., & Berry, T.R. (1997). Enhancing the educational impact of residence halls: The relationship between residential learning communities and first-year college experiences and persistence. *Journal of College Student Development, 38*, 609–621.

Rago, M.A., Moore, J.V., III, & Herreid, C. (2005, June). *Disengaged and ignored: Are working students a lost cause?* Paper presented at the annual meeting of the Association for Institutional Research, San Diego, CA.

Reddy, M.A. (Ed.). (1993). *Statistical record of native North Americans*. Washington, DC: Gale Research.

Riggert, S.C., Boyle, M., Petrosko, J.M., Ash, D., & Rude-Parkins, C. (2006). Student employment and higher education: Empiricism and contradiction. *Review of Educational Research, 76*(1), 63–92.

Rudolph, F. (1977). *Curriculum: A history of the American undergraduate course of study since 1636*. San Francisco: Jossey-Bass.

Sedlacek, W.E. (2004). *Beyond the big test: Noncognitive assessment in higher education*. San Francisco: Jossey-Bass.

Stern, D., & Nakata, Y. (1991). Paid employment among U.S. college students. *Journal of Higher Education, 62*(1), 25–43.

Stinebrickner, R., & Stinebrickner, T.R. (2003). Working during school and academic performance. *Journal of Labor Economics, 21*(2), 473–491.

Terenzini, P.T., Pascarella, E.T., & Blimling, G.S. (1996). Students' out-of-class experiences and their influence on cognitive development: A literature review. *Journal of College Student Development, 37*(2), 149–162.

Tinto, V. (1975). Dropout from higher education: A theoretical synthesis of recent research. *The Journal of Higher Education, 45*(1), 89–125.

Tracey, T.J., & Sedlacek, W.E. (1987). Prediction of college graduation using noncognitive variables by race. *Measurement and Evaluation in Counseling and Development, 19*, 177–184.

Tracey, T.J., & Sedlacek, W.E. (1988). A comparison of white and black student academic success using noncognitive variables: A LISREL analysis. *Research in Higher Education, 27*, 333–348.

Tracey, T.J., & Sedlacek, W.E. (1989). Factor structure of the noncognitive questionnaire revised across samples of black and white college students. *Educational and Psychological Measurement, 49*, 637–648.

Tuttle, T., McKinney, J., & Rago, M. (2005). *College students working: The choice nexus* (IPAS Topic Brief). Bloomington, IN: Project on Academic Success.

Umbach, P.D., Kinzie, J., Thomas, A.D., Palmer, M.M., & Kuh, G.D. (2007). Women students at co-educational and women's colleges: How do their experiences compare? *Journal of College Student Development, 48*(2), 145–165.

Umbach, P.D., Palmer, M.M., Kuh, G.D., & Hannah, S.J. (2004, June). *Intercollegiate athletes and effective educational practices: Winning combination or losing effort?* Paper presented at the Forum of the Association for Institutional Research, Boston, MA.

Zhao, C.M., Kuh, G.D., & Carini, R.M. (2005). A comparison of international student and American student engagement in effective educational practices. *The Journal of Higher Education, 76*(2), 209–231.

EMPLOYING AND RETAINING TRADITIONALLY UNDERREPRESENTED STUDENTS

by Larry Lunsford

Much research has been done regarding the impact that working while attending college has on students (Astin, 1998; Dundes & Marx, 2007). Many articles have been written about students who work full- or part-time to supplement other sources of income, including scholarships, grants, and aid, to help meet college expenses (Dundes & Marx, 2007; Nunez & Cuccaro-Alamin, 1998; Pascarella, Bohr, Nora, Desler, & Zusman, 1994). One area that has had little research and attention is the employment and retention of traditionally underrepresented students on campus. Often they have been lumped into the general category of "students who work while attending college."

Researchers who have studied minority students and first-generation college students have largely focused on aspects of their college matriculation (Chen & Carroll, 2005; Choy, 2001; Inman & Mayes, 1999; Lundberg, Schreiner, Hovaguimian, & Miller, 2007; Nunez & Cuccaro-Alamin, 1998). In terms of employment, the literature has considered focused on what happens after graduation: recruitment and hiring of minority students by employers and minority student enrollment in graduate and professional programs (Chen & Carroll, 2005; Choy, 2001; Inman & Mayes, 1999; National Association of Colleges and Employers, 2006). The missing area is that of underrepresented students who work while attending college, why they work, where they work, and whether they are treated fairly and equally with majority students in the recruitment and hiring process.

University and college administrators, faculty, and staff have not developed or implemented specific recruitment methods and mentoring programs that will attract minority students to employment opportunities. However, there are exceptions at several institutions, such as the University of Kentucky, where Antomia Farrell, an African-American student, is employed as an assistant in the Agricultural Economics Department. Farrell, a junior majoring in agricultural economics, works 15 hours weekly. Farrell said that by working in the department of her major, she has the opportunity to become knowledgeable about her future career firsthand as well as get acquainted with her current and future professors (personal communication, July 21, 2008).

Farrell is a prime example of a student who has benefited from a program that targets underrepresented students. Her mentor is the diversity recruiter for the University of Kentucky, who recruited her while she was still in high school in Louisville, Ky. After she matriculated at the university, he assisted in matching her with a position within her major department. She wanted to work on campus so that she could have a flexible work schedule and work between classes. She said:

> I have learned much about agriculture in general by working there. I help the professors with various tasks and have met the professors that I will have for my classes. Working in that office has been much more beneficial for me than working in any other office on campus not related to my major. (personal communication, July 21, 2008)

Farrell also has an internship at the Lexington Farmer's Market, which led her to make one significant career decision: she eventually wants work in the business aspect of agriculture and not the farming sector.

Although Farrell was specifically recruited to the university and her job because she is a minority student, she believes that she had the same opportunity as other students to obtain her employment on campus and that her skills and major matched the department's needs. She said that she loves her job and attributes her positive attitude and success at the University of Kentucky to her mentor.

Do minority students view on-campus employment opportunities differently? Do jobs in the student's major department or areas that can provide experience toward a potential career offer more advantages for minority students than other positions on campus? How might college and university administrators work with members of underrepresented populations to be successful for both the institution and as students? What role does mentoring play in on-campus employment? These and other questions regarding employment and retention of traditionally underrepresented students on campus are explored in this chapter.

Fiscal and demographic realities

The cost of attending college has increased dramatically in recent decades, even factoring in inflation. These rising tuition and other college-related costs have put a drain on available grants, loans, and scholarships, regardless of the source. An increasing number of students find it necessary to work while in college (Pascarella et al., 1994).

According to the College Board (2008), for the 2008–09 academic year, average annual costs for undergraduate tuition, room and board, and fees were estimated at $14,333 for four-year in-state public colleges; $25,000 for four-year out-of-state institutions; and $34,132 for private, four-year colleges. This was at least a 5.2 percent increase in each area from 2007–08. But this increase was part of a growing trend. With inflation, the published tuition and fees for public, four-year institutions rose at an annual rate of 4.2 percent from 1998–99 to 2008–09. This compares to a 4.1 percent increase during the previous decade and is much higher than the rate of increase from 1978–79 and 1988–89 (College Board, 2008).

Financial concerns have resulted in record numbers of students getting jobs to pay for college; many of them are finding it necessary to work full-time. In 2006, 46.5 percent of full-time students were employed, and 8.1 percent worked 35 hours or more per week. For part-time students, 81.0 percent had jobs, and 45.5 percent worked 35 hours or more per week (National Center for Educational Statistics, 2008a). Also in 2006, for black and Hispanic students, the percentage of full-time college students working full-time was higher than the average (10.1 and 9.7 percent, respectively).

Astin (1996) noted that both employment off campus and full-time employment negatively affect students' academics. He found that first-generation college students work more hours off campus and have more nonacademic demands than other students. More students have begun to select a college on the basis of cost and available financial aid rather than the quality of programs offered (Astin, 1998).

Many students choose to work off campus because the availability of jobs is greater than on campus and the salary may be higher. Other students choose on-campus employment because they can conveniently work when not in class, while some work on campus because they are eligible for a federally funded work-study position. Students who work off campus tend to be older than those who work on campus or do not work at all (Pascarella et al., 1994).

Terrance Burgess, a black sophomore at the University of North Carolina at Chapel Hill, chose to work while attending college as a means to keep busy versus earning money to assist with his college costs (personal communication, June 27, 2008). He works on campus because he does not have a car for transportation to an off-campus position. He works an average of six hours weekly in a campus chemistry lab, ensuring that the lab is cleaned, stocked, and prepped for classes. Burgess said his on-campus job is not connected to his geology major, so it has not provided a mentor or interaction with other administrators, faculty, or staff who have assisted him with academic or personal concerns. He believes that he had as much an equal opportunity to get the job as any other student, regardless of underrepresented or majority status (personal communication, June 27, 2008).

Stage and Manning (1992) noted that "there is no longer a typical mainstream college student" (p. 9), and the influx of nontraditional and minority students continues in higher education institutions almost two decades later. Underrepresented students include black non-Hispanic, Asian, Pacific Islander, Native Hawaiian, Hispanic, American Indian, and Alaska Native. Data from the Cooperative Institutional Research Program (CIRP) covering the 2007–08 academic year indicate that in fall 2007, 10.7 percent of new college students were African-American/Black or Non-Hispanic, 9.18 percent Asian or Pacific Islander/Native Hawaiian, 8.8 percent Mexican American/Chicano or Puerto Rican or Other Latino, and 2.1 American Indian/Alaska Native (Hoover, 2008). Minority enrollments rose by 50.7 percent to 4.7 million between 1993 and 2003 (Marklein, 2006). Chen and Carroll (2005) reported that race/ethnicity also is related to first-generation status, as students of color make up 36 percent of first-generation students, but only 16 percent of continuing-generation students. "The general college student body has evolved from a homogeneous, predominantly white population to one that is culturally, racially, and ethnically diverse" (Stage & Manning, 1992, p. 1). Black student enrollment has increased more than 37 percent since 1991, and Hispanic enrollment has grown more than 75 percent, the largest of all racial/ethnic groups. Hispanic enrollment at two-year institutions has increased more than 82 percent (ACE report, 2005).

According to a American Council on Education (2006), 63.4 percent of students that attended class and also held a job were working to pay tuition, fees, or living expenses. It is disputed what, if any, consequences this dependence on a job has on student academic performance. There is, however, consensus that working full-time has an adverse effect on students' academics (see Chapters 2 and 5 for more information). Astin (1993) found that holding a full-time job during college had a significant negative impact on student grades. Furr and Elling (2000) found that on-campus employment is positively associated with attaining a bachelor's degree and with satisfaction with college. In a study of 500 19- to 24-year-old Midwestern university undergraduates, Kulm and Cramer (2006) found that the more hours students work, the lower their grade point average. However, on-campus employment showed that increased time on campus correlated with student success, possibly due to students feeling connected to peers and faculty.

Many underrepresented students must work to meet college expenses because financial aid, scholarships, and grants are not sufficient to cover tuition and the associated costs of college attendance. Seventy-five percent of the 2.7 million full-time, first-time college students received financial aid in 2005–06 (NCES, 2008b). These students also vie with their traditional counterparts for highly sought on-campus jobs. In citing studies by Inman and Mayes (1999) and Nunez and Cuccaro-Alamin (1998), Lundberg et al. (2007) noted that "when compared with others, first-generation students are employed more hours, have lower incomes, and have more financial dependents than their continuing-generation counterparts" (p. 58).

Teresa Taylor, a senior history and English dual major at Emory University in Atlanta, said that she works 20 hours per week in the campus life office during the summer but works 10 hours in that office during the school year and 10 to 12 hours as a manager at Emory's Telefund (personal communication, June 17, 2008). The campus life job is a federal work-study position. The federal work-study program allots money to colleges, which they match on a 25 percent to 75 percent ratio, to pay students for part-time work, either on the campus or with local nonprofit agencies (Lipka, 2007). The first in her family to earn a college degree, Taylor, who is Hispanic, said it is necessary for her to work part-time to help meet other expenses in addition to the private institution's high tuition.

Taylor believes that her on-campus jobs have helped her to develop time management and interpersonal skills that enable her to work well with others. She also has developed relationships with staff members who now serve as mentors, both personally and professionally. Taylor's personal philosophy derives from a quote from Madame C.J. Walker (1867–1919), a black businesswoman, entrepreneur, philanthropist, and the first female to become a self-accomplished millionaire: "I had to make my own living and my own opportunity. Don't sit down and wait for opportunities to come; you have to get up and make them." Taylor believes that being a minority student made no difference in her finding on-campus jobs. She said that she was hired because she had the skills that met the job qualifications (personal communication, June 17, 2008).

Desmond "DJ" Whatley, a junior business accounting major at Morehouse College, a historically black college in Atlanta, also is a work-study recipient. Whatley said he works while attending college because he has no other source of income to help meet his expenses (personal communication, July 2, 2008). He chose on-campus employment because of the proximity of his classes to the technology department where he works 10 hours per week. His job is not related to his major, and he said he has not identified with anyone within the department who he considers a mentor. Because Morehouse has a predominantly black enrollment, Whatley did not have to compete with traditional majority students for on-campus employment. He said he is glad that he did not have to do that because he can succeed on his own merits and believes he is more prone to advance career-wise and in higher education.

According to Rick Kincaid (in Lipka, 2007), associate director of career services at the State University of New York at Brockport, "Work-study students employed on campus with a moderate number of hours are much more likely to finish school" (p. A40). Kincaid believes it is the only form of aid that has demonstrated a positive impact on retention. Traditionally underrepresented students may find it necessary to work while attending college more than their majority counterparts because many are first-generation college students and family socioeconomic factors require that they work. Today, first-generation students comprise almost half of all college students (Choy, 2001).

Work-study provides learning opportunities

The work-study program is an area where administrators can design positions to better complement the student's education rather than serving merely as a job. Sharon Welsh, director of student employment at Rutgers University, noted that many students decline loans in favor of a work-study position at that institution (in Lipka, 2007). She is overwhelmed by matching 3,500 students in Rutgers's work-study program with open jobs and helping those left out of the program find other employment. While administrators should conceptualize work-study jobs as learning opportunities, when matching students to any position, they can be cognizant of students' course of study and align employment opportunities with these interests.

Elizabeth Primero, a 2008 graduate of the University of Arizona, was a beneficiary of the work-study program at that institution. A Hispanic first-generation college student, she generally worked 25 to 30 hours per week on campus while attending classes. She said that many of her positions were within the university's Undergraduate Initiative Department, including New Start Summer Program, Pathways, and Student Support Services (personal communication, June 24, 2008). The Undergraduate Initiative Department is located in the Department of Multicultural Affairs and Student Success within the Division of Student Affairs and provides academic retention programs, courses for credit, and other services that help students succeed in college. Primero believes that her participation in the Undergraduate Initiative Department programs and services played a direct role in her getting a job in that department. Primero, who worked to help meet college expenses, chose to work on campus because she did not have transportation to an off-campus job, but, she said, "the biggest benefit was having supervisors and co-workers understand that I was a student first" (personal communication, June 24, 2008). This exposure to working with her collegiate peers led her to declare a minor in educational leadership and later decide to pursue graduate work in student affairs administration. She spent the summer of 2008 in an internship in the Dean of Students Office at the University of Arizona prior to enrolling in graduate school at Northern Arizona University.

Primero attributed her change in career interest to mentors with whom she worked in her jobs on campus. "I consider the people I worked with my mentors because they played a vital role in my development as a student, person, and potential professional in student affairs," she said (personal communication, June 24, 2008). Primero also believes that her minority status did not play a role in the hiring process on campus and noted that the leading factor in getting the jobs she held was having been previously engaged in the services of the Undergraduate Initiative Department. She said that working in an off-campus job would not have been as valuable as the positions she held on campus.

Complementary positions beyond work-study

Designing positions that complement academics does not have to be limited to work- study. Academic departments should strive to attract students majoring in their areas. These students can then interact with faculty and administrators and be advised and mentored about their career interest while on the job.

This opportunity is not limited to academic departments. For example, at Florida International University, an engineering student may not be aware that the campus student-run radio station is a place to gain valuable engineering experience as a part of a paid job versus being a student member of the staff. However, most student-run stations are required to have a student engineer to maintain and update equipment.

In 2008, Florida International University completed a two-year project to install complex translator equipment to enable the radio station to be heard on multiple frequencies. Electrical engineering major Tom Morris, an American Indian, obtained a job at the radio station as a paid student engineer and worked closely with the contracted professional engineers throughout the lengthy installation process. His administrative supervisor and director of student media said that the experience Morris gained was unparalleled to any hourly office position elsewhere on campus (R. Jaross, personal communication, June 24, 2008). Because the university is a majority-minority institution, Morris said he does not believe he was in a situation of competing for a campus job with traditional majority students. He said he was specifically attracted to the radio station job so that he could not only use but also enhance his engineering knowledge and skills (personal communication, August 12, 2008). Casella and Brougham (1995) noted that "work experience before graduation provides more than practical job training and skills; it also contributes to an individual's personal development in a number of ways. … Such opportunities develop self-reliance, self-confidence, and responsibility" (p. 26).

Tim Brown, a black senior at The University of Texas at Arlington, is another example of a student who has benefited academically, and potentially professionally, from his on-campus employment. Brown, a theater arts major, said that his first work-study employment on campus was in the university theater ticket office until the director of the scene shop encouraged Brown to transfer to that department. "Acting is risky," he said. "I can always find a job building sets if I have difficulty getting acting jobs" (personal communication, July 19, 2008). He said the experience he has gained working in both offices has been invaluable in exposing him to many aspects of the theater environment. His goal is to move to Hollywood after graduation, and he believes that his work experience while a student will complement the academic training that has prepared him for an acting career.

Brown said mentoring has played a major role in his development at The University of Texas at Arlington. In 2008, he changed employment to the Student Governance and Organizations Office where an administrator encouraged him to get involved and convinced him that he could make a difference. "He told me to take advantage of all opportunities and that leadership will take me everywhere," Brown said (personal communication, July 19, 2008).

Mentoring proves valuable

Employment programs and positions specifically designed to attract underrepresented students may interest individuals who believe that such opportunities are not available. These positions can ultimately help students develop skills and knowledge that benefit them personally and professionally. Additionally, as a major benefit of these specifically designed jobs, mentoring can occur, as it did for Farrell at the University of Kentucky and Brown at The University of Texas at Arlington. Students mentored on the job not only have the opportunity to improve academic performance, but they also produce learning outcomes that serve as experiential tools in their maturation and development. On-campus employment provides an excellent opportunity to demonstrate that cross-racial mentoring not only is possible but also culturally beneficial to the participating students.

If administrators implement specific recruitment, retention, and support mechanisms for underrepresented students in on-campus jobs, their efforts could result in higher enrollment and success rates. In a study by Furr and Elling (2000), 73.9 percent of working students said that working never negatively affected their academics, and only 4.3 percent said it frequently interfered with their academics. Supervisors and other staff have the opportunity to serve as mentors for these students. Mentoring occurs when more knowledgeable and experienced individuals assist the development and growth of others (Caffarella, 1992). Seepersad, Hagood-Elliott, Lewis, and Strickland (2007) said that "by recognizing the cultural perceptions and differences that exist, mentors and protégés may develop a better understanding of each other's culture so as to enhance mentoring outcomes and student success" (p. 102).

On-campus employment may foster involvement with other students and with faculty and enhance the student's integration into the college (Pascarella et al., 1994). Regardless of the type of work experience, Casella and Brougham (1995) noted that exposure to a professional working environment benefits students because they are "building networks, improving self-organization, establishing a greater sense of responsibility, expanding work skills, learning more about personal strengths and values, and gaining self-confidence" (p. 25). Developing these experiences and skills is particularly important to minority students in preparing to enter the job market or graduate school. Their background and past experiences may not have provided such educational opportunities. Their outlook toward gaining the best on-campus jobs as well as future professional opportunities may have been influenced by perceived or inherent prejudices, which cause them to view employment opportunities differently than majority students. Administrators should recognize that underrepresented students sometimes believe that most on-campus employment positions are closed to them. It is important to develop a means to capitalize on students' abilities and actively recruit them for employment.

Dee Wood, former diversity director for Delta Airlines and former manager of Career Network Development for General Electric, said, "The value of providing mentors is absolutely invaluable. Mentors are ones who can open a plethora of doors for the mentee. Accessibility to leaders and mentors provides bigger and better doors to open in the job market and work place" (personal communication, August 15, 2008). Wood added that if underrepresented students are recruited to on-campus jobs when they enter college, this early introduction to university leaders, professors, and administrators allows quicker and better assimilation to the university and learning processes.

Batchelor (1993) discussed studies about the effect of mentoring on underrepresented individuals, noting that both informal and formal relationships between mentors and mentees can provide diversity and breadth to professional growth. The support mechanisms created by the supervisors/mentors prepare students for the work world through reality- and reflection-based activities. Many of these underrepresented students will eventually become the first members of their families to hold a full-time professional position. Understanding what this means is a large part of designing a recruitment and mentoring program for this population. Understanding how culture intertwines with this dynamic is important. For example, the Hispanic family unit is known to be close-knit (Ortiz, 2004). Moving away from home to accept a professional position elsewhere often is not an option—or at least not an easy one. Black students may come from single-parent homes or from homes with a grandparent as the head of the household. Helping students form new connections with employers who are serious about recruiting minority graduates is one way administrators can assist with recruitment and retention efforts. And, helping employers understand students and their cultural nuances—essentially increasing employers' cultural competence—can help both employers and students.

In citing research by Galbraith and Cohen (1995), Seepersad et al. (2007, p. 104) noted that because black students are often the first in their family to go to college, they often "experience difficulties when confronted with cultural values and norms that contradict their own, and can benefit from the guidance of a mentor in these instances."

Seepersad and Bailey-Watson (2007) noted that "mentoring occurs when a more experienced person, or mentor, supports and guides another, the protégé. It is a learning relationship that develops knowledge and empowerment" (p. 96). The protégés can connect this knowledge to new information and skills and construct meaning for them by interacting with the mentor (Kerka, 1998). Administrators, faculty, and staff who serve as mentors have the ability to impart to student workers knowledge that can be transformed to improving time management skills, dealing with stress, developing effective study skills, improving written and verbal communications skills, and dealing with personal matters such as health, finances, and relationships.

Audrey Murrell, professor of business administration, psychology, and public and international affairs at the University of Pittsburgh has built a career studying why whole groups of people have been "underutilized" or hindered in their ability to succeed in careers. In Gill (2008), Murrell asks, "What can we do to facilitate connections between people who are different? What can we do to help women and people of color break through the glass ceiling or the concrete ceiling? What can we do?" (p. 36). Murrell found answers to these questions in her personal history of having role models and mentors:

> Mentoring is clearly a tool to help across all aspects of the workforce value chain—to develop employees, leaders, and organizations. You have to tie people's fate together. Mentoring ties you to another. When that happens, it facilitates understanding. It bridges differences. It's a powerful tool for learning. (Gill, 2008, p. 36)

Mentoring underrepresented students, particularly first-generation college students, can result in their persistence toward meeting academic challenges. First-generation students are "at a disadvantage in terms of their access to, persistence through, and completion of postsecondary education. Once in college, their relative disadvantage continued with respect to course taking and academic performance" (Chen, 2005, ¶1D). With the added pressure of securing sufficient financial aid and doing well in the classroom, minority students also face the daunting task of getting a job while attending college. They face obstacles both off and on campus, depending on whether they have the qualifications for the position and, in some cases, become a victim of prejudice in the hiring process.

After graduation

Positions on campus that complement the student's major and potential career will be beneficial should the student decide to apply for graduate school in that specific major. Students with practical work experience or an internship in their chosen career also have a real advantage in the interview process. Diversity recruiting is one of the most important challenges facing employers (NACE, 2006); therefore, the National Association of Colleges and Employers (NACE) asked college career services departments to identify employers that do outstanding work with diversity recruiting. IBM was one company identified. Bill Lawrence, senior diversity staffing program manager at IBM, told NACE:

> Make diversity recruiting a business imperative. Diversity recruiting through programs such as Project View gives IBM the ability to have its workforce mirror the marketplace. Project View brings together hiring managers and African American, Asian, Latino, and Native American students and students with disabilities from colleges and universities across the country. (NACE, 2003, ¶ 2)

Employers like IBM recognize students who have gained valuable experiences that can be transferred to the workplace.

America's Dynamic Workforce (U.S. Department of Labor, 2007) indicated that the workforce will be more diverse in the coming decades. As the white workforce declines in numbers, the minority workforces will increase. In 2005, minorities made up 18.4 percent of the workforce; this number is continuing to grow (U.S. Department of Labor, 2007). The U.S. Department of Labor estimates this percentage will increase to 26.9 percent by 2050, with black workers constituting 13.8 percent and Asian workers 8.3 percent (2007). Additionally, the Hispanic worker population is expected to grow to 17.3 percent by 2020 and 24.3 percent by 2050 (U.S. Department of Labor, 2007).

Underrepresented students, particularly first-generation, may view employment opportunities differently because their needs are different than majority students. Despite uncertain and unpredictable future job markets, students' unique backgrounds influence their opinions about employment, employment opportunities, and employers in ways that recruiters need to recognize. Recruiters, such as IBM, that are most successful at recruiting a diverse workforce pay attention to this idea and capitalize on their ability to meet each applicant's questions with confidence. It is easy for recruiters to provide fancy, glossy brochures to minority students, but it requires learned skills and knowledge to connect with them on a personal level.

On-campus job benefits

There is much more racial and ethnic diversity on most campuses than ever before, and minority students indicate they believe that there is better racial understanding on college campuses than in the past (Smith, 2007). Although underrepresented students may feel lost when they first arrive on campus and be reluctant to look for an on-campus job, minority students may be less likely to encounter prejudice in on-campus employment than off-campus. In on-campus positions, these students are exposed to administrators and faculty who serve as valuable resources for them in choosing classes, determining career paths, deciding on graduate and professional programs, serving as references, and assisting with networking. According to Lundberg et al. (2007):

> Engagement with faculty and other university personnel may be especially beneficial for first-generation students as those people can provide the necessary information, perspective, values, and socialization that may compensate for cultural capital that was not available to first-generation students in their families and broader social networks prior to the college experience. (p. 59)

Every student interviewed for this chapter said that faculty, staff, and/or administrators with whom they worked became valuable contacts and sources of information, advice, and counsel during their matriculation. Emory's Taylor said the influence of her professional mentors in the campus life office was so strong that she had considered changing majors and applying to a graduate program in higher education administration. Arizona's Primero actually made the change in major and career plan.

Furr and Elling (2000) found that developing an important relationship with faculty helps students remain in college. Students, such as the University of Kentucky's Farrell, who work and establish a relationship with faculty, are significantly more likely to state that this relationship helped them remain in college. Employment on campus does have a positive effect on involvement with professors. "Students working on campus frequently work in their major department and may have more opportunities to interact informally with faculty and to learn about opportunities outside the classroom" (Furr & Elling, 2000, p. 464).

Summary

The prevailing motivation for working while in college is simply that students have to work to help meet expenses—not because they want to work. Although there are exceptions like North Carolina's Burgess, who works to keep himself busy, other students must work to contribute to their educational costs and various personal expenses. Students prefer the convenience of working on campus versus off campus even though off-campus jobs may pay more. Although off-campus jobs can provide tangible skills that students may utilize in their major discipline and potential careers, on-campus positions that complement the student's skills and major prove more beneficial in the student's academic success, graduate and professional school applications, and job interviews.

Students also endorse the role of mentors in their personal, academic, and professional development. It is well documented that mentors educate student employees about many aspects of their major discipline and assist them by providing important reference letters, building an academic and professional network, and locating internships and co-op opportunities that enable them to further build their resumes (Batchelor, 1993; Casella & Brougham, 1995).

Regardless of geographic location, minority students interviewed for this chapter indicated they believed they had an equal opportunity to secure an on-campus position as their majority counterparts. None of the students indicated they were not hired for a position because of their minority status or that it was a benefit in getting their respective positions. The students believed they were hired based on qualifications, particularly if the job required personal characteristics such as leadership skills or was related to their major. Smith (2007) reviewed the 2006 CIRP data and noted that "only 34 percent of college freshmen rated the objective of helping to promote racial understanding as 'essential' or 'very important,' a decline from a high of 46.4 percent in 1992, the year of the Rodney King-related riots in Los Angeles" (p. 1). Minority students employed in their major department on campus overwhelmingly responded that they were hired based on their major.

Even though underrepresented students indicate they believe they have as much an equal opportunity to seek and obtain on-campus jobs as majority students, college and university administrators could do more to actively recruit and serve this population. For the most part, on-campus jobs are posted, and students are hired at random, although work-study positions often are filled with referrals from the financial aid office. Specific attention should be paid committing to and implementing a plan that specifically educates students with knowledge and skills that can benefit them academically and professionally. Pascarella and associates (1994) recommended that first-year college advisors use evidence gleaned from research when counseling students so that students understand that working does not necessarily negatively affect their studies. They learned that student employment may even facilitate dimensions of growth and maturation in college. This concept is particularly important for first-generation students who might not have parents or family members who experienced working during college. Further, educating parents through orientations, publications, or other forums can help deliver the positive message that working during college can be beneficial for students.

One departmental area that executes an action plan to recruit and educate students in a specific academic discipline is the campus life or student activities office. There, students enjoy working with their peers and are attracted to a career in student personnel or higher education administration (both Emory University's Taylor and University of Arizona's Primero commented on this connection). Academic departments are another exception where students majoring in a department's specific discipline are sought as part-time workers. These students have the basic skills and knowledge that complement the work of the department and provide an opportunity to further their development on the job. Academic departments employing students in their major find that students develop relationships with administrators, faculty, and staff who provide valuable assistance. Opportunities for underrepresented students serve as a recruitment tool for future students and increase the retention rate of continuing students. On-campus positions should be designed to be learning opportunities for students versus simply constructed as jobs. These learning opportunities for minority students can lead to increased interest in academics and persistence in the often difficult and challenging academic routine.

It is clear from the research that underrepresented students, particularly those who are first-year college students, face various disadvantages and challenges when entering college. It is often a struggle to conform and adjust to the academic environment's demands. Since many underrepresented students find it necessary to work to meet educational and personal expenses, working while adjusting to academic rigors only adds an extra burden to these students' already heavy load.

College and university administrators can ease minority individuals' transition by designing a specific strategy for recruiting, training, and helping minority students understand the world of work into which they will need to be prepared to enter when they graduate. Personal counseling, academic advising, and advice on things like how one should dress on the job, how one should talk to others, and how one should interact with co-workers can be provided to the student at his or her on-campus employment. These support mechanisms prepare students through reality- and reflection-based activities. Understanding the dynamics of this special population will enable the employing administrators to better recruit these students. Both the student and the department reap the benefits of the relationship. The department will have loyal and dedicated students who see their role as more than a job. The students will be better prepared to meet the demands of graduate or professional school or the workplace. They also will have the opportunity to gain long-lasting relationships with faculty, administrators, and staff with whom they work.

References

ACE report: Minority college enrollment climbs, but gaps persist. (2005, March 10). *Black Issues in Higher Education, 22*(2), 10.

American Council on Education. (2006, May). Working their way through college: Student employment and its impact on the college experience. Retrieved February 2, 2009, from http://professionals.collegeboard.com/profdownload/trends-in-college-pricing-2008.pdf

Astin, A.W. (1993). *What matters in college.* San Francisco: Jossey-Bass.

Astin, A.W. (1996). Involvement in learning revisited: Lessons we have learned. *Journal of College Student Development, 37*(2), 123–133.

Astin, A.W. (1998). The changing American college student: Thirty-year trends, 1966–1996. *Review of Higher Education, 21*(2), 115–135.

Batchelor, S.W. (1993). Mentoring and self-directed learning. In M.J. Barr & Associates (Eds.), *The handbook of student affairs administration* (pp. 378–389). San Francisco: Jossey-Bass.

Caffarella, R.S. (1992). *Psychosocial development of women: linkages of teaching and leadership in adult education.* Information Series No. 350, Columbus, OH: ERIC Clearinghouse on Adult, Career, and Vocational Education, Center on Education and Training for Employment, The Ohio State University. (ERIC Document Reproduction Service No. ED354386).

Casella, D.A., & Brougham, C.E. (1995). Work works: Student jobs open front doors to careers. *Journal of Career Planning and Employment, 55*(4), 24–27.

Chen, X., & Carroll, C.D. (2005). *First-generation students in postsecondary education: A look at their college transcripts* (NCES 2005-171). U.S. Department of Education, National Center for Educational Statistics. Washington, DC: U.S. Government Printing Office.

Choy, S. (2001). *Students whose parents did not go to college: Postsecondary access, persistence, and attainment* (NCES Statistical Report 2001-126). Washington, DC: U.S. Government Printing Office.

College Board. (2008). Trends in higher education series: Trends in college pricing. Retrieved February 3, 2009, from http://professionals.collegeboard.com/profdownload/trends-in-college-pricing-2008.pdf

Dundes, L., & Marx, J. (2006-2007). Balancing work and academics in college: Why do students working 10 to 19 hours excel? *Journal of College Student Retention, 8*(1), 107–120.

Furr, S.R., & Elling, T.W. (2000). The influence of work on college student development. *NASPA Journal, 37*(2), 454–470.

Galbraith, M.W., & Cohen, N.H. (Eds.) (1995). *Mentoring: New strategies and challenges, New directions for adult and continuing education, No. 66.* San Francisco: Jossey-Bass.

Gill, C. (2008, Spring). The m factor. *Pitt Magazine*, pp. 34–37.

Hoover, E. (2008, February 1). Colleges face tough sell to freshmen, survey finds. *The Chronicle of Higher Education*, p. A1.

Inman, W.E., & Mayes, L. (1999). The importance of being first: Unique characteristics of first-generation community college students. *Community College Review, 26*(4), 3–23.

Kerka, S. (1998). *New perspectives on mentoring.* ERIC Digest 194. (ERIC Document Reproduction Service No. ED418249).

Kulm, T.L., & Cramer, S. (2006). The relationship of student employment to student role, family relationships, social interactions and persistence. *College Student Journal, 40*(4), 927–938.

Lipka, S. (2007, January 26). More students seek campus jobs as work-study positions dwindle. *The Chronicle of Higher Education*, p. A40.

Lundberg, C.A., Schreiner, L.A., Hovaguimian, K.D., & Miller, S.S. (2007). First-generation status and student race/ethnicity as distinct predictors of student involvement and learning. *NASPA Journal, 44*(1), 57–83.

Marklein, M.B. (2006, October 29). Minority enrollment in college still lagging. *USA Today*, p. 5D.

National Association of Colleges and Employers. (2003, January 9). Best practices for diversity recruiting: IBM. Spotlight Online. Retrieved May, 29, 2008 from http://www.naceweb.org/pubs/broadcast/2003/e010903.htm

National Association of Colleges and Employers. (2006, Summer). Diversity recruiting: How career services can help employers. *Journal of Career Planning and Employment*, 37–40.

National Center for Educational Statistics. (2008a). The condition of education 2008: Indicator 43, Employment of college students. Retrieved February 2, 2009, from http://nces.ed.gov/programs/coe/2008/pdf/43_2008.pdf.

National Center for Educational Statistics. (2008b). Enrollment in postsecondary institutions, fall 2006: Graduation rates, 2000 & 2003 cohorts; and financial statistics, 2006. Retrieved February 2, 2009, from http://nces.ed.gov/pubs2008/2008173.pdf

Nunez, A.M., & Cuccaro-Alamin, S. (1998). *First-generation students: Undergraduates whose parents never enrolled in postsecondary education* (Report No. NCES 98-082). Washington, DC: National Center for Education Statistics.

Ortiz, A.M. (2004). Promoting the success of Latino students: A call to action. In A.M. Ortiz (Ed.), *Addressing the unique needs of Latino American students, New directions for student services, No. 105* (pp. 89–97). San Francisco: Jossey-Bass.

Pascarella, E.T., Bohr, L., Nora, A., Desler, M., & Zusman, B. (1994). Impacts of on-campus and off-campus work on first-year cognitive outcomes. *Journal of College Student Development, 35*(5), 364–370.

Seepersad, R., & Bailey-Watson, M. (2007). Mentor in the third age: A learning perspective. In S.M. Nielsen & M.S. Plakhotnik (Eds.), *Proceedings of the Sixth Annual College of Education Research Conference: Urban and International Education Section* (pp. 96–101). Miami: Florida International University.

Seepersad, R., Hagood-Elliott, K., Lewis, K., & Strickland, S.L. (2007). Cross-cultural mentoring: Exploration through the lens of African American students. In S.M. Nielsen & M.S. Plakhotnik (Eds.), *Proceedings of the Sixth Annual College of Education Research Conference: Urban and International Education Section* (pp. 102–107). Miami: Florida International University.

Smith, L. (2007, April 9). Four decades of survey data on American freshmen reveal widening socioeconomic gap. *The Chronicle of Higher Education: Today's News*. Retrieved February 2, 3009, from http://chronicle.com/daily/2007/04/2007040906n.htm

Stage, F.K., & Manning, K. (Eds.) (1992). *Enhancing the multicultural campus environment: A cultural brokering approach, New directions for student services, No. 60*. San Francisco: Jossey-Bass.

U.S. Department of Labor. (2007, August). America's Dynamic Workforce. Retrieved January 16, 2009 from the U.S. Department of Labor website: http://www.dol.gov/asp/media/reports/workforce2007/ADW2007_Chart_Book.pdf

WHEN STUDENTS ARE IN CHARGE: A MULTIPLE CASE STUDY OF TWO CALIFORNIA UNIVERSITIES

by Jerry Mann & Nadesan Permaul

Not all models of student employment on college and university campuses are overseen by the institution. Peer management and training also are effective models of leadership development in the college and university setting. At the University of California, Berkeley, and the University of California, Los Angeles, student leadership development by students for students has a long and illustrious history. This University of California model offers general notions of creating successful management opportunities for student employees regardless of organizational structure.

Case 1: University of California, Berkeley

Evolution of student-managed programs

From the outset, the University of California developed under what was known as the German model of higher education and strove to become a research and scholarly institution. State funding was restricted to those efforts, and services and programs for students were strictly within the purview of the students to provide. As a consequence, and with Berkeley's then-remote location on farmland north of Oakland, Calif., students began creating their own service model early. The Cooperative Store, established in 1883, was a perfect example, aimed at providing sundries and materials that students could not otherwise easily obtain without going by horse trolley to Oakland, miles away. Over time, the creation of student-run services, programs, and businesses became a campus hallmark.

Running the business

For more than 100 years thereafter, students hired and fired their own employees. They provided benefits and maintained their own retirement program and worker's compensation. The businesses were overseen by an auxiliary director with whom they contracted directly and who answered to them—both the strength and weakness of student-managed services. The on-the-job experience was substantive and fundamental, but it also led to complexities associated with the rapid turnover of student governments and a loss of business continuity. Nevertheless, students managed these affairs directly until 1998.

The ASUC Auxiliary

Under the original management of Associated Students of the University of California, Berkeley (ASUC) from 1887 to 1998, students directly oversaw the ASUC's business operations. The 1994 "Statement of Understanding" between the ASUC and the university stated the following in recognition of that historic and longstanding structure: "The ASUC shall maintain its own personnel system and shall be responsible for the wages, hours, working conditions, hiring, and termination of its employees" (University of California, Berkeley, n.d.a, p. 2, ¶ 4.1). This structure was replaced in 1998 by a new business model, the ASUC Auxiliary, which became the ASUC fiduciary agent. The role assigned to the Auxiliary was the same as that previously held by the ASUC business operation prior to 1998. In the Commercial Services Agreement, the role of Auxiliary is defined as:

> The Auxiliary shall negotiate and manage leases and other contracts with third-party providers of the ASUC Commercial Activities pursuant to the direction of the ASUC Store Operations Board; provide landlord services to such providers; and carry out such other functions, including those described in Section 6, below, as directed by the board. (University of California, Berkeley, 1998, Section 1, p. 2, ¶ 1.1)

The Store Operations Board has a simple and direct purpose: "The board shall establish policy and standards for, and provide oversight over all ASUC Commercial Activities in a manner consistent with all applicable university policies..." (University of California, Berkeley, 1998, Section 1.2). The board consists of 11 voting members, appointed as follows: the ASUC president and executive vice president; two enrolled undergraduate members serving two-year terms; two enrolled graduate student members serving two-year terms; three at-large university representatives appointed by the chancellor, serving two-year terms; two faculty members nominated by the Academic Senate of the University of California, Berkeley and appointed by the chancellor. This structure allows students to maintain a majority of votes on the Store Operations Board in its role of recommending commercial activities policies, contracts, and the budget of the ASUC Auxiliary, to the chancellor. This majority gives student leaders primary say over the kinds of businesses, the philosophy of commercial development, and the approval of contracts and budgets (including the budget of the Auxiliary). This approach reinforces the historic authority that students have exercised at the ASUC since the 19th century.

In addition, the Auxiliary oversees all services provided to student government for the management and operations of its programs that involve professional staff, the oversight and accounting of its funds and student government advising. The ASUC Auxiliary director sits as an ex-officio member of the Store Operations Board and makes regular reports to both the board (once per month or as directed) and the ASUC Senate (weekly). The director also advises graduate student government in its relations with the campus.

The Auxiliary has only 27 professional staff and is distinct from the campus-managed Undergraduate Student Affairs. The Auxiliary receives no funding from the Berkeley campus, its operations are fully funded by student revenues, and its budget is approved at the Store Operations Board prior to submission to the campus for administrative review and approval. The degree to which student leaders work with the Auxiliary staff is often a function of ideology. Some student governments believe fundamentally in their own exigency. Others wish to collaborate and learn how to navigate the administrative process as a team. Both can be effective, but take on a different appearance and set of responses from the Auxiliary professional staff. In the former, administrators act as an influence. In the latter, administrators may perform the role of teacher. In both, a partnership is sought.

For example, the growth of liability insurance issues has created a complex problem of authority at the Berkeley campus. Students have traditionally volunteered as ASUC organizations at concessions operated by Intercollegiate Athletics on game days. But the need for liability insurance and a form of worker's compensation for the "volunteers" who receive donations from the concession vendor has created not only contract and business issues that could affect the funds students receivefor their volunteer efforts, but also a question of independence of student management in certain affairs. The director of the Auxiliary is the navigator for the student government with its general counsel for the 501(c)(3) and for the university in its dealings with the student government. The director must both represent the interests of the university and assist the students in making their case to campus administrators.

While the Auxiliary takes leadership in maintaining the fiduciary health of the ASUC businesses, it does so on the students' behalf. For example, the Auxiliary presented to the Campus Executive Planning Committee, including the chancellor, a proposal to enhance the commercial development of ASUC businesses at the Student Union complex. This was done in conjunction with both the ASUC president and the Graduate Assembly. At the conclusion of the meeting, when authorization to proceed was requested, the committee looked to the ASUC president, rather than the Auxiliary director, for the final word on support for the project. While the director will be responsible for developing and implementing the plan, the decision to proceed was based on student support after fulfilling all campus requirements and expectations.

The mission of the Auxiliary as defined by the university is: "To create a student-centered environment that provides the campus community with programs, activities, services, and facilities that extend student learning beyond the classroom" (University of California, Berkeley, 2007, ¶ 1). In this sense, the Auxiliary is the student government's partner, operating its facilities and making its programs available on behalf of student government. The Auxiliary's principal operational duty is to ensure that the students' fiscal resources are adequate to meet their financial obligations. Therefore, the Auxiliary is the student government's fiduciary agent at Berkeley. As fiduciary agent, the Auxiliary keeps student government apprised of the financial condition and available options and makes recommendations to the Store Operations Board on the Auxiliary's perspective on how to best proceed in the commercial operations that generate revenue. The university manages its bank and investment accounts administratively, but students make all the financial decisions on their own. The student government budget is completely separate, and while staff provide valuable historical input in how to approach the management of the budget, the students oversee that portion through their own finance committee, finance officer, and administrative leaders.

Conclusion

The University of California, Berkeley's kind of assertive and affirmative student leadership is part of the business of educating students to manage their affairs and resources. At the 2008 annual banquet student government leaders hosted to recognize their own efforts over the course of the year, speakers emphasized the importance of autonomous and experiential student development. As students manage their own self-initiated programs in community outreach, mentorship, and academic course development, student governance at Berkeley has shaped both the campus and the student culture and identity.

Case 2: University of California, Los Angeles

The Associated Students University of California, Los Angeles (ASUCLA) is a unique enterprise. Born in the early 20th century, it has retained a number of historical delegations to operate the campus retail, food, college union, and licensing and trademark franchises inside a structure governed and controlled by students. With total gross sales in excess of $75 million, the self-operation of the campus bookstore and cash (non-board or residence hall) food service is unique in an overall education environment that leans heavily on outsourcing and the use of third parties to run campus retail services.

According to its mission, "The Associated Students UCLA, as a responsive student-centered organization, provides innovative and excellent services, programs, products, and facilities for the entire UCLA community," describes "its role as the center of campus collaboration, connection, and service to enrich the experience of the entire UCLA community" (ASUCLA, n.d.a, ¶ 1).

Essentially, ASUCLA is a real learning laboratory for students. From involvement in student government and student organizations, to meaningful student employment, to a chance to help direct a multimillion-dollar enterprise, ASUCLA develops students by helping them acquire tangible skills under real circumstances.

ASUCLA structure

Given its long history, ASUCLA's structure has no duplicate. Originally legally defined as an unincorporated not-for-profit student association, its status now is more closely aligned with that of a 501(c)(3). ASUCLA comprises four separate and distinct entities, separately governed, that file a consolidated tax return. These four entities are the (1) undergraduate and (2) graduate student governments, (3) student media, and (4) Services and Enterprises. Of the four, Services and Enterprises is the largest, comprised of retail operations, food services and licensing, and the college union (see Figure 7.1).

A board of 14 members, with 10 voting, governs Services and Enterprises. Its constituents are four Undergraduate Students Association Council-appointed undergraduates, four Graduate Students Association-appointed graduates, two chancellor-appointed UCLA administrators, one Academic Senate-appointed faculty member, and two Alumni Association-appointed alumni (see Figure 7.2).

FIGURE 7.1 ASUCLA ORGANIZATIONAL CHART

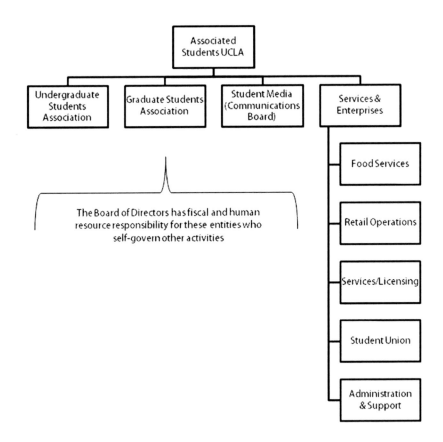

With a nearly $75 million enterprise to operate, this mixture of appointees ensures that the student voice, while in the majority, is tempered with a steadying influence of administration, faculty, and alumni. In addition, in an organization that relies on the purchasing activity of all members of campus, and that serves those members with a variety of other services, a representative board considers all opinions when evaluating strategic direction, service delivery, and facility development and renovation.

The board relies on a robust committee structure to perform the many functions necessary to keep an enterprise of this magnitude functioning, without bogging the board itself down in the minutiae (see Figure 7.3).

ASUCLA's management structure reflects its status as a large employer of students. With student employment as a cornerstone of its mission and operating philosophy, ASUCLA relies on a somewhat small cadre of career managers and employees to oversee more than 1,200 student employees. The three major reporting divisions rely on similar structures for their day-to-day operation.

FIGURE 7.2 SERVICES AND ENTERPRISES BOARD

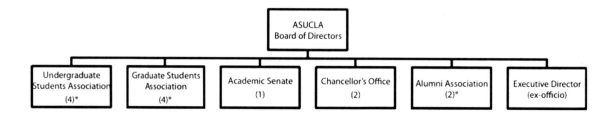

*One of these is an alternate who votes only in the absence of the other member(s)

FIGURE 7.3 BOARD OF DIRECTORS COMMITTEE STRUCTURE

BOARD OF DIRECTORS			
Finance Committee	**Services Committee**	**Personnel Committee**	**Executive Committee**
• Review budget & recommend to board • Recommend auditor, review audit • Review financial statements • Consider action on other financial/budgetary items	• Approve facilities allocation policies • Review/recommend planning, development of facilities • Review/recommend new & termination of services • Review customer satisfaction	• Evaluate executive director • Make recommendations on personnel issues • Review/approve compensation policies	• Act as board's proxy between meetings • Consult with executive director • Serve as nominating committee • Serve as conduct committee

Operational management structure

Simply put, a thin layer of management (director, division area manager, service area manager, student managers, and student employees) oversees a largely student-run workforce. The common practice is for students to become employed as first-year students in entry-level positions, usually front-line customer service (e.g., cashiers, servers, loading crew, and administrative clerks). During the next year or more—assuming they are retained, as many move on to other employment and employers—they receive training and experience enabling them to move up the supervisorial ladder.

By the time they achieve the level of senior student supervisor, they perform work that is often within the scope of a career-level employee. They manage food service and store locations (open and close operations, create work schedules, hire student employees, and participate in the employee performance review cycle), run the buildings as building managers, oversee events as event managers, or perform sophisticated office functions as management assistants.

As with many other campuses, ASUCLA relies on this structure to help keep its labor costs within reason, to populate its workforce with intelligent and creative employees, and to provide a pool of potential entry-level candidates who may find a home with the Association after graduation.

A glance at ASUCLA's management ranks finds a substantial number of UCLA graduates and former ASUCLA student employees, who continue to dedicate their considerable talents to the enterprise, benefiting the campus with which they so closely identify.

Role of the executive director

ASUCLA's executive director must be many things to many people. To UCLA's administration, the role is twofold. On one hand, the executive director must act as the CEO of a successful business auxiliary by operating a financially solvent enterprise, maintaining adequate capital reserves, and continuing investment in ASUCLA's facilities so that they are a credit to the institution. On the other hand, he or she must also actively participate as a member of a student affairs division that supports, as so many others do, the university's teaching, research, and public service functions through programs, services, and out-of-classroom educational experiences.

To UCLA's students, the role is also twofold. First, the executive director has to act as the CEO of the business auxiliary on campus that most often touches their lives (outside of housing); he or she needs to ensure that students have first access to its facilities and that it delivers the broadest array of products and services at the lowest prices and continues to be the employer of choice offering the highest paying jobs on campus. Second, the executive director must challenge ASUCLA at every turn—that is, act as a voice for students, particularly in matters of social responsibility where the enterprise's perceived power can carry weight and influence behavior beyond the boundaries of the campus.

For ASUCLA's employees, the executive director provides the leadership necessary to guide a multifaceted enterprise with many competing divisions and, with the executive management team, to formulate the enterprise's strategic direction (separate from the board's strategic efforts). Not to be diminished is the role of the executive director as ASUCLA's employees' representative to the board.

Juggling this multitude of roles is an art form, requiring a talent for and tolerance of ambiguity. The challenges are many; first and foremost is that the executive director reports to a student-majority board of directors. In a normal board setting, directors are appointed or elected to the board of a business with which they share an affinity. They possess real-world experience, and there is rarely a question of where their true interests lie (with no doubt that their fiduciary responsibility lies in the ongoing well-being of the enterprise they oversee).

The one aspect of student governance with the greatest potential to affect ASUCLA is its decision to be a socially responsible enterprise. While many for-profit and non-profit organizations have some element of social responsibility or good citizenship as part of their corporate charter, few would consider damaging the company's financial viability to adopt a socially responsible course of action. With shareholder return as the primary gauge of corporate effectiveness, any diversion of profit to nonprofit pursuits must be judged on the ultimate goodwill it brings to the company, and goodwill is usually associated with increased shareholder return at some time in the future. However, under a student governance model, the prioritization of social responsibility versus financial health—

and the identification of goodwill actions' return on investment—can be different than the ordering a more experienced-managed board might choose.

Student employment

Given the unique governance model of ASUCLA, it might be assumed that student employment practices differ greatly from those found on other campuses. This is not the case. More significant are operational, social, and environmental factors that directly influence ASUCLA's student employment model.

A commitment to maximizing student employment opportunities has long been an important part of ASUCLA's student employment philosophy, now codified as one of its core values:

> One of the Associated Students UCLA's core missions as a student-centered organization is exemplified in the professional development of our student employees. ASUCLA is the largest employer of students on campus, providing good-paying jobs tailored to student schedules in convenient locations around campus. For ambitious students, ASUCLA offers management experience in retail operations, facility management, and administrative services. Many of our student leaders become career employees who continue our tradition of providing a workplace environment that fosters respect, empowerment and individual development. (ASUCLA, n.d.b, ¶ 4)

Given the overall scope of its operations, ASUCLA employs a large number of students (1,200–1,500 at any given time). In many respects, this is a direct reflection of its commitment to self-operation of the student store and food service. Generally, when those functions are outsourced, third-party providers tend to rely more on full-time employees than part-time student employees.

In addition, California is a state where labor unions play a strong role and at ASUCLA, its food service, housekeepers, maintenance, and security personnel are all members of a union. The incremental costs of converting large numbers of student jobs to full-time jobs—particularly considering higher wage costs attendant to the Los Angeles area and generous benefits available to employees—would make a shift toward a full-time employee model financially untenable for the association.

Student employment at ASUCLA is governed by fairly detailed policies and procedures that provide guidance and structure for all student employees in general, and store employees specifically (ASUCLA, n.d.c). As an independent auxiliary on campus, defined by the "Statement of Understanding," ASUCLA provides its own human resources delivery, with a dedicated department that handles all elements of the employment experience.

With a large contingent of student employees, many engaged in jobs that support retail functions, food service delivery, and union facility operations, a formal development program would be too large and cumbersome to manage, let alone to deliver meaningful growth opportunities to the bulk of the student employees. Indeed, the employment ASUCLA offers is not much different than that found off campus, with students performing cashiering/clerking functions at a retail outlet, preparing food in a restaurant, or serving to customers across a counter. Turnover can be high in these types of positions and for many students who hold these jobs, development opportunities are neither expected nor desired.

The primary focus of ASUCLA's development philosophy is to encourage student employees to move up through the ranks to supervisory positions (see Figure 7.4, which shows hierarchy). As described earlier, the management structure is lightly populated and the bulk of unit supervision on a day-to-day basis is left to students. The common path for a student so motivated would be to work for some period of time—as little as six months in some cases—and upon showing merit and promise, be promoted to a first-level supervisor. The path to a more senior supervisory position generally follows until graduation. It is a source of pride for the association is that of the approximately 100 ASUCLA career managers, 40 percent were formerly student employees (ASUCLA, n.d.d). In ASUCLA's case, it could be argued that one of the best learning outcomes is meaningful employment with an opportunity for advancement upon graduation.

Given the "bottom line" nature of operating retail and food service outlets, the presence of smoothly functioning units that produce budgeted revenue is the measure used to assess students' development. For a board like ASUCLA, assessment has to be more structured and is probably most effective when included as part of the annual retreat. In this setting, former, current, and future board members come together over three days to orient new members, team-build, discuss forthcoming challenges and opportunities and the strategies to be employed for them, and review the just-finished year. Often the review focuses more on the performance of the association itself, but this too can lead to an examination of the board, the role it played in that performance, and the overall effectiveness of the board.

As for the board's relation to student employment, its primary concern is the executive director, who is its only employee. All employees, career and student, are the executive director's ultimate responsibility, and as such, the board helps to establish goals and broad-based policies to enable the executive director to ensure that the employment experience is as good as it can be. The board also plays an active role in assisting the executive director in establishing performance goals and bonus criteria, employee recognition programs, and—through the budget process—annual salary increase percentages.

When outside events occur that challenge the association's employment paradigm, the board acts in conjunction with the executive director to guide the enterprise to a successful outcome. One such example would be the unionization of eligible career staff (food service, housekeeping, etc.) in 2002, which had a negative net income impact of nearly $1 million. In addition, in 2007, the food service workers union attempted to convince ASUCLA's student employees of the need to unionize. The board, through the executive director and with the assistance of university resources, determined that it was illegal for the food service workers union to do so and issued a statement to that extent (ASUCLA, 2007). To more fully gauge student satisfaction with their employment at ASUCLA, the board asked management to commission a survey of its employees, the results of which were uniformly favorable.

FIGURE 7.4 ASUCLA EMPLOYEE REPORTING

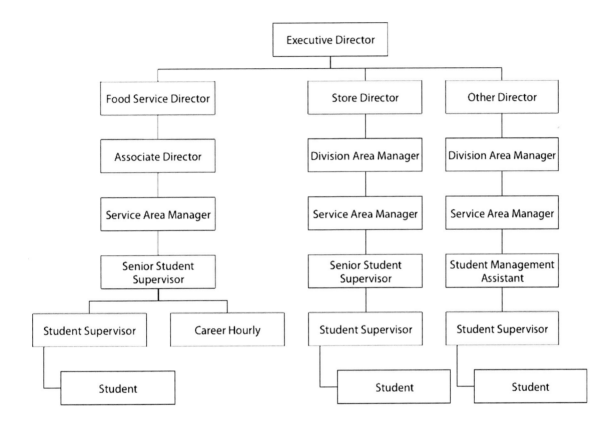

Conclusion

As stated at the beginning of this section, ASUCLA's unique structure and role on campus in operating the major retail and food service operations under a model of student control is one not likely to be found elsewhere or duplicated anytime soon. This model can and does have weaknesses: if management, particularly the executive director, is not informed and engaged, the board can and will make decisions that will not be in the best interests of the association; allowing for the time it takes to orient, inform, and mentor students delays decision-making and adds another layer of administrative expense; and philosophically, if it is believed that students should not dictate how their educational content is delivered, they similarly should not control student services.

But when the organization functions as it should, the overall benefits to the campus are numerous. First, control of the retail enterprises and food service ensures that profits from those businesses stay on campus and that service decisions are made with the best interests of the campus, not that of third-party shareholders, in mind. Next, self-operation of these functions means that student employment is a key component of the labor model, which leads to student development based on skills obtained through real-world operating environments. Finally, fully oriented student board members (operating within the constraints of well-crafted guiding documents and peer mentorship), veteran board members, and dedicated staff make decisions with real consequences and gain an understanding of the complexities of running a business.

In the end, the positive consequences would seem to outweigh the risks. Profits stay on campus, students experience employment and board membership, constituents have a voice in service delivery, and within appropriate parameters, socially responsible corporate behavior can have an outlet.

Implications

The "students in charge" concept broadens and potentially changes paradigms. How can this student-led orientation be used to frame a developmental perspective in the workplace? In the models presented here the primary focus is on students gaining skills and experience so that they can move up the organizational ladder to positions of increasing responsibility and pay. How can current supervisors and managers better prepare students for these expanded roles? And in what ways do the students demonstrate that they are ready for these supervisory positions, in skills, knowledge, and development?

Non-U.S. models

In many higher education organizations students supervise other student employees. And, many people working in these organizations have witnessed students who excel at their positions and who accomplish as much as some full-time or more seasoned employees. By providing guidance, opportunity, training, and trust, students can flourish in these roles.

Student-majority boards hold decision-making and fiduciary responsibility for many types of organizations, such as those explained here. At many overseas universities, the "student government" is known as the "students union" and is akin to the structure and purpose of U.S. student governments. Under these models, the organization may also encompass responsibility for the college union facility and other auxiliary operations, such as bookstores and basic student services. In this way these international structures mirror the California models described in this chapter.

There are often no direct reporting lines of a professional staff member to one particular student; rather, the individual reports to a student-run board. What is more customary is that a student governance structure will have elected and/or selected or appointed leaders. In this case as well there is no formal supervisory relationship one way or the other. The common concept of shared governance where students and staff work together for the advancement of the organization is prevalent throughout the United States. The ambiguity that surrounds these relationships can make the workplace uncertain and tense.

Managing students in charge

Managing students for whom no formal management or supervisory relationship exists is difficult at best. Often, supervising or advising students in this type of situation requires managing by relationship, and guidance comes in the form of role modeling, regular formal and especially informal meetings with students, and well-placed and well-timed suggestions and feedback. Prompt, direct, and constructive feedback delivered from a caring individual and colleague is an essential form of guidance for students in supervisory roles. Giving appropriate input on critical issues is probably the most critical aspect of providing guidance to students who are in charge and is not an easy task; how this is done is likely to vary from student to student and relationship to relationship. Many professionals take a significant portion of their entire careers developing the skills necessary to provide feedback, mentoring, and guidance to students where these overtures are met with acceptance and plausibility from students. It might even be argued that development and use of these skills, in combination with student development theory, is the foundation of the student affairs profession.

Retention

Maintaining clear paths to career goals, higher paying positions, and student roles that involve supervisory responsibility can be a mechanism for retaining students and helping them move through an organization. This employment ladder can be a benefit for both the student and the organization. The student continues to gain skills and experience through increasing responsibilities and the organization retains good employees, retains students in general at the institution, and allows for high-level positions to be filled by qualified and knowledgeable employees, who understand the ethos, mission, and resources of the organization. More research is needed in this important area to help individual organizations and higher education better understand the power of college employment in relation to persistence and graduation rates. This is especially significant when students constitute the primary leadership structure and, in theory, are performing high-level tasks and responsibilities.

Trust and accountability

As students move through the organization and take on new and additional roles or enter the organization already in leadership roles, trust becomes a critical element of the relationship with students in charge. Certainly, trust goes both ways, and is essential in any employment relationship, whether students are in charge or not. In many situations, students work autonomously with little direct oversight from full-time and/or professional staff. Mechanisms need to be in place for basic accountability, yet a good deal of trust must exist in these situations. An example of the power of this concept is when a supervisor took a two-way radio home to monitor the student staff traffic during their evening management of a facility. When the students were informed of this in a nonchalant way, they were put off by it and it took a good deal of time for the supervisor to regain their trust; the message sent to the students was that the supervisor did not trust them in their roles.

Students who hold significant responsibility or decision-making authority for any organization must realize and fully understand the extent and impact of their actions and decisions. Students who are in charge require a high level of accountability. The responsibility to check on this level of accountability frequently falls to full-time administrators. If systems are in place to regularly evaluate performance and monitor accountability (as addressed in the case studies), the task of holding students accountable becomes simpler as it is a regular part of doing business or a standard operating procedure of the organization.

Training

The role of training in any employment setting cannot be overlooked and is critical when positioning students for success, particularly if they will be supervising others and/or full-time staff. And, when students are in major leadership roles, it is essential to their success to learn the organization as rapidly as possible, acquire new and relevant knowledge, and develop and sharpen critical skills. As is the case with the two California examples, as well as in many other settings on college campuses, students may directly supervise or direct the work of full-time, often older employees. For example, college union building managers, dining services managers, maintenance/grounds crew supervisors, in addition to the governance and fiduciary roles outlined in this chapter, all may have direct influence on, and responsibility for, the work of others. These significant responsibilities must be taken seriously by the organization and mechanisms for consistent training and evaluation in place. (For general information on training programs, please see Chapter 11.)

While students have significant roles on many campuses, institutional policies and procedures and federal rules and regulations can sometimes get in the way of fully empowering students. Promoting students to supervisory or managerial roles in some areas can prove difficult. For example, in areas where the Family Educational Rights and Privacy Act (FERPA) and the Health Insurance Portability and Accountability Act (HIPAA) are integral to the work of the employee, special training and "certification" may be required. The training and awareness necessary for employees serving in these roles is not just for students, but some educational institutions maintain policies where students cannot serve in roles that have access to, or need to transmit, information regulated by these acts.

Conclusion

In many ways, working with students who are in charge is much like working with administrators who are in charge. Subtleties exist in working with people overall and can be amplified when a student is supervising or leading others. Age difference can play a role in perceptions and feelings among employees, and doubts about ability and relative experience may be an issue. If students are not sensitized and made aware of these possibilities, their performance can suffer; thus, the organization may also suffer as a result. With increased responsibility comes increased ethical and moral judgment that staff of colleges and universities need to demonstrate and teach to students in charge.

In addition to the concepts covered here, having clear expectations, setting boundaries for behavior, and caring about each individual is necessary in all healthy employment environments. While there may be a tendency to reserve some positions for non-students, these California case studies illustrate that students can be in charge of major organizations and operations that are vital to the campus. High-level fiduciary and governance responsibilities, in addition to major supervisory and management roles, can be entrusted to students. This reciprocity between students and administrators in the post-secondary educational environment seems fitting. Working with student employees is not always easy, and many of the common trappings can be amplified in situations where students are in charge. However, when handled appropriately, the synergy between college student employees and their educational institutions can endure over time.

References

Associated Students, University of California, Los Angeles. (n.d.a). Mission statement. Retrieved October 31, 2008, from http://www.asucla.ucla.edu/mission.asp

Associated Students, University of California, Los Angeles. (n.d.b). Our core values: Employee investment. Retrieved August, 25, 2008, from http://www.asucla.ucla.edu/corevalues.asp

Associated Students, University of California, Los Angeles. (n.d.c). Student employment policies. Retrieved on August 25, 2008, from http://www.asucla.ucla.edu/jobs/curremp.asp?ref=polstu

Associated Students, University of California, Los Angeles. (n.d.d). What role do student employees have at ASUCLA? Retrieved on August 25, 2008, from http://www.asucla.ucla.edu/bod/faq.html#2

Associated Students, University of California, Los Angeles. (2007, April 20). Board of directors statement on student employment unionization. Retrieved August 25, 2008 from http://www.asucla.ucla.edu/bod/statement.html

Chang, J. (2005). *Can't stop, Won't stop: A history of the hip hop generation.* New York: St. Martin's Press.

The Daily Californian. (2008). Information. Retrieved November 24, 2008, from http://www.dailycal.org/about.php#information

Ferrier, W.W. (1930). *Origin and development of the University of California.* Oakland, CA: West Coast Publishing.

University of California, Berkeley. (2007). Organizational chart. Retrieved November 24, 2008, from http://asuc.berkeley.edu/asinside.aspx?uid=24

University of California, Berkeley. (n.d.) Statement of understanding between the university and the ASUC. Retrieved November 14, 2008, from http://asuc.berkeley.edu/cahiers/20088133952.pdf

University of California, Berkeley. (1998) Store operations board. Retrieved November 24, 2008, from http://asuc.berkeley.edu/cahiers/20087934426.pdf.

Teoh, S.H., Welch, I., & Wazzan, C.P. (1999). The effect of socially activist investment policies on the financial markets: Evidence from the South African boycott. *Journal of Business, 72,* 35–89

INTERNATIONAL MODELS
OF STUDENT EMPLOYMENT:
IRELAND AND AUSTRALIA

by Linda Croston & Andrew O'Brien

Countries worldwide provide employment opportunities for students whilst attending university. This chapter provides a global perspective on student employment in the higher education sector. The first half of this chapter explores the general structures of the higher education systems of two countries, Ireland and Australia. This macro look at each country's educational framework creates the context for the second half of the chapter and provides information on student demographics and different types of employment in each country.

An institutional level of analysis is presented in the second half of the chapter, which provides a fresh look at the support and structural mechanisms in place at higher education institutions in the two countries. Cultural perspectives are explored as they relate to student work on campus, off campus, and upon graduation. Pertinent issues facing higher education in Ireland and Australia are addressed.

It is important to note the cultural influences on employment and the attitudes that drive context for students. Student motivation and perspectives on work during university can be significantly affected by the country's culture, mores, norms, etc.

Section I: Global perspective

Ireland

Irish education has an enduring history in Europe. The following section accentuates the importance of "third-level" education in Ireland and explores the fundamental motivations that influence Irish students to seek part-time employment whilst studying at third level. The framework for this work is rooted in the structure of the education system and the governmental provisions made to aid Irish students' progression from the primary and secondary levels to third-level education. Readers will be informed about Irish student employment and are encouraged to draw comparisons to their own approach and frame of reference.

Educational system

Education is regarded as one of the core contributors to the economic, social, and cultural developments in contemporary Irish society. Even in historic times of great political, economic, and social complexity, the desire to educate was always important (Department of Education & Science, 2005). The Irish government and the social partners of the national development strategy, such as the Irish Business and Employers Confederation, perceive education to be purposely connected with the nation's planning, and a vision exists that providing a highly skilled workforce is beneficial to Ireland, both economically and socially (Department of Education & Science, 2005). In the early 2000s, economic success could be attributed to the well-educated workforce available in Ireland as it provided a competitive advantage over other countries (Department of Education & Science, 2005).

McIndoe (2004) stated that for decades the Irish government has prioritized education as a foundation of the state's contribution to national development and as a method of achieving equity. The focus of the government's educational policy is rooted in raising participation levels of all socioeconomic groups at primary, secondary, and tertiary education levels. The 1990s saw strong developments to counteract educational disadvantage in Irish educational institutions. A more recent spate of economic success in Ireland—"The Celtic Tiger"—acted as a major catalyst to the cultural shift toward progression to third-level education and continuing adult education in Ireland.

The social benefit of third-level education to which McCoy and Smyth (2004) referred has helped lead to this shift in attitude toward the importance of education in Irish society:

> In the Irish context, initial qualifications are highly predictive of employment chances, quality of employment and pay levels. ... The benefits of education accrue not only to individuals but to the broader society with increased educational investment associated with a reduction in welfare costs and crime levels. (p. 92)

The high level of public interest in Irish higher education has guided the government to adopt a consultative approach to formulating education policy with the Higher Education Authority. On an international level, Irish students perform in the higher echelons of academic achievement as is evident from studies and evaluations conducted by the Organisation for Economic Co-operation and Development (2008, 2007). The Times Higher Education QS World University Rankings (2008) positioned seven of Ireland's third-level institutions in its top 400 universities—Trinity College Dublin was listed No. 49—demonstrating that the standard of third-level education is relatively high in world comparisons.

Additional data from Education Ireland (n.d.) suggest that 81 percent of Irish students complete second-level education and approximately 60 percent progress to higher education, one of the highest educational participation levels in the world. The Irish government is largely responsible for the investment in the development of commercially orientated skills, and there are currently more than 100,000 full- and part-time students enrolled in third-level education in Ireland (Higher Education Authority, 2009).

Structure of third-level education in Ireland

Traditionally, the system of third-level education has encompassed the university sector, the technological institutions sector, and the colleges of education, all of which are largely state-funded. However, recent years have seen the emergence of independent, private colleges, which provide a vast range of courses, adding to the existing supply within the third-level sector.

Article 13 of the United Nations International Covenant on Economic, Social, and Cultural Rights (1966) denotes that "Higher education shall be made equally accessible to all, on the basis of capacity, by every appropriate means, and in particular by the progressive introduction of free education" (¶ 2.3). Incongruent to tuition and fees in the United States, the Irish state funds student tuition through public taxation, leaving the student to pay capitation (similar to student fees) and registration fees only. Under the Free Fees Initiative, introduced in 1996, the Department of Finance pays the tuition fees of undergraduate students who meet appropriate course, nationality, and residence requirements. A registration fee is paid at the start of each academic year, which covers the costs associated with registration, administration of student records, and student examinations throughout the academic year. Students pay a capitation fee to provide for student services such as the students union (similar to student government in the United States), college union facilities, gym membership, etc. For example, in 2008–09, an annual registration fee of €900 was required to study an undergraduate course (full-time student, several classes) at University College Cork, along with a capitation fee of €145. These fees are moderate in comparison to many other countries.

Without the Irish government's Free Fees Initiative, third-level education would likely be financially unattainable for the majority of Irish students. However, due to the recent economic downturn in the Irish economy, the university debate has reopened and some government officials believe that the government should examine the advantages of the Australian fees system, introduced in 1989. This fees system requires that all students entering third-level institutions be charged higher education fees. Students can defer payment of the student contribution by applying for support under the Commonwealth's Higher Education Loan Programme, which is interest-free. The cost of the contribution is taken from student earnings once earnings are above a pre-set minimum amount, but there is an incentive of a 20-percent reduction for those who make immediate payment. Elimination of an upfront fee applies to third-level education and could help Ireland assist students in their continued interest in and pursuit of a third-level education.

Ireland's state-funded tuition fees are one significant difference with the U.S. system as well, making the motivations for employment somewhat different in Ireland than in the United States. To aid students who wish to pursue a third-level education, the Irish government introduced maintenance grants to give financial aid to eligible students to assist them with the costs of the academic year.

Maintenance grants

Maintenance grants for Irish university students are made available by the Higher Education Authority. The program is aimed at providing an incentive to students who come from disadvantaged, low-income households who otherwise may not have the necessary funds to attend a third-level institute. For the academic year 2008–09, the higher education maintenance grant provided €3,420 to students residing more than 15 miles from college and €1,370 to students' resident within 15 miles of college—this is the full amount of the grant sent to students paying full maintenance (Limerick City Council, 2008). Students (or a student's family) who pay less than full maintenance are eligible for less grant money.

Maintenance grants are beneficial and favorable to students at third level. Nonetheless, the funding often fails to be adequate in supporting students for the academic year that stretches from October to May. Students and families who fall short of the maintenance grant income thresholds are often forced to seek term employment to maintain their place at a third-level institute.

FIGURE 8.1 PROPORTION OF IRISH STUDENTS WORKING DURING TERM TIME

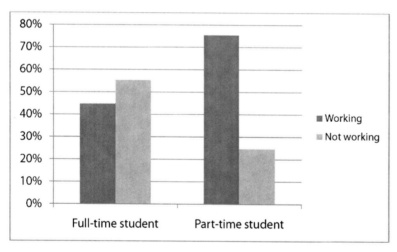

SOURCE: Delaney, L., Bernard, A., Harmon, C., & Ryan, M. (2006–2007). *Eurostudent Survey III: Report on the social and living conditions of higher education students in Ireland.* Dublin, Ireland: Higher Education Authority.

Student demographics

With more than 100,000 students in third-level education, participation continues to increase (HEA, 2009). The Higher Education Authority (2008) showed that there is a higher female participation ratio in third-level education than male; figures from 2006–07 indicated 59 percent female participation and 41 percent male. The average age of a third-level student in Ireland is between 18 and 25 years. Data indicate that in 1998, 23 percent of students from lower-income households participated in third-level education compared to 33 percent in 2004 (Ring, 2008).

Current Irish students are likely to experience changes or uncertain times as a result of the economic global and national downturn in 2008. The Minister for Education, Batt O'Keeffe, is campaigning for the reintroduction of third-level fees to reduce expenditure in the educational sector. The potential reintroduction would mainly affect those households in the higher income echelons, where those who could afford to pay would do so (Ring, 2008). Foskett, Roberts, and Maringe (2006) documented that the Union of Students in Ireland (USI) oppose such policy as it is felt that the proposal neither assists in widening involvement nor solves the current financial crisis within the universities and technical institutions. It is widely considered by students to create a commercial higher education system at the expense of users who will be burdened with debt.

Minimum wage and types of employment

Relative poverty figures largely in contemporary Irish society, whereby a serious disparity exists among the various socioeconomic groups. To target this ongoing problem, the Irish government adopted a national antipoverty strategy of which one such tenet was to introduce a minimum wage. This poses a decree on all employers in Ireland to pay a minimum wage to the entire workforce, hence incorporating the working rights of students.

The National Minimum Wage Act 2000 ensures that the minimum wage rate for an experienced adult employee from 1 July 2007 is €8.65 an hour, an increase from €8.30. The fact that workers' rights are protected to a large degree in Ireland entices students to take up part-time employment.

The relationship between the national minimum wage and third-level student employment is imperative to students. At a glance, the main sector of employment that incorporates student employment in Ireland is the service sector. The average Irish third-level student obtains employment in areas such as retail assistants, waiters in restaurants and cafes, and also service personnel in bars and nightclubs. These part-time jobs pay on or just above the minimum wage.

Australia

This section provides an overview of the Australian higher education sector and student employment arrangements in the country. After providing an outline of the sector and an overview of student demographics, this section considers the types of student employment; university employment services; attitudes to student employment including on-campus work, student perspectives on employment, and an outline of other relevant issues, such as challenges for international and domestic students; employability skills; and information on student wages and salaries. A short conclusion provides a summary and highlights a number of key differences with the United States.

Higher education and student demographics

Higher education in Australia is overwhelmingly provided by public institutions, with 39 public institutions and two private institutions (Bond University and University of Notre Dame Australia). Public institutions are established under state and territory legislation and are located in all Australian states and territories. Teaching and research are the prime activities of Australian universities, with the older institutions being recognised as the leading research universities. The balance of the higher education sector comprises one overseas institution with a branch in Australia, four self-accrediting institutions, and state and territory self-accredited institutions, which are small, mostly private, and tend to specialize in areas such as theology, business, information technology, natural therapies, hospitality, health, law, and accounting.

Funding for Australian universities comes from a variety of sources, including the federal government, tuition fees from international and post-graduate students, university commercial activities, donations, bequests, and nongovernment grants. Limited funding comes from state governments with the federal money comprising the Commonwealth Grant Scheme. This fund provides for a specified number of government-supported places each year: the Higher Education Loan Programme (HELP) arrangements providing financial assistance to students; the Commonwealth Scholarships; and a range of grants for specific purposes including quality, learning and teaching, research, and research training programs (Department of Education, Employment, & Workplace Relations, n.d.).

The federal government recoups part of its contribution to higher education from the Higher Education Contribution Scheme (HECS). Under HECS, each domestic undergraduate student is required to contribute to the cost of tertiary education by paying an annual fee. In 2008, HECS fees per year of study varied from $3,988 per year for education and nursing; $4,966 for humanities and arts; $7,188 for accounting, commerce, engineering, science, and health science; and $8,333 for law, medicine, and veterinary science. The annual charge is a combination of cost, demand, and national priority, with the annual average cost of a course (full-time load) in Australia estimated at $12,000 AUD per year (StudyLink, 2008). HECS operates as a loan scheme; a key aspect of HECS is that students are not required to (re)pay these fees until their annual taxable income reaches $38,150.

In the first semester of 2007, there were 899,021 higher education students, of which 76.2 percent were domestic and 23.8 percent were from overseas, with 96 percent of students attending public institutions (Department of Education, Employment, & Workplace Relations, 2007). Forty-five percent of students were male and 55.3 percent were female, with 71.5 percent of students studying full-time and 28.5 percent of students studying part-time (Department of Education,

Employment, & Workplace Relations, 2007). Approximately three-fourths of students were undergraduates and one-fourth were postgraduates, with the majority of students located on the Australia's east coast—31.5 percent in New South Wales, 26 percent in Victoria, and 18.3 percent in Queensland.

Types of student employment

Undergraduate students in Australia work an average of 15 hours per week in paid employment (McInnis, 2003), and this has changed little between 2000 and 2006 (Universities Australia, 2007). In 2006, 85.5 percent of undergraduate students and 90 percent of postgraduate students were in paid employment, with most students working for a single employer; however, 20 percent had more than two places of employment each week (Universities Australia, 2007).

Students in Australia have a multitude of reasons for working, which McInnis (2003) says is a significant contrast to Britain where 75 percent of students claim they must work to remain at university. In Australia one in three students claims that money worries distract them from study, but the remainder of young, full-time undergraduates work to maintain a lifestyle and some financial independence from their families (McInnis, 2003).

A range of employment approaches can be found among Australian higher education students.

Part-time and casual employment

In Australia, part-time work is usually paid pro-rata with full-time work, and casual work is paid on an hourly basis and usually lacks holiday pay, sick leave, and the ongoing status of full-time and part-time employment. This type of work ranges from traditional, student part-time hourly work in supermarkets, food service, hotels, retail, entertainment, fitness, and other entry-level positions to more advanced work where students have specialist skills and can perform middle management roles.

For some students, casual employment is vital for paying their way through university and meeting basic living expenses such as food and accommodation. For other students, especially those still living in the family home, casual employment can provide income for social activities, travel, cars, and other items not provided by the family.

Part-time and casual employment are often not directly related to students' courses of study and are primarily seen as a sources of income rather than career strategies—although there is wide recognition that this type of work provides a background in basic employment skills. These concepts are revisited again in Section II of this chapter.

Full-time employment

With 28.5 percent of students studying part-time (Department of Education Employment & Workplace Relations, 2007), many are in full-time employment and studying in the evening or during the day with employer support. Students working full-time fall into two major categories: those studying and working in their chosen profession and seeking to improve their career progression, and those seeking to change careers or move into a different field of employment. Students working full-time whilst attending university can be found at both the undergraduate and graduate level.

Vacation employment

Australian higher education has a long break over summer that gives many students the opportunity to work on a full-time or on an extended basis from late November until late February. For some students, vacation employment enables them to earn and save as much money as possible so as to pay tuition and living expenses throughout the academic year. For other students, vacation employment represents the opportunity to work for organisations in their field of study and to develop their skills for graduate employment. University career services are increasingly supporting this approach to vacation employment by developing connections between students and employers and running vacation employment fairs on campus.

Internships

Internships are not widespread in Australia when contrasted with the United States. A number of degrees require students to complete internships (e.g., law, engineering, and accounting at some universities) or on-the-job placements (e.g., teaching, nursing, medicine). And where these types of work placements occur, the faculty involved will normally assist students in providing internships. Alternately there are a number of commercial providers that assist students in finding internships in return for a considerable service fee.

There are, however, signs that internships may become increasingly important in Australian higher education. Universities Australia, the peak body representing universities in Australia, released a discussion paper proposing a national internship scheme (Universities Australia, 2008). As part of the paper it was recognised that more work-ready skills are sought and that, as well as providing income, a national internship scheme would enhance employability skills and workplace flexibility (Universities Australia, 2008).

Graduate employment

The major focus of university support related to student employment is graduate employment, and other student employment policies and practices are designed to support employment upon graduation. On-campus employer visits, employer databases and resources, interview and resume skill development, and on-campus graduate career fairs are some of the key practices designed to assist students to achieve graduate employment.

Section II: Institutional insights

Ireland and Australia have distinct systems of higher education and vary in many ways. Whilst the first half of this chapter sets the stage for employment in each country, the second half approaches student employment from an institutional level. The policy efforts of government agencies and regulatory organisations provide guidelines for colleges and universities, yet the individual institutions must interpret and implement the policies. The following section begins with information about Irish institutions and culture and presents data gathered from students. The second part of the chapter continues with information about institutional support for student employment in Australia. Attitudes toward student employment and other critical Australian issues are explored.

Ireland

University services and programs

Most universities in Ireland provide and generate student term-time employment. One example is within the Student Centre in University College Cork whereby, without the assistance of student staff, the centre would not be operational. Students are employed in most areas of the centre, such as the information desk, coffee shops, bar, and shop. All of the aforementioned positions are part-time contracts and pay above the minimum wage. University College Cork has introduced a student employment policy by placing a ceiling on the amount of hours worked; currently students in campus positions are prohibited from working in excess of 20 hours per week. This policy, however, fails to stretch to the private sector, making it extremely difficult to monitor students who work off campus, and making off-campus employment attractive to students desiring to work more than 20 hours per week.

Other areas of the university seek to employ students both throughout the year and during busy or high times of activity. For example, during the two-week orientation program at the start of the academic year, the admissions office requires student staff to give campus tours and information to the incoming undergraduates to ease the transition from second-level to third-level education. And the career services office employs part-time student help to assist with open days, recruitment fairs, and orientation days. Many other areas of Irish institutions employ students throughout the term in various roles.

Cultural aspects of student employment

Fahey, Russell, and Whelan (2007) highlighted the economic growth of the Celtic Tiger, which commenced in the early 1990s and resulted in increased employment rates and living standards throughout the Irish nation. Disposable income increased significantly during this time whilst absolute poverty was sufficiently reduced. The need for a larger labor force resulted in the exploitation of student staff to fill the expanding employment opportunities on a part-time basis. This shift in attitude toward student employment provided students with financial independence and the ability to spend more liberally on their social activities. McCoy and Smyth (2004) expressed that the typical Irish student is motivated to work to finance a generous and improvident lifestyle, which has recently become a recognized aspect of Irish culture in relation to college students overall.

The general shift to a less economical lifestyle has allowed part-time, term-time employment to be seen as conventional among Irish perceptions. The hours of work mainly take place in the evening or during the weekends (thus not interfering directly with lectures).

Irish parents tend to advocate for students seeking part-time employment, as it somewhat relieves the financial burden of a third-level education from parents and shifts some responsibility to the students themselves. Even though the cost of tuition and fees for third-level education in Ireland is relatively low, parents and students alike appreciate of the overall cost of attendance.

Student motivations

There is a wide array of underlying principles that motivate students in Ireland to assume college term-time employment, the most prominent of these being to earn much-needed money to assist

FIGURE 8.2 STUDENT EMPLOYMENT IN IRELAND: RELATIONSHIP OF JOB TO STUDIES

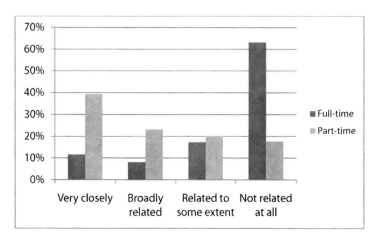

SOURCE: Delaney, L., Bernard, A., Harmon, C., & Ryan, M. (2006–2007). *Eurostudent Survey III: Report on the social and living conditions of higher education students in Ireland.* Dublin, Ireland: Higher Education Authority.

with basic survival whilst attending university. For all the success resulting from the Celtic Tiger, a negative consequence for college students has been the post-boom increase in the standard of living and concomitant increase in the cost of living. Lewis and Contreras (2008) explain, in their literature on connecting student employment and learning, that working part-time may not be a student's favorite aspect of college life, but many deem it as being a necessity. The need for such basic essentials such as food, accommodation, light, and heat are often the driving factor toward obtaining a student job. Irish inflation rates stood at 4.7 percent in 2008, an increase from rates between 3 percent and 4 percent in previous years (Burke-Kennedy, 2008). As a result, day-to-day living necessities such as food, light, and heat prices tend to be expensive, compelling students to enter into part-time employment.

Another element that acts as a motivator to students is being able to afford accommodation whilst at college. A majority of students attending third-level education in Ireland do not reside in close proximity to the campus. The student-rented housing sector in Ireland is a lucrative market for landlords, as demand often exceeds supply. The high demand for student housing near any Irish college propels landlords to hugely increase rent prices during term time, compared to out-of-term time, when rent prices decrease by almost half. On-campus accommodation also houses a large segment of third-level students; however, these facilities can be expensive, too. This is due to their on-campus location, the added benefit of onsite security, and their pristine living conditions. On average, the monthly term-time rent rate for an Irish student ranges from €400–500 exclusive of bills, and students also are required to give a deposit of one month's rent. Consequently, students engage in part-time employment, enabling them to pay for rented accommodation.

Place of residence affects Irish students' choice of work environments. Students who live with their parents often drive a significant distance to their educational institution and tend to work for off-campus establishments, frequently in the areas where they and their parents reside. This is in contrast to students who live in the communities directly adjacent to university, and those who live in university-sponsored housing who are frequently attracted to on-campus employment. Transportation and the associated commute are important to Irish students and often weigh heavily into their employment choices.

Irish culture is one that factors largely around enjoying a busy social life. This holds true for college students as well. "Pub culture," as it is termed, substantially permeates Irish society across all sectors. By law, the legal age of alcohol consumption is 18 years, making it accessible to third-level students because the majority are 18 years or over. Pub culture originates from the Irish custom of frequenting public houses (pubs) and still plays a predominant role across all realms of Irish society as the primary venue for socialising. This does not necessarily imply that students are consistently consuming large amounts of alcohol. Pubs provide various social events, such as quiz nights, Gaelic Athletic Association football and hurling match viewings, etc. However, it would be naïve not to acknowledge the results of the Organisation for Economic and Cultural Development Health Data (2005): Ireland has a problem with over-consumption of alcohol and ranks the third-highest alcohol-consuming nation in the world. This is reflected on Tuesday and Thursday nights during the college terms. Certain pubs and nightclubs are often thronged with students who are "partying" the academic pressures away. A large number of students see term-time employment as a means to an end and a way to fund their social activities and fully embrace the college experience.

A final important motive inherent in Irish society relates to students wishing to pay off loans received from financial institutions whilst studying at third level. Many Irish financial institutions are student-friendly and make money readily available to students by offering pre-approved bank loans, overdrafts, and student credit cards. Slogans such as Bank of Ireland's "When you start making it, we start making it too" are common in the execution of financial institutions' marketing throughout Ireland. This highlights the belief that banks' investment in undergraduate and postgraduate students whilst studying initiates the development of customer loyalty. The view that this customer loyalty will be retained once the student enters full-time employment is extremely favorable to the financial institution. These funds often assist students with costs incurred during the academic year and provide extra money for personal endeavors, such as the J1 summer working holiday visa to the United States, a popular experience for many Irish college students who are interested in both earning money and travelling abroad. Although interest rates are relatively low for students, repayments have to be made so as to prevent them from falling into extreme debt. This reason alone propels students toward obtaining part-time term-time employment.

Survey administration

To present a clearer picture from the Irish perspective, an informal survey was developed and distributed to 50 students currently in third-level education at University College Cork. The aim of this informal survey was to gain a sense of the motivations of these students relative to part-time, term-time employment.

The convenience sample of students included males and females, ranging in age from 20–27; the average age was 22, with 70 percent male and 30 percent female, and all were full-time students. All students solicited responded to the survey (providing a 100 percent response rate), and all worked in part-time, term-time employment and studied full-time at third level. One hundred percent of survey respondents had jobs in the service or tertiary industry in Ireland. This is logical as employment is readily attainable in bars, nightclubs, cafes, and some on-campus areas. The average hours worked per week was 15.9, whilst the amount of lecture hours per week averaged 12.3. Sixty percent of the sample group worked a mixture of weekdays and weekends, whilst the remaining 40 percent worked only during the week. Thirty percent received maintenance grants, leaving the remaining 70 percent to pay fees and support themselves during the academic year. Forty percent had no other sources of income, whilst 30 percent received regular funding from their parents. The primary motivation for having a part-time job was money for living expenses, which accounted for 60 percent of the respondents. The remaining 40 percent included money needed for socialising, paying rent, and the costs associated with running their cars, and traveling.

The data establish that 60 percent of the respondents believed that working part-time is detrimental to their academic achievement at third level and interferes greatly with their studies. However, survey respondents felt that without part-time employment, they would be unable to survive. On-campus student employees indicated that the on-campus aspect of the job was convenient and made it easier to organise study time and attend lectures.

Summary

Sean Lemass's dictum "A rising tide lifts all boats" can be applied to the evolving viewpoint of education in Ireland. The economic surge of the 1990s directly affected the number of students progressing to study at third level. In turn, a direct consequence has been the increasing cost of studying in the country, thus motivating students to enter part-time employment to ensure remaining at third level. Even those qualifying for maintenance grants may find those funds falling short of keeping them at third level. Contributing motivators to part-time work, such as socializing, student debt, and car maintenance, are also factors at work in Irish culture. The concept of students holding part-time, term-time employment in Ireland is a social norm. It is regarded as acceptable if it does not consume too much study time and academic achievement is not affected. Part-time employment in Ireland remains a consistent opportunity for students seeking to attain a degree from third-level education.

Australia

University support for student employment

In Australia, part-time work by students is not generally seen as important other than as preparation for full-time "real" work following graduation (Korczynski, 2005), although McInnis (2003) suggests this is changing as universities are now accountable for the development of work-related skills. One way this accountability can be noticed is with increased government scrutiny and the introduction of various ranking schemes.

Australian universities are not big employers of students; however, universities are becoming increasingly mindful of ranking systems and the perception among students, potential students, parents, government, alumni, and industry with regard to the employability of graduates. The increased focus on graduate destinations—as measured nationally by the Graduate Destination Survey—and the comparisons among universities have resulted in some universities providing increased resources for student employment and student employability initiatives. Increased focus on student employability can be seen at both the central and faculty level, with individual faculties introducing employability skills programs, alumni mentoring schemes, and faculty-guided employment services.

As a general approach, university support for student employment is at the graduate employment level, although some universities provide limited support for students trying to find work whilst they study. The rationale for assisting students in finding employment whilst studying is seen as assisting students to earn an income so as to support their studies.

University employment services

There are a number of administrative approaches taken to student employment in Australia. At some universities the career and employment service is a stand-alone service, and at other universities it is associated with the broader counselling portfolio. With a focus on graduate employment, the range of employment services provided include:

- Career counseling.
- Graduate employment, which assists students in finding work upon graduation.
- Job search, including resume writing and interview skills.
- Vacation employment.
- Internships.
- Part-time employment.
- Casual employment.

A combination of central administration and faculty services is provided, and at some campuses the college union or student government provides the part-time and casual student employment service. The terms "part-time" and "casual" employment are often used in the same context, and many organisations use them interchangeably. In general, the distinction relates to tenure and rates of pay. Part-time employment is closely related to full-time employment; however, the hours are fewer than full-time. In this context salaries are paid on a pro-rata basis with full-time salaries, include sick and vacation entitlements, and usually involve continuing employment. Casual employment, on the other hand, involves hourly tenure and the payment of an hourly rate that includes all entitlements. For example, it would be assumed that any entitlements would be paid as part of the hourly wage rather than being provided above and beyond the hourly rate. Casual employees are rostered on a short-term basis and rarely have sick and annual leave entitlements.

Attitudes toward student employment

Working part-time whilst studying full-time is now the norm for young Australian students, with the majority of Australian workers initially entering the workforce through part-time work whilst studying (Smith & Patton, 2007). This applies equally for high school, university, and technical and further education students. And despite this, it is noteworthy that whilst student employment is important to students, support from universities is mixed.

On-campus work

Student work on campus in Australia is not as significant as in the United States, and Australian universities are not known for employing large numbers of students on campus nor for pursuing policies that encourage student work on campus. Government policy in Australia does not provide incentives for universities to employ students, as students must be paid the same wages as all other wage earners and the university does not receive any funding assistance for employing student labor.

As a consequence of the Australian government policy situation, university managers often choose nonstudent workers because, without cheaper wages or employer incentive subsidies, students do not offer any obvious cost advantages to university employers. In addition to the lack of cost advantage, some university managers argue against employing students on the grounds of perceived lack of experience, limited availability, confidentiality concerns, student time off for exams, and the need to continually recruit and retain student employees.

There are, however, notable exceptions with college unions, sports associations, libraries, and computer information desks often seeking student employees to staff their operations. In the case of college unions and sports associations, student government policies are designed to employ students as much as possible. Popular locations for student employment within the areas mentioned include food service, information desks, retail outlets, fitness centres, and student organisations. Despite the high percentage of student workers in these services on some campuses, the overall percentage of roles for student workers on campus in Australia is very low.

TABLE 8.1 EFFECT OF WORK ON STUDY
(percentage of employed students studied who agree or strongly agree)

Statement	Undergraduate	Postgraduate
My work commitments adversely affect my performance	43.1	47.8
I regularly miss class or study because I need to attend paid employment	25.7	26.7
The type of work I do is not related to my studies	59.9	21.7
I do the work I do because it will help progress my career and help my career goals	30.1	59.7

Source: Universities Australia (2007)

Impact of employment on study

McInnis (2003) suggests there is an optimum level of paid work that varies from student to student; however, researchers have been unable to pinpoint the level at which too much work puts study at risk. A number of insights into student attitudes toward paid work have been outlined by Universities Australia (2007) and are summarised in Table 8.1.

A contrasting finding related to student employment is that students who do not work at all are, among other things, less likely to be as well organised in their study habits and generally less satisfied with their university experience (McInnis, 2003).

There is also a wide range of views on the role of the university in assisting students in gaining employment. At one end of the debate there is the view that a university education should focus on learning and the ability to learn regardless of employment outcomes. At the other end of the debate is the view that university education should prepare students for the workforce. In the middle of these two extremes is where universities search for balance; however, the diverse views within the sector and across disciplines combined with fighting for research dollars lead to a situation where student employment is poorly resourced and lacks clear policy direction.

Domestic student challenges

Students around the world, including Australian students, face the major challenge of balancing work and study. Employer support also is seen as a major challenge—especially when it comes to exam time with many employers taking different approaches ranging from time off for exams to expecting students to maintain normal shifts. Table 8.2 shows that whilst some employer support is provided on key issues, even with flexible working hours employer support represents a number of challenges with less than half of all students receiving any form of employer support.

TABLE 8.2 ASSISTANCE PROVIDED BY EMPLOYERS
(percentage of employed students studied)

	Undergraduate	Postgraduate
Unpaid study leave	16.5	15.9
Paid study leave	6.6	21.2
Flexible working hours	46.0	37.5

Source: Universities Australia (2007)

International student challenges

Department of Education, Employment, and Workplace Relations (2007) data indicate that 23.8 percent of Australian students attending public higher education institutions are from overseas, making the employment of international students an issue of some magnitude. In addition to the challenges of balancing work and study, international students in Australia face three additional challenges associated with student employment. The first of these challenges relates to language skills, with some employers reluctant to employ students with poor spoken English. The second challenge for international students relates to long-term employment prospects. Some employers like to test students as casual employees before they graduate with a view to offering them full-time employment upon graduation. When students are on visas, employers take the view they will return to their home country at the end of their study and therefore are not available to become long-term employees; as a consequence, employers do not consider these students for casual employment. Third, international students are subject to visa requirements that limit the amount of work they can do (Department of Immigration and Citizenships, 2008). Key restrictions prohibit international students from working prior to commencing classes or from working more than 20 hours per week during the semester. International students can work unlimited hours in semester breaks; however, family members accompanying them to Australia are limited to working no more than 20 hours per week.

Employability skills

A number of reports have been prepared in Australia in recent years with the focus on enhancing employability skills (Australian Chamber of Commerce and Industry & the Business Council of Australia, 2002; Precision Consulting, 2007; Universities Australia, 2008). These skills have been identified as:

- Communication.
- Teamwork.
- Problem solving.
- Initiative and creativity.
- Planning and organising.
- Self-management.
- Learning skills.
- Technology.

A number of universities have introduced additional noncredit programs to assist students with development of these skills whilst others have reviewed graduate attributes and subject outlines to ensure employability issues are addressed. Where this occurs, student learning outcomes are directly linked to achieving employment-related skills.

Student employment wages

Students in Australia are paid the same rates as all other workers. The minimum hourly adult rate as of October 2008 was $14.31 AUD (Australian Workplace Authority, 2009). Some employers pay junior rates for employees under 20 years of age. As a result of students being paid at the same level as other workers, students do not provide a cost advantage to employers in Australia.

Summary

With 85.5 percent of undergraduate students and 90 percent of postgraduate students in paid employment (Universities Australia, 2007), a case can be made that Australian students do well in accessing student employment. Universities Australia (2008) has reported that Australian students have higher workforce participation than their peers in other industrial countries. The majority of the work opportunities for students come from organisations not affiliated with any university.

On this basis, the groundwork for an enhanced employment skills approach is in place (Universities Australia, 2008). However, there is little evidence to suggest that Australian universities play an active role in encouraging students either to find part-time work or to gain maximum educational benefits from this approach to student employment. This is an area that could benefit from an increased research focus.

Conclusion

This chapter provides an overview of the higher education systems in Australia and Ireland. Policy initiatives and economic trends have affected both countries' current higher education environment. Student characteristics and demographics provide insight into the realities of employment in this sector of education in the two countries. This systemic backdrop provides the framework for the colleges and universities in each country, and, consequently, the student employment context.

More localized information in terms of individual institutions and student affairs/services divisions sheds light on general levels of support, prevalence, and acceptance of the employment concept for students and ameliorates the mechanisms in place to facilitate student positions on campus.

Cultural influences of both countries are strong, and figure significantly into the provision of student employment. Many funding schemes and various other environmental and individual factors affect the employment landscape. Students' financial, family, and residence situations are all prominent aspects of their realities that influence their employment motivations and desired outcomes.

Donnchadh O'hAodha and Liz Carroll contributed to this chapter.

References

Australian Chamber of Commerce & Industry & Business Council of Australia. (2002). Employability skills for the future. Retrieved March 1, 2009, from http://www.dest.gov.au/sectors/training_skills/policy_issues_reviews/key_issues/es

Australian Workplace Authority. (2009). The federal minimum wage. Retrieved March 1, 2009, from http://www.workplaceauthority.gov.au/rates-of-pay/federal-minimum-wage.asp

Burke-Kennedy, E. (2008, June 13). Inflation rate rose to 4.7 percent in May, CSO says. The Irish Times. Retrieved June 13, 2008, from http://www.irishtimes.com/newspaper/finance/2008/0613/1213262335573.html

Department of Education, Employment, & Workplace Relations. (2007). Summary of students 2007 (First half of year). Retrieved April 22, 2008, from http://www.dest.gov.au/NR/rdonlyres/F1BB7BB3-82B2-4B81-A9C3-F19EF5AF5172/20529/SummaryofStudents2007 firsthalfyearselectedhighered.pdf

Department of Education & Science. (2005). Educating Ireland's workforce. Retrieved June 20, 2008, from http://www.business2000.ie/cases/cases_9th/case11.htm

Department of Immigration and Citizenships. (2008). New permission to work arrangement for student visa holders. Retrieved May 15, 2008, from http://www.dimia.gov.au/students/_pdf/permission-to-work-students.pdf

Education Ireland. (n.d.). Irish education system. Retrieved February 18, 2008: http://www.educationireland.ie/index.php?option=com_content&view=article&id=12 &Itemid=16

Fahey, T., Russell, H., & Whelan, C.T. (2007). Best of times? The social impact of the Celtic Tiger. *The Economic and Social Review, 39*(2), 157–169.

Foskett, N., Roberts, D., & Maringe, F. (2006, June). *Changing fee regimes and their impact on student attitudes to higher education. Report of a Higher Education Academy Funded Research Project 2005–2006.* Southampton, England: University of Southampton & The Knowledge Partnership.

Higher Education Authority. (2008). *Higher education: Key facts and figures 2006–07.* Dublin, Ireland: Author.

Higher Education Authority. (2009). *Higher education: Key facts and figures 2007–08.* Dublin, Ireland: Author.

Korczynski, M. (2005). Skills in service work: An overview. *Human Resource Management Journal, 15*(2), 3–14.

Lewis, J.S., & Contreras, S. (2008, January). Research and practice: Connecting student employment and learning. *The Bulletin of the Association of College Unions International, 76*(1), 30–38.

Limerick City Council. (2008). Higher education grants. Retrieved February 17, 2009, from http://www.limerickcity.ie/HEG

McCoy, S., & Smyth, E. (2004). Educational expenditure: Implications for equality, Budget Perspectives 2004. Retrieved March 2, 2008, from http://www.esri.ie/pdf/Budget04chp_McCoy_Eduational percent20expenditure.pdf

McIndoe, T. (2004). A case for re-introducing third-level fees? An econometric analysis. Student Economic Review of Trinity College Dublin. Retrieved March 1, 2009, from http://www.tcd.ie/Economics/SER/pasti.php?y=04

McInnis, C. (2003, August). New realities of the student experience: How should universities respond? Proceedings of the European Association for Institutional Research, Limerick, Ireland, 24–27.

National Minimum Wage Act, House of the Oireachtas, S.I. No. 99/2000 (2000).

Organisation for Economic Co-operation and Development Health Data. (2005, June). Alcohol consumption in litres per capita (age 15+). Retrieved March 1, 2009, from http://www.ecosante.org/OCDEENG/812010.html

Organisation for Economic Co-operation and Development. (2007). Education at a glance 2007: OECD indicators. Retrieved March 1, 2009, from http://www.oecd.org/dataoecd/36/4/40701218.pdf

Organisation for Economic Co-operation and Development. (2008). Education at a glance 2008: OECD indicators. Retrieved March 1, 2009, from http://www.oecd.org/dataoecd/23/46/41284038.pdf

Precision Consulting. (2007). *Graduate employability skills*. Melbourne, Australia: Business, Industry, and Higher Education Collaboration Council.

Ring, E. (2008, October 24). College fees review to be completed within 6 months. *The Irish Examiner*. Retrieved March 1, 2009 from LexisNexis.

Smith, E., & Patton, W. (2007, April). *A serendipitous synchronisation of interests: Employers and student-working*. Proceedings of the Evolution, Revolution or Status Quo? The new context for VET, AVERTA, Melbourne, Australia.

StudyLink. (2008). Study in Australia. Retrieved March 1, 2009, from http://studylink.com/australia/index.html.

Times Higher Education QS World University Rankings. (2008) The complete rankings. Retrieved February 18, 2009 from http://www.topuniversities.com/worlduniversityrankings/results/2008/overall_rankings/fullrankings

U.N. General Assembly, International Covenant on Economic, Social and Cultural Rights, 16 December 1966. United Nations, Treaty Series, vol. 993, p. 3. Online. UNHCR Refworld, available at: http://www.unhcr.org/refworld/docid/3ae6b36c0.html

Universities Australia. (2007). Australian student finances survey 2006 final report. Retrieved March 1, 2009, from http://www.universitiesaustralia.edu.au/content.asp?page=/publications/policy/survey/index.htm

Universities Australia. (2008, May). A national internship scheme: Enhancing the skills and work-readiness of Australian university graduates. Position paper No. 3/08. Retrieved March 1, 2008, from http://www.universitiesaustralia.edu.au/documents/publications/discussion/National-Internship-scheme-May08.pdf

SECTION III

ADMINISTRATIVE CONSIDERATIONS

ADMINISTRATIVE ASPECTS OF STUDENT EMPLOYMENT

by Z. Paul Reynolds

Student employment program administration can be rigid or nebulous, but most programs are on a continuum of intentionality between these two extremes. Some organizations may utilize an administrative structure based on deliberate planning. However, in attending to administrative concerns, the significant philosophy of cocurricular education can be lost. Does it matter? Is not any program better than none? Yes, any program is better than none—even if the only thing it accomplishes is offering students a way to earn money while they are going to school. But if given the chance to make the program more than this—to make it educational, rewarding, preparatory, and grounded in theory—this approach is beneficial to both employer (i.e., the university or department) and employee (i.e., the student).

With more and more emphasis on accountability and a focus on integrating all institutional programs to the academic mission, it seems that there really is no question at all. Administrators must make student employment programs relevant and substantive if students are to achieve success and if institutions are to offer more than just a paycheck to students. With this in mind, a student employment program can be organized, administered intentionally, and have significant thought behind what happens on a daily basis. Especially when facing the challenge to do more with less, it is good practice to design employment programs from start to finish and have a goal in place for each stop along the way.

Creating a common organizational philosophy

Like most things in the working lives of higher education administrators, understanding boundaries and roles that make a team successful is important. Such is the case with student employment programs. The program cannot only exist in one person's mind; it must be recognized, manipulated, written, and reconstituted with input from all of the key stakeholders. It has to be a shared vision of what a student employment program will look like. Senge (1994) described the organizational discipline of a shared vision as moving beyond simple compliance with ideas that a group might share and toward a team commitment to get the work done to achieve its ultimate goals. This issue can be discussed during regular staff meetings to determine whether the administrative assistant feels the same way about the employment program as the director. Although each person in the organization plays a different role, if they understand the whole of the program and its key components, they will be more effective at serving in their individual capacities. Everyone must come to a consensus. What should the program accomplish? A small school that does not have abundant physical or financial resources might have a lean program. Likewise, larger institutions might have a program so intricate and complex that even individual stakeholders might not understand all of the details. Having a shared vision or philosophy will assist in getting from the basics to a holistic employment program that serves students' needs.

It is helpful to adopt at least one of the student development theories and connect it to the employment program. The organization can be more intentional with the various parts of the program by grounding it in theory and can ensure that all important components are included. For example, the seven vectors of identity development (Chickering & Reisser, 1993) can be used as a foundation for student employment programs, striving to connect components of the program back to these theoretical concepts. Each piece of this theory can be linked to a particular aspect of a student employment program. In fact, even in basic programs, the linkages are probably already there, but they might just need to be explicitly stated and integrated more purposefully. If a program is conceptualized with this approach, it will help to organize and streamline efforts, leading to better administration, operation, and student learning. (For more options and explanation related to this topic, see Chapter 1.)

Centralized versus decentralized administration

Much of the way in which a student employment program is structured is in accordance with institutional or division guidelines. For instance, some schools have a career services department (or an office with a similar name and function) that is responsible for all administrative aspects of the employment process. Likewise, some schools participate in a centralized process via their human resources department or financial aid office. For example, the University of Alaska Fairbanks handles all student employment centrally through the university's human resource office (J. Maxwell, personal communication, March 11, 2008). Individual offices throughout the university work with the human resources office to recruit and hire student employees. Paperwork and employment verification is done centrally through that department and then the human resources office authorizes departments to make a job offer.

Decentralized administration is more common and occurs when multiple departments manage their own student employment programs. Examples of schools that operate under this model are Texas A&M University–Corpus Christi, The University of Texas at San Antonio, Rice University, Texas Tech University, the University of Pennsylvania, The University of Toledo, and Bowling Green State University. Many schools that operate under a decentralized model still rely heavily on other departments to aid and assist in the employment process. For example, at Rice University, each individual department is responsible for its own program but relies on the financial aid department, which centralizes the recruiting process in concert with the Texas Guaranteed Student Loan Corporation (B. Beckwith, personal communication, June 9, 2008).

Much of what dictates the way in which each campus administers its programs comes from tradition, philosophy of the administration, financial considerations, and human resource regulations. However, no matter what version of student employment administration a campus adopts, it is vitally important to create and sustain relationships with offices that can help in the program's daily management. Even if institutions have centralized models that touch many departments, individual administrators can be the driving force to develop and maintain a shared vision of how the program looks and acts.

For instance, Texas A&M University–Corpus Christi has a decentralized model of student employment. Individual departments are responsible for administering their own programs. However, each of these departments is dependent—and really, interdependent—on a number of offices to help make the program successful. First, the human resources department helps everyone understand applicable local, state, and federal employment laws. Second, the career services department provides functions such as job postings, consulting services, supplemental staff training sessions, and work-study eligibility. Third, there is interaction with the payroll department to ensure that students are compensated for the work they have performed. Several other departments are relied upon to enhance the program (e.g., police department, environmental health and safety office, identification card office, financial aid, employee relations, counseling center, and student health). All of these offices assist with annual training, one-time trainings, electronic access control, and consulting services, to name just a few services. It is critically important to the success of the program that staff members be on more than good terms with these offices. These university offices create added value for student employees and help define the student employment program. Working with other departments on a regular basis keeps the program fresh and sets this unique program apart from other employers on the campus—and most certainly from off-campus employers.

The employment process

There are as many different models for a student employment program as there are actual programs. However, successful student employment programs should have the elements contained within Figure 9.1. These components, as well as others, are discussed in the following section.

FIGURE 9.1 ELEMENTS OF SUCCESSFUL STUDENT EMPLOYMENT PROGRAMS

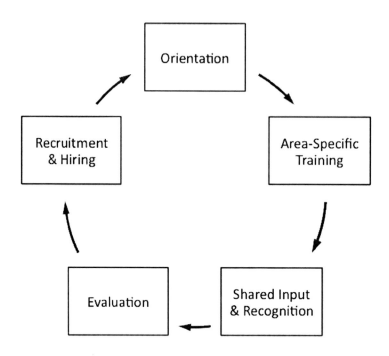

Domachowski, S. & Jacobs, K. (2005, March). Risk and reward: The rewards of creating a developmental student employment program. Presented at the annual conference of the Association of College Unions International, Reno, NV.

Recruitment

Recruiting can be defined as any activity associated with the solicitation of students to work in an employment program. Recruitment is a three-step process that allows for positions to be filled on an ongoing basis. Recruitment consists of advertising, identifying employees for consideration, and then interviewing the prospective employees.

A helpful guideline is to begin to solicit potential candidates at least one month prior to the time that the position(s) need to be filled. The reason for the one-month period is to collect applications from as many interested students as possible through broad advertisement. Soliciting one month in advance also gives ample time to schedule interviews, review and narrow the search, check references, and make a hiring decision. Having an application deadline will give students the opportunity to know by when they must apply.

Once applicants have been solicited, it is time to review and narrow the applicant pool. For most student employment positions, there are few, if any, inflexible qualifications. For this reason, look through applications and select those students who portray a willingness to learn and who show the promise of being an exemplary employee.

The application screening process can be an opportunity to engage student employees who are in a leadership or management position. The screening process is also a way to build relationships with other professionals in the office or even those elsewhere who work closely with the hiring department. For students who are leaders or managers, this involvement will give them an additional sense of purpose and will allow them to have "buy-in" when interviewees are chosen. It also benefits the hiring manager with much-needed help; if student assistants have a clear understanding of the hiring manager's expectations, they can pre-screen applicants so that there are not as many applications to review. In any case, consider the screening process and think about having more than just the hiring manager involved.

Interviewing

Once the applicants are screened, it is time to schedule interviews. Interviews are critically important in the employment process. It is the first sign that student employment positions are taken seriously and that it is not as simple or easy as hiring the first person who completes an application. Formal interviews provide an important service to the students selected. This could be the first time they have had a formal interview, and the experience of going through the process is good for any student regardless of the outcome.

Ideas for Posting Student Employment Opportunities:

- Post signs/fliers/notices in career services, human resources, and financial aid offices

- Use social networking media sites to advertise or post links to more information

- Post advertisements to on-campus bulletin boards and classroom chalk/bulletin boards, etc.

- Advertise on campus electronic signage

- Work with the career services and/or financial aid office to post openings externally

- Have informational sessions for students interested in employment

- Discuss the job with current student employees

- Post large posters on an easel near the director's office or information desk so students can pick up job descriptions and applications

- Hang banners in your union and/or in other buildings on campus

- Post to campus-based electronic distribution lists

- Post the job in your community or off-campus locations at which students regularly visit

- If the position is above an entry-level student employment position, post the position with all students in lower-level positions

It is important that the interview be an exchange between the interviewer and the interviewee. Much like professional interviews, this is a time for the hiring manager to assess the students' abilities as much as it is an opportunity for students to learn about the organization and consider more fully whether they really want to be a part of it.

Of equal importance is that the hiring manager or committee fully prepares for the interview. It is helpful to document questions and record answers in written format. Craft questions in such a way that prompts students to communicate why they are interested, what they can contribute to the organization, and how they might be able to think through a process. For upper-level student employment positions, it can be helpful to design certain questions in the form of a scenario. This allows assessment of how students think on their feet and gives an indication of what kinds of decisions they may be able to make.

During the interview, it is important to share with the student a complete position description, wages, expected schedule and total hours expected to work, and the general position expectations. It is also helpful to briefly summarize the department's organizational structure so that the students might better understand the context of their role.

Make sure that questions are written to comply with federal and state laws, particularly regarding discrimination. For legal purposes, as well as to ensure fairness to all of the candidates interviewed, develop and use an interview assessment questionnaire (See Appendix 1 for an example). This will ensure that the hiring manager does not stray from the pertinent questions, that the same questions are asked of each candidate, and that there is a way to objectively rate candidates against themselves and others.

Checking references and hiring

Before a hiring decision is made, it is an absolute requirement that references be checked. To have students treat their new job with respect and give it the serious regard desired, checking references goes a long way in communicating the fact that this is a serious employment opportunity that pays real money and comes with real responsibilities. Not only that, checking references on potential student employees gives students an opportunity to understand what it is like to search for a job and go through a comprehensive hiring process. It is possible to give them a realistic experience from start to finish. Reference checks inform the hiring manager and department about their potential employees. Checking references can confirm the feeling of a good hire, and it also can raise flags about a potential bad hire.

When checking references, the same general rules apply as when asking questions during the interview. Keep questions pertinent to the position, be careful to ensure that questions are legal (the human resource department can verify this), and use a form to ensure the same questions are asked of each reference. To comply with the Federal Educational Rights and Privacy Act (FERPA), have every student who applies for a job sign a waiver giving their consent for reference checks. See Appendix 2 for a sample of a Student Reference Request and FERPA/Liability Release.

Once a hiring decision has been made, individually let the students know that they have been selected for employment and ascertain if they are still interested in the position. If they are, this would be a good time to confirm the wage discussed during the interview and schedule orientation.

Orientation and training

Even if an institution handles its employment process via one central office, there is likely at least one person at each employment site who will be responsible for coordinating with that central office. An orientation checklist can assist in ensuring that all necessary information is covered with each new employee. See Appendix 3 for a sample checklist.

There are some general suggested steps that might help with any student employment orientation:

1. If there is one person in an office responsible for processing new-hire employees, there must be notification that a new employee has been hired. This can come in the form of a paper or form notification, the use of an Intranet site form, e-mail correspondence, etc. Make sure that the student's personal information such as name, address, and phone number are noted. Additionally, note the position, pay rate, potential physical building access needs for the new employee, and any other information the institution requires.

2. Schedule an appointment between the central coordinator and the new employee to review and sign any pertinent documentation. This is an appropriate time to request e-mail accounts, forward access control information, review office-wide or institution-wide employment standards or manuals, and review the department's organizational structure, including the department's relationship with any pertinent professional organizations.

Once the student has gone through departmental or institutional orientation, the hiring manager can set up area-specific training and orientation.

Before the area-specific training begins, there are two major items that need to be discussed with new employees: training expectations and content and learning outcomes assessment. While training is covered at length in Chapter 11, it is germane to point out a few concepts here.

Document the training process so that there is proof that students have been trained in the necessary areas for their positions. One simple method for documentation is a training matrix (see Appendix 4). A training matrix is simply a list of training topics or details, along with space provided for the dates the training took place as well as space for the trainer to "sign off" that the training has occurred. The training matrix allows everyone involved in the training to view the progress and to easily add training topics or details. It is also important to indicate on the training matrix when training began and the expected completion date. This gives the new employee a goal toward which to work, and it also conveys a message of personal responsibility. If students have a training matrix along with a "due date," they are much more apt to actively seek training from their peers and supervisors in an effort to complete their matrix on time. Additionally, it can be effective to issue an "end of training" raise to employees when they complete the training process. Most want to be recognized for the work that they do, and if they understand that they will be monetarily rewarded, in general, they will strive to stay on task and complete their training within the prescribed time period. Ultimately it is the manager's responsibility to see that the student receives appropriate training to be successful on the job.

Shared input and recognition

Encouraging input during decision-making processes provides a way for employees to support the organizational goals and objectives and promotes positive relationships between managers and employees. "Strong workplace teams enhance both employee well-being and productivity" (Baker, 2007, ¶ 15). Student employment is no different. Students want to have a say in how they do their jobs and in creating policies and procedures. They want to be involved in the management of the program of which they are a part. Input mechanisms will support positive work environments for both professional and student staff.

Organizations that employ students can promote this shared input in a number of ways. One way would be to create a student advisory committee on employment. When changes are made to policies or procedures, take these desired changes to the students themselves and solicit input. Another approach is having more senior-level student employees participate in the training and evaluation of lower-level student employees. This not only provides a mechanism for input, but as stated previously, helps the senior-level students develop skills and abilities in managing human resources. Provide opportunities for students to give input on a routine and regular basis. Encouraging students to feel comfortable discussing problems, issues, or concerns they may have demonstrates a willingness to listen and make changes based on their desires and ideas. Fresh perspectives are helpful for the students, the managers, and the overall organization.

High-quality employment programs also seek to recognize performance excellence and learning on a regular basis. Recognition Professionals International (2008) stated: "Employee recognition is the application of a scientifically confirmed behavioral psychology principle: employee performance and retention are strongly linked to consistent, appropriate positive reinforcement of behaviors that promote the organization's goals" (¶ 1). So, recognition is not only the right, humane thing to do; it actually benefits the organization at the same time. Performance recognition must be swift and regular to be most effective. A way to accomplish this task is to connect an organization's recognition process to its disciplinary program. Recognize strong performance and weak performance in unison. Allow students to regularly see what they have done well and areas in which they need to improve.

In the Office of the University Center and Student Activities at Texas A&M University–Corpus Christi, a progressive disciplinary and recognition program called "Slams and Kudos" is used. Employees who do something wrong or have a disciplinary issue are assessed a certain number of slams for the infraction. Likewise, if students assist in a project or task that is beyond the scope of their job responsibilities, they get a certain number of kudos. Monthly totals are tabulated. If a student amasses five or more slams in a given month, he or she is disciplined via a written warning and an accompanying verbal discussion with the supervisor. Once a student has been issued two written warnings (i.e., 10 slams), the problem is again discussed, and the student is notified that a third written warning could result in probation or termination. Any kudos received in a month act as a counter-balance to the slams assessed; however, once a written warning is issued, it stays on the student's record for the remainder of the school year. The two students—one from the facilities department and one from the activities department—with the highest number of kudos for the month are chosen as the student employees of the month. Their photos are displayed in a perpetual display, and they are rewarded with a monetary gift on their campus access card. The two students with the highest number of kudos at the end of the year are chosen as the student employees of the year and are again featured on a perpetual plaque and given an even larger monetary award. Employees of the Month are awarded $25 each and the Employees of the Year are awarded $250 each. This program is successful in that it gives immediate and long-term feedback to students and recognizes their performance excellence.

There are numerous other ways to recognize student achievements and exemplary performance. Having employee luncheons where full-time staff members cook for students is a way to thank students for their contributions. Recognizing students on their birthday with a staff-signed birthday card is a nice touch, while not specifically aimed at performance. Again, there are countless ways of achieving the goal in this area.

Evaluation (and separation)

Employee evaluation is the last step in the employment process. Organizations need to demonstrate that learning has occurred through employment, so assessment measures are critical. The impact of regular and routine employee evaluation is paramount to ensuring that employee development is occurring and that students are afforded the opportunity to learn from their mistakes and improve their performance. Although annual, formal evaluations are a necessary and functional part of an employment program, it also is helpful and progressive to review performance on a regular, routine basis. Again, immediate and regular evaluation helps students to understand concretely how they can improve their performance and further build their skills. Additionally, when it is time for managers to conduct a formal yearly evaluation, they are able to review employee files for the whole year and formulate a comprehensive evaluation. The two components to the program complement one another. Moreover, if employees' performance is evaluated formally at the end of the second term, having a less formal evaluation during the first term is helpful in giving students an idea of their performance. It gives them time to make improvements so that their development and improvement can be noted on their formal evaluation. An assessment tool can be administered to students before their training begins and then again after a designated period of employment. However, this is only one of many methods that can be implemented in a student employment setting. More information, specifically related to measuring student learning, is available in Chapter 12.

Increased accountability and increased understanding that the cocurriculum is part of the learning and development process have amplified the importance of clearly stated learning outcomes for each student employment position. Evaluation forms should be modeled after position descriptions, measuring learning outcomes and performance. Evaluations must indicate what goals and developmental opportunities can be considered between now and the next time a student is evaluated. It is best for each successive evaluation to be linked to the previous evaluation by looking at performance improvement, promotions, and overall development. (For more information on creating and/or modifying position descriptions see Chapter 3.)

Whether students separate from the organization voluntarily or involuntarily, it is a good idea to conduct some sort of exit interview. Devise a form that can be used to assess how exiting students view the organization. This gives students a chance to say what they really feel and believe without the fear of retribution. It also gives the organization an opportunity to learn from the students' experiences. Exit interviews can be reviewed by every level of the organization and used as a tool to effect positive future change. Exit interviews must be conducted by someone in the organization other than the direct supervisor so that, again, students feel comfortable enough to discuss any problems or issues that arose during their employment. See Appendix 5 for a sample exit interview form.

Process and procedures development

As is the case in any organization, documentation is essential for successful student employment programs. Even where signed contracts do not exist, written documentation provides both parties (the employee and the employer) with written records concerning matters that may be subject to interpretation or dispute at a later time.

Administrators are encouraged to review documentation from other institutions and adapt them for their institution. Of course, credit must be given where credit is due, but there is no reason to create all new administrative materials when so much useful material already exists. Higher education is a sharing community, and this is an area where that sharing can significantly affect business operations while saving time.

Written position descriptions are among the most significant documents for a student employment program. They serve as a kind of road map, explaining the basics of a job and allowing the employer to express expectations clearly and concisely. Position descriptions encompass four basic parts: a brief overview, duties of the position, qualifications for the position, and expected learning outcomes.

1. A brief overview contains the basic purpose and responsibilities of the position. It includes from whom the position receives direction and whom the position might be responsible for supervising. The overview might also include the pay range for the position and any associated grade or level.

2. Clearly enumerate the duties of the position in the description. Usually, a bulleted list will suffice but it must include all major responsibilities of the position. List the duties as action

statements (e.g., "Student building managers will be responsible for the opening and closing of the facility").

3. Position descriptions need to include the qualifications for a position. Include skills that a person must already possess in order to qualify for the job. Also include any qualitative qualifications sought (e.g., "Students interested in this position must be willing to learn management skills via on-the-job training").

4. Position descriptions need to include expected learning outcomes. As indicated earlier, position descriptions need be reviewed with each student during the interview. This is a appropriate time to communicate to students that there is an expectation of significant learning through their employment. There is no better way to do this than to state expectations in written format from the very beginning of the process. (See Chapter 3 for further details and see Appendix 6 for a sample position description.)

Individual institutions may have additional requirements for position descriptions.

Employment manuals can be some of the most extensive and informative documents developed in the administration of a student employment program. They act as a set of guidelines for employees to use as a resource and in clarifying expectations for employment. Employment manuals can be categorized into three basic areas: general employee handbooks, position-specific handbooks, and technical handbooks.

General employee handbooks can be seen as office- or division-wide handbooks. They seek to contain all of the pertinent rules and guidelines for all employees no matter in what area of an organization they are employed. General employee handbooks include items such as a welcome from the director or department chair, general employment guidelines such as drug-free workplace standards, harassment laws, disciplinary procedures, grievance procedures, payroll information, time-off request procedures, customer service philosophy, discrimination-free workplace standards, and equal employment opportunity policies. Again, depending on the structure of a student employment program, and depending on the structure of the organization, this general employee handbook could be for one single department, a division made up of many departments, or an institution-wide manual that applies to every student employee.

Position-specific manuals describe the policies and procedures for a particular position or set of positions. For example, in a college union, a manual might exist for set-up crew members alone or a manual may include all student operations positions. Position-specific manuals are obviously more detailed than general employee handbooks. An operations manual might include items such as the proper procedure for opening and securing a facility, locations of safety and security equipment, location and contents of storage rooms or facilities, and abbreviated directions on using relevant software. These manuals also typically include more detailed position descriptions and organizational charts.

The last type of manual is a technical or daily operations manual. These manuals are even more prescriptive than a position-specific manual and will most likely contain more dynamic information. For example, a technical manual for an information desk might include items such as frequently called phone numbers, a list of the building tenants and their locations, home/emergency phone numbers of key staff members, and daily reports. A technical manual for student building managers might include material safety data sheets, alarm and access codes, common settings for sound and lighting equipment, and room capacities and set-up types. Technical manuals can be seen as reference guides that will aid student employees in the day-to-day performance of their job-related responsibilities. It is important to note that because these manuals may contain sensitive or privileged information, they may need to be kept in a secure location or, if electronic, have restricted access.

Pay plan and equity considerations

Most students are not working on a volunteer basis—they are working to make money to support academic, living, or personal leisure expenses. To attract and retain quality employees, it is imperative to have a well-thought-out compensation plan. Not only are wages a primary interest to employees, they directly correlate to budgetary ability to provide meaningful employment and learning experiences for students.

Pay banding is a concept by which many or several positions are lumped together because of their likeness to one another or the similarities that exist in position responsibilities (Pay Band, 2008). For example, there may be 20 total student employment positions within an organization, and because of the similarities and differences between the positions, four may end up in Band 1, four in Band 2, six in Band 3, and six in Band 4. Further, grades or levels may exist within these bands to account for years of service and/or raises based on superior performance. If there are four bands and four grades within each band, there are a total of 16 different grades in the organization.

Pay banding is simply a way to structure a compensation plan to account for differences in job responsibilities, length of service, and/or performance. It is a structure to ensure objectivity and equity among position types, positions, and years of service performed. The popularity of pay banding student employment programs or positions comes from the fact that, in most cases, salaries for full-time and professional positions are banded as well.

A note of caution is in order here. Pay banding a student employment program must be done with care to ensure that the bands do not encroach upon the pay bands for full-time staff. If this does happen, it could cause serious equity issues between the student employees and the full-time staff. If this is unavoidable or even if the manager knowingly wishes for this to happen, there must be communication to all regarding the reasons for this overlap. For example, it might be appropriate for the highest paid student managers to make more money per hour than the lowest level full-time position. There are certainly instances where this is appropriate and fair. However, it is almost certain that the full-time staff will feel this is inappropriate and unfair. Care must be taken to explain the reasons for this overlap and to remind everyone that there are other compensation issues at hand other than just salaries and wages. Other nonmonetary compensation may be involved such as vacation and sick time, retirement benefits, and insurance benefits. (See Appendix 7 for a sample student employment pay plan.)

Scheduling

Effective employee scheduling requires addressing several variables: necessary routine coverage; additional coverage based on special circumstances, needs, or events; and the students' availability to work.

Before a department or organization can seek to create a workable employment schedule, administrators must consider what the philosophy is regarding the number of hours student employees will be allowed to work. A department or organization might be bound by institutional policy that dictates the maximum number of hours a student may work. Research shows that students working 15 or fewer hours per week either on campus or in a field that supports students' degree has a positive effect on persistence and degree completion (King, 2006). (For more information about impact of work on students, see Chapters 2 and 5.)

Routine coverage is the next variable that must be considered. A manager needs to look at all of the work hours necessary for the organization to function in an efficient and effective manner. For instance, consider when only one office assistant is necessary and when it might be prudent to have two on duty at the same time. Once a decision has been made regarding the number of hours employees may work and once an outline of a schedule is completed, one will know exactly how many staff members needed to fill a schedule. For more active organizations or those in which frequent schedule modifications are necessary, managers might consider scheduling additional staff.

There are other, perhaps secondary, considerations for creating a routine schedule. As part of a scheduling policy, one can consider students' longevity at work, students' preferences for hours worked, and the strengths of students' abilities and fitness for particular positions. Remember, however, that students often decide to work on campus because scheduling is more flexible and because campus departments generally tend to support students in their persistence to obtain a degree. These are non-monetary incentives that on-campus employment environments can offer to students at little to no cost, advancing the goals of both student employees and the institution. It is an area in which off-campus employers find it more difficult to compete.

For those organizations or departments that have a multitude of positions available and who have a large number of students to schedule, the actual employee scheduling process is a significant undertaking. There are many dilemmas to be solved. For instance, thought must be given to fairness so that the available hours are spread out in an equitable fashion. Consider, also, the process by which students trade and substitute shifts, how the schedule is published, where the schedule is published, and how often the schedule is reviewed for changes. Software and websites are available to assist in the scheduling process, easing some of these administrative concerns.

Timekeeping and payroll

Timekeeping standards are more than likely prescribed by an organization's payroll department. However, a few notes and highlights might be helpful. While the legal requirements on records retention differ by state and institution, it is important to document time worked by students as well as other staff. At the very least, students need to record the time that they have worked. More desirable would be to have students punch in and out on a time clock or use an online or software application to record their time. This is important because it is always better to have an objective system that is free from potential security issues. Timekeeping is not only something that maintains legal compliance—it is an opportunity for students to see, first-hand, the causal relationship between working and getting paid.

This is also an area where process is important. Consider who is responsible for the completion of payroll on a regular basis and what roles other staff members in the organization play in making sure that time records are accurate and completed in a suitable manner. For most organizations, it makes sense to have one central payroll administrator. This suggestion is made because it is important to have one person whose job it is to monitor policy and procedural changes related to payroll matters and one person who can administer the program to everyone. This one person is, many times, in a clerical position, so everyone in the organization must understand that this individual is the final authority on payroll issues and has the ability to make procedural changes when necessary.

Supervisors, however, also have a role to play in the payroll process. These are the people who ensure that payroll is turned into the central administrator and who certify students' time records. Additionally, individual supervisors are the most appropriate personnel to counsel students regarding any mistakes or oversights that may surface in the review process.

Conclusion

It cannot be emphasized enough that the methods of administering a student employment program are as wide and varied as there are programs. Administrators can "shop around" and find ideas and approaches that can be modified and made to work for individual organizations. With this said, however, a few parting comments can help anyone charged with the oversight and administration of a student employment program.

Communication is absolutely vital. From talking with student candidates during a hiring interview to hearing from former employees during an exit interview, every communication is an opportunity to have a positive and lasting effect on students. Be clear about expectations and listen when students have something to say. Clearly articulate goals and objectives of programs, and hold students accountable for learning and growing in their positions. Much of the way students feel about their employer is determined by how they are treated and the communication they receive on a daily basis (Carnegie Mellon University, n.d.).

Communicate with students on their level and in ways to which they best respond. For example, drafting a memo, posting it on a bulletin board, and having everyone indicate understanding by initialing the paper is probably not the best way to communicate with students today. In an electronic, on-the-go world, the challenge is to communicate via methods with which students are familiar, including new technologies. These preferences are always changing, so it is important for supervisors to find a consistent and appropriate method that is effective in their context.

When training students, engage them in the learning process. This not only is good pedagogy but also is applicable and makes sense for student employee populations. Simply standing at the front of a room and training or conducting a meeting via lecture is not going to cut it. Today's students must be actively involved. (See Chapter 11 for more information about training.)

Learning outcomes are here to stay. With students, parents, and other stakeholders demanding accountability, administrators responsible for student employment programs must demonstrate employment opportunities' relevance. Student employees who understand their learning gains will be better prepared to take on future responsibilities as working, contributing members of society. Make the decision now to craft learning outcomes in a way that illustrates that student employment is not only beneficial, but necessary. (See Chapter 4 for further details about crafting learning outcomes.)

Once a program is in place, it is probably time to begin revising it. Student employment program administrators must always seek ways to be more relevant, always look to better prepare students, and always reach for continuous progress. It is useful not only to review policies and procedures on a regular basis, but also to assemble a group of students and staff who can help parse through all of the information and make suggestions for future improvement. If students are intimately involved in the process, they are more likely to become significantly invested in the program.

Additionally, thought can be given to developing a successful student employment alumni program. Many former student employees will welcome the opportunity to be involved in campus activities after they have graduated, and this gives current employees potential sources for advice. It also perpetuates an organization and more fully underscores the fact that, once students accept a position with an organization, they will be forever attached to something great. What better mechanism to build loyalty to a student employment program while maintaining lasting friendships and professional contacts from which an organization can draw for years to come? It is a win-win proposition.

Finally, be willing to share successes and failures with colleagues and partners worldwide. As indicated earlier in this chapter, with the myriad student employment opportunities available on campuses today, our collective knowledge is more powerful than any one department's isolated program.

References

Baker, B. (2007, July 10). Pass the pasta, Please, hold the stress. *The Washington Post*. Retrieved June 8, 2008, from http://www.washingtonpost.com/wp-dyn/content/article/2007/07/09/AR2007070901305_pf.html

Carnegie Mellon University. (n.d.). Supervising and managing. Retrieved August 2, 2008, from http://www.studentaffairs.cmu.edu/career/campus_employment/supervisors/ supervise.html

Chickering, A.W., & Reisser, L. (1993). *Education and identity* (2nd ed.). San Francisco: Jossey-Bass.

King, J.E. (2006). Working their way through college: Student employment and its impact on the college experience. Retrieved May 4, 2008, from http://www.acenet.edu/AM/Template.cfm?template=/CM/ContentDisplay.cfm &ContentFileID=1618

Pay band. (2008). Retrieved August 3, 2008, from http://en.wikipedia.org/wiki/Pay_Bands

Recognition Professionals International. (n.d.). Employment recognition. Retrieved May 1, 2008, from http://www.recognition.org

Senge, P. M. (1994). *The fifth discipline: The art & practice of the learning organization.* New York: Doubleday Business.

PARTNERING WITH OUTSOURCED SERVICE-PROVIDERS TO CREATE LEARNING OPPORTUNITIES FOR STUDENT EMPLOYEES

by Maggie Towle & Denny Olsen

Higher education has been seeking ways to be more efficient and transparent for decades. Abundant literature supports the importance of collaborative efforts within the campus community (Association of American Colleges and Universities, 2002; Keeling, 2004). Student employment is a prime area for academic, student affairs, auxiliary departments, and others to create partnerships focusing on student development. New possibilities have emerged for higher education to embrace student employment beyond the traditional campus opportunities. With the increased level of collaboration between higher education institutions and for-profit companies, the time is ripe to capitalize on these relationships for the benefit of students, individual institutions, and the private companies doing business with higher education. Can higher education institutions be proactive and intentional about asking outsourced service providers to incorporate student development?

"Learning Reconsidered: A Campus-Wide Focus on the Student Experience" (Keeling, 2004) emphasizes that the entire campus be considered a learning community. However, what about asking that for-profit companies partner with educational institutions to support the mission of student development and growth? Is it possible and reasonable to collaborate with service-providers for increased developmental gains of students? Can we expect for-profit companies to place the same premium on student growth as the academy? This chapter explores these philosophical questions and illustrates that it is possible and desirable for service-providers to play a larger role in educating and developing college students. Current practices and trends illustrate that these companies have taken steps toward being critical partners in student development and are already moving toward a more developmental approach.

For the past two decades many services, especially in the auxiliary and support areas on American campuses, have been outsourced to for-profit companies. These include dining services (e.g., ARAMARK, Sodexo, andChartwells), bookstores (e.g., Follett and Barnes & Noble), printing/mailing services (e.g., FedEx/Kinkos and UPS), travel agencies (e.g., STA), and residential life (e.g., Campus Living Villages and American Campus Communities). These companies, in turn, hire large numbers of student employees to complete their labor force. Most of these companies have programs such as leadership training and education (Campus Living Villages) or sustainability education and marketing internships (ARAMARK) in place, which illustrate that they already are a key player in supporting the educational environment on campus.

Reoccurring fiscal constraints in higher education have led institutions to explore outsourcing to provide previously self-operated services. Another perceived and often real advantage of outsourcing is that hiring companies with expertise and experience in operating auxiliary areas allows universities to focus on their educational mission. While companies provide university-requested deliverables related to service, quality, and finances, they also are able to offer their training programs as a benefit to student employees.

Orientation and training opportunities in a for-profit operation provide a more hands-on skill-building experience beyond the academic environment. Follett Higher Education Group offers skill-building courses on topics such as selling skills, loss prevention, and harassment prevention as well as customer service, marketing, and environmental awareness. Many outsourced companies provide internships and graduate assistantships for student managers that are experiential and include academic credit.

Can institutions partner with companies?

"Learning Reconsidered 2" (Keeling, 2006) gives several examples of how to incorporate student learning outcomes into out-of-classroom settings. There has been success with a variety of programs from learning abroad, college unions, learning communities, dining services, and housing and residential life. Readers are encouraged to reconsider basic assumptions in the academy including current structures and organizational patterns. Perhaps it is time to think beyond the current university structures and organizations and expand thinking to for-profit companies on campus.

It is possible, as Steffes and Keeling (2006) describe, to "create a spectrum of new and healthy cultural norms that can transform working relationships and refocus energy away from competition and the maintenance of silos and toward cross-functional planning and shared responsibility for learning"(p. 69). Steffes's and Keeling's ideas can be expanded to working toward cross-functional planning, training, and shared responsibility for educating and developing students.

Even if it is possible for service-providers to partner in students' education, is it reasonable? Why should administrators expect for-profit companies will be motivated to be more intentional about developing their student employees, when students are already in an academic environment? Can institutions move beyond the assumption that academia, not the outside sources, provides the education expertise? And can these entities work together for the benefit of students? Though these ideas need to be put in practice and researched, a model is proposed that could be translated for non-campus partner use (see Figure 10.1). If successfully implemented, the value of the model may be

FIGURE 10.1 STUDENT EMPLOYMENT PROGRAM LEARNING OUTCOMES: CONCEPTUAL MODEL FOR HIGHER EDUCATION & OUTSOURCED SERVICE-PROVIDERS

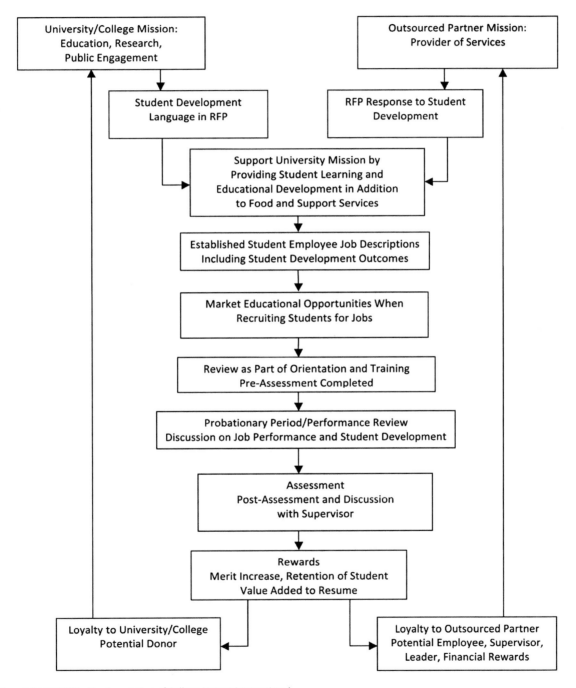

understood through staff retention, improved morale, improved customer service, additional revenue, and increased student success.

Implementing a specific student development component into the outsourced partner's daily operations and practice will be perceived as value-added when competing during the request for proposal (RFP) process. Institutions expect that outsourced RFP proposals will include deliverables on financial performance and quality of products and services. However, illustrating that the company plays a vital role in the students' holistic education could be perceived favorably by the university when determining the final RFP award.

Service-providers need to think of the benefit to their company if they are seen as important collaborators in students' education. In turn, this will decrease perceptions that corporate America is intruding on the hallowed grounds of academia or using student employees as a source of inexpensive labor.

Best practices of service-providers

Many partners providing services to colleges and universities already have well established student development programs in place. One example is Follett Higher Education Group's student internship program. Follett has individual development plans and expected learning outcomes for all of its student associates. Its program consists of six values: focus on customers, innovation, integrity, teamwork, accountability, and valuing each and every associate. These values are used in a developmental approach when training student employees. The values also are consistent with what higher education espouses via student learning outcomes and illustrate that service-providers have an interest in a holistic educational approach toward their student employees.

In addition, Follett's Customer Service Reward and Recognition Program recognizes associates who demonstrate a passion for exceeding customer expectations and are proactive, approachable, and responsive in their relationships with external and internal customers. Again, these are characteristics that demonstrate a developmental approach.

Many companies have programs that tie directly into educational programs. Campus Living Villages at Northwestern State University in Natchitoches, La., collaborates with the student personnel services master's degree program faculty to provide practicum experiences and internships at their sites. Campus Living Villages develop a learning contract and have the students function as direct service-providers. Students are engaged in entry-level professional activities and gain experience in a specific counseling or student development setting.

These service-providers are to be recognized and appreciated for their practices in developing students. However, many of these programs, similar to many university programs until recently, do not articulate their contribution to individual student learning outcomes or growth. They realize the value of developing student employees; however, their perceived outcome may relate to students becoming members of their company post-graduation and starting in management positions within their company as an ultimate career goal. This is mutually beneficial to the companies and the students, but there is also value in focusing on student learning for general success in life and work.

More intentional student development programs may assist with students' retention and graduation and can still provide more post-graduation employees for the companies involved. Intentionality around student development programs could also increase morale, which may translate to better customer service, less absenteeism, and increased revenue generation.

Current trends

One key assumption is that students learn throughout their collegiate experience, whether in or out of the classroom. "Learning Reconsidered" (Keeling, 2004) has called this transformative learning, the idea that learning "must include the full scope of a student's life" (p. 11). "Learning Reconsidered" suggests that higher education institutions should define specific learning or developmental outcomes for their students and suggests a list of seven desired learning outcomes for students (pp. 18–19).

One of the recommendations from "Learning Reconsidered" (Keeling, 2004) is that "Student affairs professionals and faculty must commit to assessing the campus environment for specific learning experiences in each of the overall student learning outcome categories" (p. 28). On-campus student employment is an excellent opportunity to structure what could be a routine student experience into a transformative learning experience. Lewis (2008) posited that "Student affairs officers and researchers have sought to better define, understand, and promote learning within our cocurricular and extracurricular programs. Student employment has the potential to be a significant development experience for many students" (p. A56).

University departments, including student affairs units, have traditionally had various student employee programs in place. These programs typically incorporate job knowledge and customer service training, involvement in student employee governance functions, and recognition programs. A recent trend has been the incorporation of student development or learning outcomes into student employee programs.

The University of Minnesota story

The process in which the student learning outcomes program was started at the University of Minnesota can provide lessons to develop a vibrant, collaborative program with service-providers. Within the Student Unions and Activities department at the University of Minnesota–Twin Cities, staff initiated a pilot program with 14 student employees in 2004 that incorporated student learning outcomes into job descriptions. These student learning outcomes are:

- Responsibility and Accountability.
- Independence and Interdependence.

- Goal Orientation.
- Self-Awareness.
- Resilience.
- Appreciation of Differences.
- Tolerance of Ambiguity.

Assessment tools were developed to measure student learning as a result of their student employment. Based on supervisor and student employee scores, student employees improved on student learning measures. Focus groups indicated that student employees thought the outcomes program was positive. Students indicated that it gave them better language in which to explain their work experience for resumes and job interviews. Further, it gave them a sense of more meaning to their jobs and an improved working relationship with their supervisors. An interesting byproduct was that supervisors tended to see themselves more as educators, teachers, and mentors, rather than just the boss.

Since its introduction, the program has expanded to all of the more than 250 student employees in the college unions. The student learning outcomes are not only the basis of the job description but also have been incorporated into the performance review process. The concept has expanded and is presented as part of supervisor training sessions for all university employees and is being developed across campus in other departments.

One example of a campus partner that has been using a student learning outcome program is ARAMARK, the campus-wide dining services provider at the University of Minnesota. ARAMARK, or University Dining Services, continues to incorporate student learning outcomes into its student employee program. University Dining Services based its program on the model Student Unions and Activities developed.

University Dining Services employs more than 650 student employees and began implementing its learning outcomes program in the 2004–05 academic year. Its first step was to revise all job descriptions to incorporate the student learning outcomes. For example, what follows is language in a student attendant job description under the outcome of "Responsibility and Accountability":

Responsibility and Accountability
- On time for shift and required to provide replacement if cannot work assigned shift.
- Adheres to basic policies and procedures and understands staff roles.
- Presents her/himself in a friendly and professional manner.
- Takes responsibility for, and learns from, errors.
- Takes responsibility for his/her learning.
- Always meets basic expectations (e.g., uniform based on location).
- Customer-focused and driven.

The rest of the job description is similarly arranged referencing the learning outcomes and providing definition to each one.

In 2005–06, University Dining Services began having supervisors meet with all student employees and complete an employee goals form. A student learning outcomes assessment tool, again based on the Student Unions and Activities model, was added to measure the seven student learning outcomes. Students took the assessment at the beginning of the year and again at the end of the year, basically self-ranking their progress on the outcomes. Listed below is an example of the "Resilience" component on the assessment.

Resilience

- Bounces back after disappointments.
- Recovers quickly from a bad experience and continues to work successfully.
- Assesses cause of a negative experience and learns how to prevent it from recurring.
- Learns from mistakes and willing to accept constructive criticism.
- Balances classes, work, volunteer activities, and personal commitments.

Each of these items is ranked on a five-degree scale from "never" to "always" and is again repeated for each of the seven learning outcomes. The assessment is written to be used as a discussion tool, with the hope that specific examples from student work experience can be related to desired learning outcomes. For example, a student employee may make a mistake at the cash register and process a credit card payment incorrectly. If the student understands the learning outcome concept, he or she may realize that the supervisor is more interested in the learning that results from that mistake than disciplining the employee for the mistake.

After implementing its program, University Dining Services discovered that not all supervisors were ensuring that the goals and self-assessment were being completed with student employees. For the past two years, the program had been a requirement for all supervisors. Meetings and discussions with student employees about their goals and learning outcomes also are required for supervisors.

The next steps for University Dining Services are to conduct more measurement and assessment of the program. Student managers also might be permitted more involvement as supervisors in this process. To determine whether having a student learning outcomes program is effective, it may be important to measure whether it improves student development and also whether it helps student employee retention, improves customer service, and enhances financial performance or the organization.

While the student learning outcomes component is a newer concept, ARAMARK/ University Dining Services has, similar to other corporate partners and other institutions, other programs to support student development. These include a student manager program, a general orientation program for all students, and a student "Green Team" that works on a recycling and composting program. Students also can participate in marketing, human resources, and nutrition and wellness internships related to career areas.

Another important component of a university/outsourced company partnership around student learning outcomes is to have administrative and corporate support for the program. Service-providers could work with the university to introduce student learning concepts and an outcomes program to a small group of supervisors. Once job descriptions and an assessment tool are in place, the program can be rolled out to students working directly with those supervisors. If the program makes sense and is successful, those supervisors and students in the pilot program will become ambassadors in supporting expansion of the program to other student employee positions.

At the University of Minnesota, the vice provost for student affairs was able to get buy-in from other administrators on the importance of student learning outcomes for the campus. He worked with the student affairs division leadership to develop the outcomes and worked tirelessly to get the word out to everyone on campus. Bookmarks were distributed across campus with the header: "As they progress toward their degree, students will develop and demonstrate:" followed by list of the seven learning outcomes. This broad campus support, and in the University of Minnesota's case, endorsement of these outcomes at the highest levels, makes implementing the program with campus partners much easier to explain and execute. Campus partners can have their higher-ranking officers work with university administrators to market and promote the learning outcomes across campus and internally within their areas. Messages about the outcomes to administrators, faculty, students, and even parents of first-year students can be coordinated with the student affairs department and/or the appropriate units. There is a perception that student jobs are little more than a form of inexpensive labor and a source of financial aid for students. Moving the perception of student employment as a developmental program for students begins with staff supervisors and administrators working together with campus partners to promote that message.

Conceptual model

According to the conceptual model of how universities and colleges can partner with service-providers for student employment learning outcomes (Figure 10.1), the following components need to be developed: integration of student learning into organizational mission and student employment jobs, marketing, training, job performance review, assessment, and rewards.

The foundation of the student employment partnership model takes into account the missions of both the educational institution and the potential partner to see where there is a match beneficial to both groups. For an institution beginning a relationship, expectations and needs can be outlined in an initial RFP. Every higher education institution has the concept of student learning explicitly or implicitly within its mission. Service providers would be advised to add learning to their mission statement or, if already implied, to reinforce it as part of their RFP response.

The first step for any outsourced partner is to convince its executives of the benefits of incorporating student learning outcomes into practice with its campus accounts. This may require a review of literature and education on successful programs that currently exist on college campuses, or it may be as simple as looking at existing practices and revising language to articulate the learning that is already occurring in most of their on-campus student employment opportunities.

The potential partner's RFP response is an opportunity to articulate its previous programs related to student development. When responding to RFPs, the company should blend the two mission statements and provide one that emphasizes student learning (partners in education) as well as quality service and financial benefits. However, the potential partner also can respond to the specific language on how it might incorporate learning outcomes and assessment into its program. Institutions understand that service-providers have financial goals, but learning outcomes programs should not by nature decrease bottom lines. Once a partner is selected, most student affairs professionals would welcome an invitation to assist partners in developing a program or the language necessary to illustrate the student development that occurs within its operations/companies.

The key stages in the student employment partnership model are:

1. RFP: Incorporate student learning outcomes language into the RFP proposal.
2. RFP response: Draft a working agreement.
3. Position descriptions: Write student employee position descriptions with the partner and student learning outcomes language.
4. Marketing program: Market employee positions using outcomes language and benefits of program.
5. Orientation and training: Provide orientation and training to supervisors and student employees.
6. Performance development process: Initiate a performance development process that reviews job performance and student learning outcomes.
7. Assessment: Assess students' performance and overall program.
8. Rewards: Communicate value and investment returns.

Use of this model is an overt way to tie the bid process to implementation and assessment phases. It helps prepare the institution for procurement and helps ensure success after a vendor has been selected.

Incorporating student learning outcomes into requests for proposals

While traditional student development or training programs have included orientations, internships, student manager positions, and other similar programs, the concept of identifying learning outcomes for student employees is relatively new, both for universities and service-providers. Since universities and corporate partners strive to work better and more collaboratively, this new developmental concept can be an excellent way for both entities to work on a meaningful and mutual endeavor that ultimately benefits universities, corporate partners, and students. Universities must take the lead on formalizing these relationships, and a logical way to do so is through RFPs and contracts. In an existing relationship, contracts or working agreements can be developed that address student learning outcomes.

The University of Minnesota recently went through a system-wide RFP process for new food and beverage contracts. As part of that process, a work group was formed to draft and recommend language for the RFP specific to college unions and needs of students. This group included staff members from Student Unions and Activities, students, and other staff members from departments housed in the unions. Among the concepts discussed within this work group were:

- Requiring the vendor to propose a student learning outcomes program for student. employees or adopt the university's program.
- Language that required respondents to have a general student development program.
- Student involvement in sustainability and green initiatives.
- Requiring a certain percentage of student versus nonstudent employees.
- Student internship/management positions.

Students on the committee proposed many of these concepts. The final language on student development in the RFP was not as specific. However, the process created a dialogue, introduced a vernacular on student learning, and established the importance of student learning in this outsourcing arena. Future RFPs could include language that would require respondents to identify how they would incorporate, measure, and assess the effectiveness of learning outcomes for student employees.

The language below is an example of how specific higher education institutions can craft RFP language, requesting that the respondents specifically outline how they will assist with student development.

> Provide a description of how respondent would collaborate with the university and incorporate the university's student learning outcomes into its student employment program. Description should include the following components:
>
> - Plan for job descriptions to incorporate student learning outcomes.
> - Plan for assessing effectiveness of student employee program in achieving desired student learning outcomes.
> - Training and orientation program for student employees.
> - Training and educational program for student employee supervisors, especially as it relates to learning outcomes.
> - Plan to work in collaboration with the university and individual departments on the student employment program.

This type of specific language facilitates clear understanding by both parties about student learning outcomes' importance in the work being bid.

RFP response

Once a vendor has been selected through the RFP process, or if the institution is already in a relationship with a vendor, a working agreement or contract should be developed. That agreement may cover many items including programmatic, financial, and facility issues and also should include a student learning outcomes component. This component of the agreement might contain the following language, which should mirror aspects of the RFP language:

The vendor agrees to work with the university and/or department to incorporate student learning outcomes into their student employee program. The university and/or department agrees to provide information on current student learning outcomes program related to student employment. This includes sharing existing job descriptions, assessments, training and performance review documents, and other information. The vendor agrees that the following components will be included in its student employee program:

- Job descriptions will incorporate student learning outcomes language.
- Student employees and supervisors of student employees will receive orientation and training on student learning outcomes.
- Performance reviews will be conducted with all student employees and review process will include discussion of student learning outcomes as well as work performance.
- An assessment program will measure the effectiveness of student employment and whether it is beneficial to bringing about desired learning outcomes.

The vendor and university agree to meet not less than annually to review their respective student employee program components and develop a plan for collaborating on efforts, where possible.

A working agreement containing specifically outlined components of a learning-based employment program sets clear expectations for all involved.

Position descriptions

Position descriptions can be developed to incorporate student learning outcomes. In the section on the University of Minnesota story, there was an example of language used to show desired outcomes for "Responsibility and Accountability" in a student employee food services attendant position description (see Appendix 8). This type of language is quite different from a position description that talks about assisting with food preparation and washing dishes. Regardless of the position responsibilities, student employees know they need to follow policies and procedures. Students also clearly see language in the descriptions that errors are not to be hidden but are educational tools to help them improve their performance. When errors are discussed in the position description students will likely understand that someone has made mistakes before and will not be afraid of errors. A job description for a games room attendant (see Appendix 9) has similar items for responsibility and accountability but also includes outcomes for general knowledge of games and game room equipment, knowledge of menu, food preparation, and safety rules, correct operation of cash register/point-of-sale system, and balancing a cash register at the end of a shift.

Outcomes for independence/interdependence can include seeking instruction from a supervisor and asking a supervisor for help when a student is unclear of tasks and procedures or how to correct errors. Resilience outcomes might be accepting instruction or constructive criticism from a supervisor and the ability to work through problems or unusual circumstances. The example position descriptions can provide corporate partners with ideas on how to structure their student employee position descriptions. Working collaboratively with the university, they may be able to replicate basic parts of the position description that are applicable to most jobs. For example, self-awareness outcomes, such as good verbal and nonverbal communication skills, and a friendly and helpful attitude with customers and peers are likely desired outcomes for all employees.

There are several other examples of desirable outcomes that are more universal in nature. The outcome for appreciation of differences may be to treat all customers, peers, and supervisors respectfully and congenially. Tolerance of ambiguity can be demonstrated by whether the student employees are able to handle a difficult customer when there is little information available to guide them in their actions. These broad-based outcomes can be adapted to a variety of student employment settings. Organizational variables such as scope and distribution (see Chapter 4) also will affect the selection of learning outcomes.

Marketing program

The outsourced partner should develop a marketing program that highlights the student development benefits in addition to learning in a for-profit environment, which will add more value to any academic degree. While this education may seem less concrete than receiving wages, it can be presented as a tangible benefit to employment.

Marketing student employee jobs as opportunities to develop hands-on management skills and direct job experience may translate to a career with the outsourced partner. Minimally, it is an opportunity to introduce students to various career opportunities in the industry.

At the University of Minnesota, there are students majoring in environmental sciences who serve on the "Green Team," a group that educates customers on recycling and other environmental initiatives. There is also a group of student interns called "The Food Dudes" that assists with the marketing and promotion of Union Dining Services. Those students are majoring in marketing and recently one of the interns was hired for a permanent full-time position with Union Dining Services. Most higher education administrators can give testimony to the many undergraduate and graduate students hired into full-time positions, helping provide a solid and consistent employee base. This could happen with service-providers, which would also positively affect student retention rates in supervisor and leadership positions on campus. At the University of Minnesota, both of these groups of students are gaining specific management and skill development pertinent to their majors.

Orientation and training

Orientation and training for direct supervisors of student employees are critical. Traditionally, student employment utilizes on-the-job training where students learn specific skills, such as how to operate a point-of-sale register or how to properly complete a report. The orientation component for both higher education and outsourced companies will typically review the department's mission and values and perhaps some history of the company or university division. Service-providers and educational institutions should consider partnering in the students' orientation and training.

Most institutions have a set of core values that closely relate to those of service providers. Development of an orientation program that includes each entity's core values is a good starting point. History and goals could be developed collaboratively. Those goals could include a statement regarding student learning outcomes as an important component of their student employment experience.

Collaborating on the student employees' orientation would help break down the "silo mentality." In fact, what would occur is a better understanding of the two cultures of higher education and corporate partners. It also would reiterate the value of students getting their education while also understanding the values of organizations beyond academia. Most students do not develop careers solely in higher education, so employment with service-providers offers a positive opportunity for them to learn more about the for-profit world.

In responding to RFPs, if for-profit companies requested that their orientation programs be merged with existing institutional programs or vice versa, it would illustrate the company's foresight in efficiency (cost savings) while showing they value and want to be part of the students' education.

The model program also should introduce the position descriptions incorporating student learning outcomes during orientation for supervisors and, later, during orientation sessions for student employees. These position descriptions then become the basis for discussions during the student employee probationary period as well as for performance reviews and assessments. The following introductory statement can be used to introduce the concept to supervisors and student employees:

> The university and its outsourced service-provider have developed a program, called Student Learning Outcomes, designed to have the students' work experience mirror their academic experience, fulfilling a clear and comprehensive student development goal. The Student Learning Outcomes program encourages supervisors to help students acquire valuable life skills within the work environment. Some behaviors are necessary for the work environment and also are aspects for personal development. For these reasons, student position descriptions include both performance and development aspects. Furthermore, our student employee performance and development process consists of evaluating students' job performance as well as their personal development.

Clearly stating expectations about training and orientation up front will help facilitate the education process when implementing the employment program, and this intentional design may lead to greater developmental outcomes for students.

Performance development process

One disadvantage to the student learning outcomes process is that it may be seen as more work for supervisors when added to their current performance review process with student employees. If the concept of learning outcomes is to be fully integrated with partners, then the performance review should not only be a separate process, but also based on the position description and incorporate the same learning outcomes. Administrators can work with partners to have similar performance reviews and timing parallels that will most benefit the student experience and minimize burden to supervisors. (There are differing views on this concept; see Chapters 3 and 12 of this book for additional discussion.)

The performance development process defines the student employee experience as a process, rather than just a job with a performance review at the end. What are the benefits to having a performance development process?

- Student Benefits:
    - Maintaining or improving job satisfaction and morale.
    - Identifying areas that need improvement.
    - Opportunity to develop a stronger work ethic.
    - Opportunity to discuss job challenges and interests.
    - Understanding that their job is not just a paycheck; it consists of gaining life skills in addition to performing their job duties on a day-to-day basis.
    - Developing the skills needed to market oneself better. Language from performance development conversations can be used to strengthen resumes and interview skills, making them more appealing to potential employers.
- Supervisor Benefits:
    - Documenting performance issues and identifying training needs.
    - Giving positive feedback and recording special talents, skills, interests, and capabilities.
    - Forging stronger working relationships.
    - Reinforcing work expectations.
    - Developing and motivating employees.
    - Achieving the university's and/or partner's overall mission and goals.
    - Satisfying university requirements.
    - Satisfying legal due process requirements (documentation necessary for terminating employees).

- Opportunity to create a vibrant and positive environment in the department and the university.

The performance review process begins by establishing expectations on the front end. One way to do this is by defining the standard for meeting expectations. This can further be defined for each of the learning outcomes. What follows is an example of defining expectations for one of the University of Minnesota's student learning outcome, "Responsibility and Accountability."

Definition of Meets Expectations:
Understands work procedures, policies, technical aspects, and responsibilities. Makes appropriate decisions to handle assorted responsibilities. Takes ownership of duties and responsibilities, ensures they are completed accurately and on time. Plans and follows through on commitments and expectations set by supervisor. Uses resources efficiently and effectively. Appropriately engages manager in prioritizing and completing critical assignments or work load. Notifies manager of information especially in regard to mistakes, incomplete work, and other critical issues (when appropriate). Amount of work produced is consistent with the needs of the job. Seeks additional assignments as time permits. Complies with departmental and university policies and procedures. Maintains confidentiality and discretion as appropriate. Reports to work on time, work absences are infrequent, and finds a replacement for shifts as necessary. Accepts and supports goals of the unit, department, and university.

These expectations can be shared with corporate partners so that they may incorporate their own expectations language where applicable.

The performance development process in action

Most university departments and some corporate partners have performance review processes for student employees. However, the actual execution of performance reviews is not always consistent. Universities can work closely with supervisors and with corporate partners to emphasize the importance of the performance development process tying together performance measures with the learning outcomes.

Discussions should occur with service-providers to have similar performance development processes so that students receive a similar experience and are exposed to learning outcomes regardless of their employer. Supervisors should meet with student employees at the start of the year to review their job descriptions, establish expectations, and explain the performance development program and the rationale for using the program. While training and informal meetings happen throughout the year, the supervisors and students meet formally during each term to discuss performance and personal development. At the University of Minnesota, supervisors use a written

"Student Performance Review Summary" (see Appendix 10) form to evaluate each student employee at the end of the year.

Assessment

Universities can work with service-providers to determine whether the student development outcomes program is effective. One way to do this is to analyze supervisor and student employee assessments of student performance or improvement related to the student learning outcomes.

Another longer-term and more difficult goal would be to evaluate whether the student learning outcomes program has affected financial performance, employee retention, or quality of service delivered. At the University of Minnesota, performance review summaries were used to assess individual performance. In addition to measuring whether the overall program is effective, the following tools were used: an assessment completed by student employees and/or supervisors, focus groups with student employees, and focus groups with supervisors.

Focus groups with student employees and separately with supervisors can be an informative assessment method for these programs. Through training and practice, supervisors realize that they are teachers, role models, and educators. Many student employees and supervisors express their relationship as that of mentors/mentees versus supervisors/supervisees. The supervisors realize what an important role they play in developing students, and they can actually see the results from the beginning to the end of the school year and from students' first year to their senior year.

By discussing results with supervisors, students take more ownership of their work and also see themselves learning and developing over time. Students want to understand how their job is more than technical skill development. They realize they are learning how to handle ambiguity, solve problems on their own, etc.

The results of assessment can be shared in RFP responses and with institutions, shareholders, and corporations. There is evidence from University of Minnesota assessment results that students see themselves improving on student learning outcomes and, anecdotally, that they see benefits in terms of developing different language to describe their experience, which can translate into better resumes or job-seeking skills. Supervisors report these same changes for student employees and that the learning outcomes program enables them to take on a different role with student employees. As suggested at the start of this section, future assessment with service-providers could focus on additional areas. This might include whether there is a link between employment and development outcomes, retention at the university, and eventual career tracks for students. It might also focus on studying impact on financial performance and quality of service. For a full analysis of methods and assessment, see Chapter 12.

Rewards

The rewards when incorporating student development outcomes into student employment are many. One is the increased engagement of supervisors as they understand the important role they have in working on the student development component with their student staff. Additionally, it can be beneficial to organizations and personally rewarding to supervisors to measure their students' development and observe them improving and mastering new skills. These rewards are augmented as student employees are retained and promoted into advanced positions, and benefits are further amplified when student employees can be recruited and hired into full-time staff positions. Such progressions reduce training time and help with the program's continuity. Former students see the value of student development as they themselves become supervisors of student staff.

Another reward is students using the language of the student learning outcomes when applying to graduate school or for their first professional position. Supervisors use the language when writing recommendations or responding to job references. They are able to articulate specific skills their students developed versus saying "they worked as a cashier in our games room." Recently an undergraduate senior mentioned that he "totally messed up" his mock interview because he forgot to focus on the skills he developed through his work. He said he focused too much on the tasks of his job and realized that he needed to promote the learning outcomes that he had mastered over the three years of his employment. Such connections are difficult if learning outcomes are not fully integrated throughout students' employment experience.

The implications of this learning extend beyond the years immediately following graduation. Lifelong loyalty to the institution or specific department where the student was employed may be observed and measured over time as campuses apply the conceptual model. Perhaps former student employees are potential donors after they begin their career and understand the important foundation they developed while working on campus.

For corporate partners, rewards and awards would be similar: retention, improved morale (for both supervisors and students), company loyalty, and potential employee, manager, or leader of their company. All of this could contribute to the bottom line, and revenue gains would be realized for both the service-provider and higher education institution.

Potential pitfalls

There are potential pitfalls for service-providers if they focus on student learning outcomes. Some may be skeptical about the need for the student development component when the focus and energy really needs to be on the bottom line or on providing quality service. There is a learning curve in training supervisors and students on the concept and incorporating it into daily practice. This translates into additional time and paying for increased hours on the front side of the curve. Many areas traditionally outsourced by higher education have high employee turnover rates so the training may be ongoing.

Moving into the program too quickly or being inconsistent in how it is implemented may result in a lack of buy-in or the feeling that the program is being forced upon supervisors. Service-providers may be wary of embracing a concept that may take time to get buy-in from staff. However, a student learning outcomes approach should be studied to see if it has a positive impact. Supervisory staff may value their jobs more if they see themselves playing an important role in the development and ultimate future of their student employees. In addition, the students will understand the value of their experience beyond receiving a paycheck. Perhaps these factors would provide motivation for staff to stay in their positions. The feeling of contributing to something greater than revenue generation might result in higher staff morale and less absenteeism. Ultimately, the goal is that participation in the learning outcomes program can translate into better service, increased retention of staff, and increased use of services resulting in improved financial performance.

Conclusion

Outsourcing on college campuses continues to be a viable way to achieve a number of organizational goals, such as enhanced performance, economic prudence, and a focus on core mission-related issues. Given the persistence of this trend, it behooves colleges and universities to capitalize on the situation by working to embrace student learning and development as part of the regular course of business with for-profit companies.

The fiscal realities of both higher education and the for-profit sector may foster a reluctance to focus on integrating learning outcomes into the student employment experience. However, many tools and resources are available that can assist in a smooth transition to provide more focus on student development while minimizing additional human or financial resources.

Formal communication between the higher education institution and the corporate entity often begins during the initial RFP process. The RFP process lays the groundwork for the working relationship and provides necessary details when implementing the final plan. Communication protocol is narrowly prescribed during a procurement process, so the clarity and conciseness of written materials becomes critical for the outsourced service-provider. The ability for the corporate partner to articulate and anticipate the institution's needs as demonstrated first in writing, and then in person, becomes central as the RFP process unfolds.

The relationship between the two organizations continues through negotiation and ultimately program implementation. It takes a willingness to surrender a certain amount of control on both sides to build the trust necessary to capitalize on the potential synergy between the two organizational types. Both sides must give and take. For example, the academy must concede some ownership, indeed embrace the company, by assisting with the implementation and measurement of learning outcomes. And service partners must take some risk on the potential investment of labor into a more time-intensive methodology around student employment. While the focus on student development may be more labor-intensive for supervisors, institutions view the adoption of learning outcomes as a positive forward step, and the potential benefits to the corporate entity are numerous.

The alignment of the missions and the integration of training and orientation programs can help bring the organizations more in sync philosophically and administratively. Expansion of existing corporate programs, use of internships, and creation of other developmentally related programs demonstrate an understanding and value of employee growth. Common sets of student learning outcomes, compatible position descriptions, and collaborative and innovative ideas and partnerships are likely to yield greater synergy in the current higher education outsourcing environment and could lead to retention of current contracts or the ability to secure new, long-term commitments.

Getting to the point where collaborative environments between higher education and service-providers is commonplace and expected may yet be in the future; however, there are many ways for these entities to enjoy common ground for the good of students, higher education, and for-profit companies.

References

Association of American Colleges and Universities. (2002). *Greater expectations: A new vision for learning as a nation goes to college.* Retrieved February 2, 2009, from http://greaterexpectations.org

Keeling, R.P. (2004). *Learning reconsidered: A campus-wide focus on the student experience.* Washington, DC: ACPA, NASPA.

Lewis, J. (2008, June 20). Student workers can learn more on the job. *The Chronicle of Higher Education,* p. A56.

Steffes, J., & Keeling, R.P. (2006). Creating strategies for collaboration. In R.P. Keeling (Ed.), *Learning reconsidered 2: A practical guide to implementing a campus-wide focus on the student experiences* (pp. 69–74). Washington, DC: ACPA, ACUHO-I, ACUI, NACA, NACADA, NASPA, & NIRSA.

ORIENTATION, TRAINING, AND DEVELOPMENT

by Eve Scrogham & Sara Punsky McGuire

Many university departments could not survive without students to provide assistance in the daily operation of facilities, programs, services, and projects. Research indicates the potential benefits of student employment during college (Gleason, 1993; Kincaid, 1996; Peters, 1997). How can supervisors move beyond the obvious reasons for employing students and make workers' experiences a valuable component of their college education? It is professional staff members' responsibility to provide student employees with an opportunity for involvement that is both meaningful and educational while assisting them in becoming successful members of an increasingly global society. College students' success is promoted "by setting and holding students to standards that stretch them to perform at high levels, inside and outside the classroom" (Kuh, Kinzie, Schuh, & Whitt, 2005, p. 269). Personal growth can be fostered through challenging experiences, and staff can be willing to help students learn from mistakes, take risks, and experiment (Gehrke, 2006).

Because so many of campus organizations' basic operations are left in student workers' hands, it is imperative that they are provided with the right tools to be successful. As part of well-constructed student employment programs, supervisors can establish standards through high-quality, learning-focused training, and they can strive to "provide opportunities for students to make the connection between their work and their personal and professional development" (Smith College Mission Statement, 2003, ¶ 1). The student employment experience is affected by the "quality of work and the attention that the employer pays to their development" (Shertzer & Doyle, 2006, p. 98). In this chapter, various student employee training programs are described, along with best practices, methods, pitfalls, and issues to consider when creating or updating student employment programs to be more developmental and learning-focused.

What is training?

Training could be defined as the education or instruction that occurs during a workers' introductory or transitional period. It provides employers with an opportunity to introduce the new employee to the organization while providing specific, job-related education. It is through this process that the employees are able to gain the skills and knowledge needed to successfully complete their job duties within a larger organization. Training and development are sometimes used interchangeably, but a subtle distinction is made here where the focus is primarily on orientation training when students initially enter and transition into an organization.

In the higher education context, institutions are responsible for creating learning environments that allow for a choice of educational opportunities and that challenge students to learn and develop while providing support to nurture their development (Miller, 2001). Training clearly focuses on learning, and this makes it an excellent opportunity for many seamless connections to students' classroom learning, personal development, and citizenship. While the primary responsibility for learning and development lies with the student (Miller, 2001), student employee supervisors can ultimately lay the groundwork for that development of personal responsibility and the whole person. Likewise, they should believe that the better the training, the better the student employee.

Training occurs in a variety of ways (see Appendix 11 for sample training timelines). It can be an extensive orientation covering a broad range of topics for a group of employees who are all starting at the same time. It can be hands-on learning that takes place on the job for a current employee with initiative to learn new skills or for a new employee hired mid-term to fulfill a need. A developmental aspect of training can be ongoing education that takes place through formal sessions or informally at staff meetings to teach new procedures, technologies, or services. Regardless, there are a number of factors that should be thoughtfully considered for an effective training program.

It is important to understand students' perspectives when it is time to train. What are their individual needs and working environment preferences? What do they want from a job? How do they work best? How much support do they need? Determining answers to these questions also should assist in building a student's personal ownership of the job, and in return the students can become a part of the employment or training process by sharing opinions and providing feedback before and during planning. Further, asking questions invites a group to examine its purpose and practices instead of thoughtlessly continuing old practices (Komives, Lucas, & McMahon, 2007). Several organizational questions also should be considered for the training of every student staff member. These include: What is the organization's purpose? How does the organization fit into the larger scope of the university? What is the organization's history? What is the organization's vision? How does the student fit in? With answers to these questions, the direction and focus of the training can begin to take shape.

Theoretical implications for training

Effective training takes student development theory and translates it into practice to enhance the students' learning experience. Theory can be used to better understand and design educationally purposeful environments (McEwan, 2003). In the opening chapters of this text, an overview of student development theory and its meaning related to personal growth through employment were described. Here, various key concepts from theory will be expanded to support the design of employee training programs.

Chickering and Reisser (1993) outlined seven vectors of college student identity development, each of which can be reexamined throughout development. The first vector focuses on *developing competence*, which really is the root of a training program—to learn the skills necessary for the job. Basic competence is vital so that student employees feel stable enough to trust their own abilities and perform effectively, especially if this campus job is their first experience working. Within this vector are intellectual competence (e.g., solving problems and mastering and applying job knowledge), manual/physical competence (e.g., moving equipment, building maintenance, and artistic ability), and interpersonal competence (e.g., communication, leadership, and working effectively with others), all of which are skills that can and should be addressed in a comprehensive training program.

While competence is key to the training process, other vectors described by Chickering and Reisser (1993) also are relevant. *Moving through autonomy toward interdependence*—the third vector—is characterized by a student's ability to be self-sufficient and take responsibility. An employee training program should provide students with the tools necessary to be effective without the constant need for reassurance and supervision. The desired result is that employees can serve the organization well by organizing activities, solving problems, and understanding how their personal goals can be achieved while also being part of a larger community where interdependence is expected for service delivery.

The fifth vector, *establishing identity*, involves a comfort with oneself, an awareness of abilities and values, and self-confidence (Chickering & Reisser, 1993). As students learn new skills and job responsibilities during training, perhaps an additional activity could involve small group discussions about personal strengths and weaknesses and how these relate to the job. This openness not only builds relationships but can help to promote comfort and self-awareness.

Another category of student development theory describes how students process and make meaning of information, known as cognitive-structural theories. Perry's (1968) theory organized positions of intellectual and ethical development into four key groups: *dualism, multiplicity, relativism*, and *commitment*. During training, these concepts are likely to come through when discussing policies and expectations. Dualistic students will accept procedures because an authority figure is saying that they are right. Students in multiplicity are likely to doubt policies (or not enforce them well) because they view all opinions as being equally correct. Students in relativism will respect an expectation within the context of the organization, especially if the policy is sufficiently supported with evidence. Often policies are either somewhat vague (i.e., leave room for interpretation) or very specific (i.e., no flexibility for special circumstances). Therefore, it is important to teach student employees how to handle ambiguous situations. To promote cognitive development, Perry (1968) suggested engaging students in experiential learning environments where they regularly discuss alternative perspectives and feel safe taking risks. Baxter Magolda (1992) suggested building community where students feel validated as learners and where their ideas can be confirmed or contradicted. Development in this area cannot occur if students' current ways of thinking are never challenged, and student employee training programs are excellent environments for this development to occur through experiential learning, customer conflict scenarios, and group discussions.

Employees also will be expected to make wise decisions on the job. Kohlberg (1976) described the development of moral reasoning—or students' rationale behind the decisions they make—as a progression from obeying in order to selfishly avoid getting into trouble, to following rules so as to be accepted, to making decisions based on values and ethical principles. When sharing job expectations with students during training, theory might suggest communicating them as being aligned with the organization's values rather than as rules with consequences. For example, students should learn that regularly browsing the Internet for leisure while at work is inappropriate—not because they will get caught, not because it is against the rules, but because they are likely to miss out on an opportunity to welcome and engage a customer. Plan activities that will allow for the modeling of higher-level reasoning to help employees learn how to use better judgment and make more ethical decisions on the job.

When designing a training program, one must identify topics to be covered, but equally important are the methods used to present the content. Every student is unique with an individual combination of personality types (Myers, 1980), learning preferences (Kolb, 1984), and vocational personalities (Holland, 1992). Therefore, training activities must be intentionally designed to appeal to different characteristics while also challenging students to explore new perspectives. Allow extroverts opportunities to actively participate, but when asking for contributions, also consider that introverts may want time to write down their thoughts before sharing. Plan the typical social, team-oriented activities but also include other artistic, investigative, or enterprising and goal-oriented options. Stick to the agenda, but be flexible within the allotted time. Because training is typically students' first experience with the organization, it is important that everyone be engaged so that they do not become dissatisfied with their employment from the start.

To help in appealing to a variety of types of students, Kolb (1984) developed an experiential learning model that described the learning process as a cycle of four stages, with individuals having different learning styles based on their preferences for the particular stages. First in the process is *concrete experience*, where students are fully immersed into an activity without having any sort of previous experience or bias. Beginning a training program with an interactive role play with little or no instruction—or by making connections to previous experiences they might have had with employment or the current organization—would be an example of this. The second stage is *reflective observation*, during which students begin to better understand the expected behaviors in the environment by watching others and considering different perspectives. Examples of this stage include observing supervisors or veteran student employees complete tasks or journaling about alternative ways to approach the experience. Third, *abstract conceptualization* allows students to develop personal theories about what does and does not work in the environment based on their observations. During training, students can brainstorm a list of ideas for how to complete particular tasks effectively or develop personal goals for the year based on their own strengths and areas for improvement. Finally, the stage of *active experimentation* puts these theories into action. While this stage might actually occur on the job, the training session could end with a hands-on activity that places students in various scenarios and gives them the opportunity to safely try out what they learned in a practical situation. The cycle repeats itself with each new experience an employee has while working, and regular staff meetings or one-on-one interactions help to facilitate the ongoing learning process.

Empowering student leadership through employment

Throughout this book, much evidence is provided for the merits of student employment as an educationally purposeful category of student engagement on campuses. While using training programs to lay a foundation for learning outcomes such as communication, management, work ethic, conflict resolution, and so on, student employee supervisors also should recognize "that students are part of a process of empowerment and transformation" (Smith College Campus Center Learning Outcomes, 2003, ¶ 3). Murrell (1994) presented six methods for empowering employees. Through these six methods, supervisors can discover the best practices for pedagogy through reflection of intended learning outcomes (see Figure 12).

Murrell's (1994) first method for empowerment is *educating*, through which supervisors provide employees knowledge, information, and development by sharing expertise within an organizational framework. To educate, supervisors must consider how to accommodate different work styles and be aware of the ways in which students acquire information and knowledge (Shertzer & Doyle, 2006). Another part of the education process is to outline the learning outcomes that should result from student employment. Through training, students are taught policy and procedure and provided with strategies for dealing with difficult situations through hands-on learning scenarios, role play, or group discussion. A common goal is to establish the importance of customer service and the avenues one should take to provide it. Other main aspects to be taught include accountability and time management, which can be illustrated by beginning training on time each day and following the schedule or agenda that has been provided. Strong work ethic can be illustrated by being organized and informative and offering students the opportunity to participate openly in discussions and training activities. Supervisors can lead by example, showing students what to do and then walking them through the process. "Model the way; don't ever ask anyone to do anything you are unwilling to do first" (Kouzes & Posner, 2002, p. 14).

The second method is *leading*. Leaders "inspire and empower by creating direction and purpose," identifying strengths in their employees instead of "keeping them dependent and subservient" (Murrell, 1994, p. 189). Supervisors can inspire students using the organization's mission and vision. Students are rewarded and directed through positive reinforcement of a task completed well, without needing to focus only on what went wrong. It can be easy to lose sight of the intentions behind the development of the student employee—or at least tend to focus only on the task-specific aspects of the job, especially when dealing with tardiness, missed shifts, service mistakes, or unfinished projects, for example. However, taking a positive approach could have a profound impact on the morale of the entire team. Students should be asked for their feedback during the training process, and supervisors should have a mechanism for logging suggestions, comments, concerns, and new ideas. These notes can be compiled after training and distributed to students as progress is made in each area. This reinforces teaching and careful, informed decision-making, as well as allows students to be a part of the transformation process.

Murrell's (1994) third method for empowerment is *structuring*, the opposite of control and restrictions. Examples include a comprehensive training schedule with clearly mapped expectations, opportunities for questions about procedures, and activities that involve participation and feedback. Additionally, training program planners can utilize the returning, experienced student employees as training facilitators rather than participants. Interactive experiences, such as role play, lead to structuring, rather than just lecturing. Structuring is a means for students to gain knowledge about how to provide an integral service to the campus community. "Enable others to act; engage all who must make the project work and all who have to live with the results" (Kouzes & Posner, 2002, p. 18).

The fourth method is *providing*, or "combining and sharing resources" for employees to be successful (Murrell, 1994, p. 190). Student employee supervisors should lead by example and model the way by being prepared. To do this, supervisors can make available concrete resources, such as student employee manuals, operations guides, online networking, and an open-door policy to ensure they are supporting students' needs. Student employees should have access to a student handbook or reference guide outlining their job descriptions, basic services or responsibilities, where to find things, and how to do things. Operating manuals can be developed to reinforce student learning throughout their student employment experience by providing them with immediate answers to their questions. Online communities can enable access to schedules, reports, documents, and contact information. The options for resources are limitless, and maintaining at least a handbook with the pertinent information students need to function in their positions will reinforce organizational commitment to them, and in turn, their commitment to the organization. "Challenge the process; search for opportunities to innovate, grow, and incorporate" (Kouzes & Posner, 2002, p. 17) your resources to benefit all involved.

Murrell's (1994) fifth method is *supporting*, or "empowering through example, advice, or counsel … as in a mentor-protégé relationship" (p. 191). Establishing a personal connection with student employees reinforces commitment to their development as a whole person. Training can include time solely for the purpose of establishing rapport and boosting team morale. Students must know that their supervisor has their best interests at heart and can help them stay focused, energized, and balanced in their work and academic lives. One option is to take students off campus or away from their "home territory" to embark upon a team adventure, such as a ropes course or an overnight retreat. Mentoring should be about getting to know each other's styles, the benefits from working together, and what it means to be a team. It is important to take time during training to focus on the team, not the task.

The sixth and final method is *actualizing*, or achieving one's full potential through "self-awareness, growth, and development" (Murrell, 1994, p. 191). This requires "a conducive environment and support from the previous five areas of empowerment" (Murrell, 1994, p. 191). Student employee training must contain a component that allows them to put their knowledge to work. This can be accomplished through team activities based loosely on television game shows, board games, or interactive activities. Challenge students to take the information they have been given and put it into practice. Create case study scenarios and keep students physically moving.

Administering a training program

Before identifying training best practices and methods, it is important to create an action plan. The key logistical elements of creating a successful training experience are staffing, timing, compensation, program costs, and risk management. Within the context of experiential education programs, Shertzer and Doyle (2006) similarly recognized the challenges linked with planning these experiences. Consider students' attitudes, dedication, and willingness to participate in the entire training process. Effective preparation for training typically leads to more successful training.

Staffing

An important factor to consider in planning student employee training is the organization's structure. Some student employee programs are led by full-time staff, some are student-led, and others are a hybrid of both types. What follows are examples of each type of program, along with a brief history and description of example programs.

Staff-run training programs can offer better continuity and more experience in planning and execution. However, it could be easy for the program to become stagnant as full-time staff could be less likely to try new things. Emory University's Dobbs University Center has had a staff-run student manager program in place for more than 30 years. The University Center currently employs between 35 and 40 student employees. While Emory conducts a three-day training session early in the academic year, student employees also participate in a short "refresher" session in the second part of the year. The students who work in the audio-visual department meet weekly to review and train.

An intriguing example of a student-run program can be found at Appalachian State University in Boone, N.C. Its college union student employees are responsible for scheduling, training, and managing the recognition process, among other duties. This program was one of the first to formally use learning outcomes and also features its own training videos for the union's more than 130 student employees.

Another example of a student-run employment program can be found at Arizona State University's college union. This organization transitioned to a student-run program in the 1990s. A shift supervisor program trains student managers to be responsible for student employee interviewing, hiring, training, payroll, scheduling, discipline, evaluation, and program development. Building managers have a 16-day training process that includes shifts during different times of day, shadowing, and being the "lead." Training also covers fire safety, security, policies and procedures, and proactive risk management.

The training program at Bowling Green State University uses a hybrid method of training. Key decisions and adaptations made related to training are the result of student input through the Employee Advisory Council and program evaluations, and full-time professionals implement the changes at the beginning-of-semester orientation session. Students and supervisors from all areas intermingle throughout the majority of the program, which includes a variety of presentations and activities facilitated by the professional staff members. Then, ongoing training activities occur throughout the rest of the semester that often are led by student staff coordinators and occur during area staff meetings or in the form of on-the-job shadowing. For example, audio-visual student staff members are required to work 40 hours with experienced employees before working an event on their own.

Another version of a hybrid program is found at The Ohio State University's college union, where the Student Staff Development Committee strives to enhance the student staff experience. Originally, the committee consisted of supervisors only, but it has grown to include students. The group meets weekly to discuss ongoing developments and plan future training. Team members created a theory-based model that is a cycle of assessment, training, and feedback.

Returning employees should be given special consideration when planning training programs. Some schools use the returning staff as facilitators, while some students may consider their seniority a privilege and a "get out of training free" card. All student employees should be involved in training, no matter the level of knowledge or years of experience. Building a team begins again each year, as the new staff is added to the existing team. It is possible to schedule and promote training dates well in advance and during hiring so that student employees can plan accordingly, or in extreme cases choose other employment or be excused from training. Excusing students from training can create a need for specialized and/or individualized training, which can require additional time and resources.

Timing

Another key element for consideration is the scheduling or timing of the training. It is essential to communicate mandatory training dates with potential student employees during the interview process. Students must be informed of their commitment before agreeing to take a position. Plan ahead for new hires to attend training; for example, if hiring a considerable number of first-year students, determine when appropriate dates and times are so they are not missing other first-year activities. Other general activities or conflicts with the date(s) being planned should be considered as well, especially if hiring many students from a similar cohort (e.g., international students) who may have similar conflicts. Some schools may need to plan around student employees' additional leadership involvement and training commitments, housing move-in dates and restrictions, large sporting events, or large weekend events on campus.

Besides making sure students can attend the training, it is important to think through the timing or flow of the event. Try to balance the fun, active experiences such as team-builders and icebreakers with the more lecture-oriented, content-heavy sections. Allow times for breaks and snacks so students are not overwhelmed with information and can resist "checking out." Training can be exhausting not only for students but also for the facilitators who are attempting to fit an enormous amount of information into a small period of time. To get the most out of an experience, there should be enough time for each part of training, and even smaller scale team-building efforts require extra time for debriefing and reflection (Shertzer & Doyle, 2006).

It would be ideal to train an entire group at the same time, only having to teach a session once. However, the size of the group and the varying positions within one student employment program may dictate the need for break-out groups. Breaking into smaller groups can be beneficial in enhancing learning (Shertzer & Doyle, 2006). If possible, utilize multiple facilitators at the same time, rotating through each phase of the training session and offering area-specific training for each position. Consider requiring that new student employees participate in a "pre-orientation" a few days earlier than the general orientation for all student employees. This allows new employees time to assimilate to a new environment and feel comfortable asking basic questions.

Compensation

Supervisors must consider how students will be paid for training. The three main options include paying students their normal hourly rate, paying a set amount or stipend for training, or not paying the students for their time in training. Most institutions require that employees be paid if they are working, even if it is training-related. Check with the institutional student financial services/payroll office as pay rates during training can vary. Budget realities will significantly impact most aspects of training.

In response to an online Association of College Unions International (ACUI) Forum question, several institutions (the University of North Dakota, Texas Tech University, The Ohio State University, the University of Dayton, and Oregon State University) reported that they pay students their regular hourly wage for training activities. The University of North Carolina Wilmington is considering a shift to paying minimum wage during training, since that does not require the skills for which they are paid for completing their regular duties. Smith College pays student employees a set stipend for each day of training. Once training is successfully completed, students assume their assigned hourly rates based on their position. The University of Akron has implemented a process where students can receive additional pay based on additional training they do outside of their regular area. This process coincides with the evaluation process. Compensation is considered in this section only from a training perspective, but is significant and varied across the broad spectrum of student employment.

Program costs

In addition to compensation, it is important to consider the overall costs of training. To adequately provide training, realistic costs must be estimated in advance. It may be helpful to use a per-person amount for supplies, food, and other services, or a total amount that can be spent in each area or category of expenditures. Also consider supplies, materials, and possibly attire (such as shirts and nametags). Remember to order all of this ahead of time, so that it arrives prior to the training. Basic costs associated with training may include:

- Housing for early arrivals, depending on when students can move into their living space for the upcoming year.
- Food or snacks, depending on when students return to campus and if dining is available.
- Supplies for training materials such as printed manuals or reference guides, schedules, folders, payroll information, and pens.
- Additional/adjusted hours for professional and administrative staff assisting with or facilitating training.
- Team-building needs, such as a ropes course or games.
- Off-site training or retreats, such as an alternate location for certain training sessions
- Uniforms and nametags.

Collaboration with other campus departments may allow some budgetary flexibility. For example, The University of Akron partnered with its athletics department to get a "deal" on student staff attire.

Most organizations incorporate free food into their training process as well. Consider doing something nontraditional or at least a non-pizza option. An emerging trend is to select healthy options for students—if not a full, wholesome meal—when food is provided institutionally. If funding is tight or nonexistent, consider finding a partner or cosponsor.

Institutional support plays a large role in this realm and can dictate how much training can be afforded. Some institutions provide no specific funds for student staff development or training, some set aside a flat amount, and some use a percentage of the total student employment budget.

Risk management

Risk management is a consideration in any training activity, whether the training is on or off campus. Leaving campus helps focus on the team-building aspect of training, but there are potential risks involved with travel to and from the site as well as while there. Liability waivers, insurance considerations, and driving institutionally owned vehicles all come into play when planning training. Student employee supervisors should be informed and prepared. Risk management is a critical topic for all of higher education and is particularly acute in the student employment realm. Many subtleties exist around students as employees, and those working with student employment programs must be well-versed in managing risk and the ever-changing legal landscape surrounding the concept. For helpful step-by-step information about risk management, see *http://www.asu.edu/studentaffairs/risk/what_is_risk_management.htm*.

Aspects of training

How do administrators move beyond the black and white of policy and procedure and encourage student employees to embrace the gray area often encountered in the higher education workplace? How much guidance and supervision is needed when the focus is on initiative? What do students want from their jobs? How are their individual needs and working styles identified? How can a balance between team-building, skill-building, and specific on-the-job training be achieved? These are all questions that can be addressed when determining what topics to include in training.

Different approaches and theory-based methods for training activities have been previously discussed. Here, curriculum and components of training are described. These include training locations, team-building, featured speakers, an introduction to the organization, job-specific content, and well-developed additional resources. Each of these components could be implemented during separate sessions or combined during a more extensive training, but all topics are essential elements of an effective learning experience for student employees.

Location of the training

The benefits of off-site retreats include better retention, as it is more difficult for students to leave early if they are not close to campus, providing a captive audience. There are less distractions because students and supervisors are removed from their typical environments and can avoid being caught up in regular activities. Likewise, it could provide students with a new experience, with students from urban areas spending time in a rural environment or vice versa. Finally, an off-site location could place students outside of their comfort zone where more learning is likely to take place.

Potential difficulties with an off-site retreat include: increased costs (e.g., transportation, food, and lodging); students being uncomfortable in their surroundings (if they have never been in a different environment, they could become too distracted to focus); lower attendance rates if involved students have conflicts; and an increase in time commitment for students and supervisors.

Some organizations choose to provide their student employees with in-house or in-service training. The benefits of that choice include lower costs, less time commitment, and a familiarity of surroundings. Difficulties for on-site training include more distractions (both for students and supervisors), being perceived as boring (same old thing), and students feeling like they can come and go as they please.

Team-building

While imparting germane and cogent information is vital to the function of any organization, it is equally important to make sure employees are enjoying themselves and learning to work as part of a team.

DIFFERENT APPROACHES FOR TRAINING

Task-based training:
Addresses the components of the specific job that are vital to the operation of the organization

- Describes basic job responsibilities
- Introduces organization policies and procedures
- Specific to the position or area

Skill-based training:
Focuses on the development of skills necessary to become an effective employee

- Interactive activities to promote communication and interpersonal skills
- Hands-on practice with relevant tools, technology, etc.
- Learning-centered, a complement to the academic mission

Hybrid training method:
Combines methods to be an all-encompassing training program primarily focused on learning

- Connects job responsibilities and practical skills with personal and professional development
- Introduces employees to the overall organization and their role within it
- Motivates students to be personally responsible for their learning and development
- Often focuses on preparing students to become successful employees and citizens in the future

Strength is not in the individuals, but in the team. Put a group of superstars together on any team and they will still lose if they operate as individual superstars. But once they start operating as a team, they become unbeatable. (Taylor, 1991, p. 124)

Team-building can be a part of any training program by building a small session into each day or taking a full day to focus on the people, not the task, of training. Teampedia is an online resource and a collaborative encyclopedia of team-building activities, icebreakers, teamwork resources, and tools for teams that anyone can edit (Teampedia: Tools for Teams, n.d.). Providing these sorts of experiences will give students an opportunity to interact with each other as well as with their supervisors. "Team learning happens in dialogue with each other and through reflection on shared experiences" (Komives et al., 2007, p. 240). There are many different lengths, types, and structures for team-building, but the focus ultimately should be on the well-being of the group of people working together, so that common interests and goals can emerge. Higher education should "teach all of us to be supportive and accountable to another; to deal creatively with competing interests; and understand that we are all in this together" (Palmer, 1981, p. 79). Taking time for team-building reinforces the importance of what each person brings to the team, as well as how they contribute to the greater good. "Inspire a shared vision; know your constituents and speak their language, understand their needs and have their best interests at heart" (Kouzes & Posner, 2002, p. 15).

POTENTIAL EXPERIENTIAL TRAINING ACTIVITIES

Concrete experience – Feeling
Students are fully involved in the experience
- Complete mock job tasks during training with little instruction
- Participate in role-play scenarios prior to formal training
- Work a shift or event prior to formal training
- Discuss previous experiences with employment with peers or supervisors
- Engage in teambuilding or leadership development activities

Reflective observation – Watching
Students consider experiences from multiple perspectives
- Observe different behaviors of professional staff and peers during activities
- Process experiences and receive feedback from others through group discussion
- Shadow other, more-experienced student employees
- Write a reflective paper or journal about job-related experiences
- Learn new job expectations and cultural norms through training

Abstract conceptualization – Thinking
Students develop ideas and theories based on observations
- Brainstorm ways to effectively complete tasks
- Organize tasks and responsibilities into a concept map or diagram
- Connect job duties with the development of intended learning outcomes
- Make suggestions about how to improve the work experience
- Develop personal goals and group goals for the year

Active experimentation – Doing
Students use new ideas to make decisions and solve problems
- Participate in role-play scenarios after formal training
- Give a presentation to other groups or departments about the job
- Complete job tasks during first scheduled shift
- Continue through the cycle with each new experience

Model based on:
    Kolb, D. A. (1984). *Experiential learning: Experience as the source of learning and development.*
    Englewood Cliffs, NJ: Prentice Hall.

Presenters

An option to "spice up" training is to provide an outside speaker. This could be a non-supervisory staff member or an outside consultant. A benefit of providing someone different to assist with training is that since the speaker is not their supervisor, students may pay closer attention knowing that they will not have ready access to this person throughout the normal course of their employment. An outside speaker can provide a fresh and different perspective, reinforcing what student employees learn from supervisors. Outside presenters could also introduce the supervisor to a new way of seeing things, helping to understand or broaden universal concepts. Potential negatives would be costs associated with paying an outside consultant and the possibility that the speaker may not have an understanding of how the organization works.

Many times, people on campus can provide excellent presentations. Most institutions have a career center and some have an office coordinating student employment campus-wide, so consider inviting representatives to share their expertise about working on campus, understanding the supervisor-employee relationship, or balancing work responsibilities with academic demands and other involvement. Staff members from outdoor adventure or recreation programs could facilitate unique team-building activities beyond the typical icebreakers. Faculty members from business or communications departments might be able to give a presentation on representing an organization or serving customers' needs. After considering the options, the ultimate decision might be that the individuals best suited to speak during all training sessions are found on the department's staff, and that is definitely a great option as well.

Introduction to the organization

Training logically begins with the indoctrination into the organization—its mission, its functions, its beliefs, and its values. From the beginning, student employees should be familiar with the organization's mission, as the mission establishes the tone and conveys educational purpose, giving direction to all aspects that foster student success (Kuh et al., 2005) and ultimately laying the groundwork for further understanding of their jobs. In addition to learning the mission, a training component might describe past events to provide a historical context for organizational policies and procedures. Also, a discussion of the role the organization's values play in its basic functions will assist students in understanding the foundation upon which their work is based.

To help students connect these larger ideas to students' individual employment responsibilities, basic information should be shared about the organization's functions. Provide statistics about the number of full-time staff, number of student employees, and population that uses the organization's services. Have the director or department head welcome the students and introduce other key professional staff members with whom the students will work. Incorporate a tour of the facility or department, being sure to point out unique features, key offices, resources, and student workspaces. If the overall training program includes students from different positions, take some time to briefly describe the duties of all student positions and how they relate to one another. Once the employees grow accustomed to the purpose and operations of the larger organization, it is time to transition into more position-specific topics.

Specific job requirements

Another vital component of training is to review specific job requirements and expectations the organization has of the student and expectations the student should have of the organization. This can be accomplished by reviewing the details of the job description and discussing the learning outcomes associated with the position. Introduce and explain the expectations for performance and attendance, including any related disciplinary procedures. Engage students with some form of an employment agreement, memorandum of understanding, or learning contract that sends a message of accountability and motivates them to take their responsibilities seriously.

There also should be time for supervisors to work with student employees individually or in small groups to cover area-specific content. Supervisors should allot sufficient time to review the specific department's relevant policies and procedures and any special applicability or considerations of broader regulations. For instance, a student working in the outdoor programming office will need to know the process required for camping gear rental as well as university-mandated limits on who can participate in campus recreation. If this orientation is conducted as an in-house training, it may be beneficial to teach employees using the equipment in the actual location where they will work. For example, in a career services setting, the supervisor can show an employee how to use the system for posting open positions. Additionally, it will be important to go over information that may seem basic but that students would not ordinarily know. For instance, an employee in the study abroad office will need to know what academic departments offer overseas study opportunities. As students prepare to begin their employment, these details are often at the forefront of their mind, so consider organizing them all into an employee manual or online collaborative document-sharing tool. Also consider incorporating role-playing scenarios or other activities that can reinforce what has been taught and learned.

Appropriate resources

It is important that supervisors provide student employees with appropriate, well-developed resources. At Carlton College, Student Financial Services (n.d.) offers a comprehensive webpage covering topics such as key points to remember, general work strategies, learning through work experience, asking questions, and dealing with difficult situations. At Jacksonville University, the Houston Cole Library (n.d.) offers student employees a checklist covering topics relevant to learning the library. This checklist includes a general overview, physical layout, website overview, equipment and shelving explanation, evaluation procedures, and an award for which all student employees are eligible. Texas A&M University (n.d.) offers students training opportunities and workshops through its Student Employment Office. Its workshops include a broad range of topics, such as workplace etiquette, preparing for the global workplace, controlling anger, and finding a balance.

Important elements to include in these resources (whether provided virtually or physically) are contact information, responsibilities, pictures and an organizational chart of staff, frequently asked questions, and emergency procedures documents. Regardless of format, access limits must be considered.

One key part of the training resources should be a binder or manual. One option for distribution is to provide a hard copy—give each student a binder (although the supply costs for this could be high) and provide space for students to keep their manual at work in a mailbox or cubby (this could be difficult if space is limited). Besides the costs associated with this and the physical space they require, there is also the issue that the information these resources contain changes too frequently for them to be consistently accurate.

Virtual manuals and an online forum could be another way to distribute the important resources covered during training and that are relevant to student employees' jobs. Lehigh University uses a wiki for its college union's standard operating procedures manual so that it is dynamic and searchable. The benefits of going virtual would be that information can be accessed and updated quickly and easily, and most students are used to getting information online rather than in paper and binders. Some detriments include the difficulty of ensuring that students read or check updates, the lack of accessibility during some emergency situations (e.g., power outage), and the substantial time and effort needed to create it.

Finally, a combined distribution method would be to provide a shortened version for all students while providing a more comprehensive set of information at main areas or online that can be updated as needed.

Evaluating training

Training evaluations often are completed immediately following the experience, perhaps not capturing applications and lessons learned (Shertzer & Doyle, 2006). One option to obtain accurate initial impressions, in addition to longer-term lessons, is to have an immediate reflection on the training itself and conduct a post-assessment later in the year to determine what information the students are retaining, how they are viewing their job, and how they would suggest improving the training and program. Depending on the length of training, students could be tired and interested in moving on to other things at the program's conclusion. Collecting feedback later allows students to relax and let the information soak in. The evaluation could be on paper or distributed to students electronically using one of the methods discussed in Chapter 12.

Virginia Tech provides a learning outcomes-based example with its Leading, Learning, Earning Program. Multiple groups participate in evaluations throughout the year through an annual retreat evaluation, workshop evaluations, annual student employee survey, exit interviews, and alumni survey evaluations. The program has developed over its 11-year existence and boasts 198 alumni.

The Ohio Union at The Ohio State University considers evaluation to be an integral part of its program. Students provide feedback at the end of the training and mandatory meetings throughout the year. At the end of each year they are provided the opportunity to evaluate themselves, their co-workers, and their supervisors. The information collected has been crucial in consistently evaluating and improving the program and the student experience.

Another suggestion for evaluation is to offer 360-degree feedback. This method could allow for peer-to-peer evaluation (see Appendix 12 for sample), student-to-supervisor evaluation (see Appendix 13 for sample), and the common supervisor-to-student evaluation (see Appendix 14). A consideration with this much feedback is to determine whether to allow anonymity. The benefit of allowing anonymous feedback is that students may be prone to provide more honest and lengthy feedback. The downside of allowing anonymous comments is that students may be hurtful and would not be held accountable for what they say. Also, anonymity does not allow for follow-up on comments from the evaluations.

STUDENT EMPLOYMENT PROGRAM
TRAINING & EVALUATION PROCESS

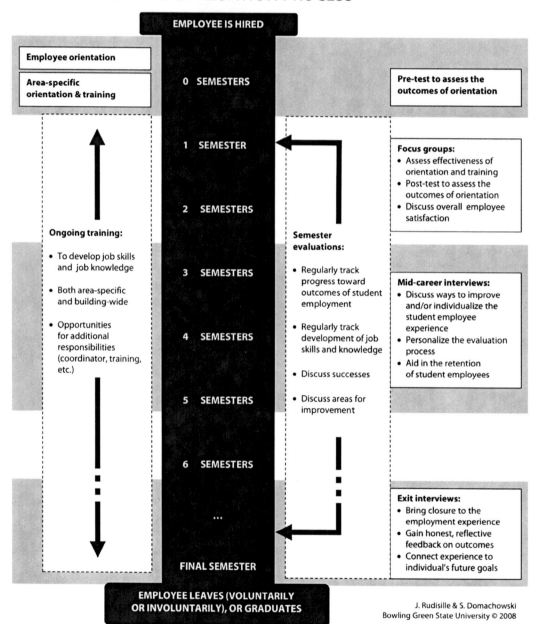

EMPLOYEE IS HIRED

Employee orientation

Area-specific orientation & training

0   SEMESTERS

Pre-test to assess the outcomes of orientation

1   SEMESTER

Focus groups:
- Assess effectiveness of orientation and training
- Post-test to assess the outcomes of orientation
- Discuss overall employee satisfaction

2   SEMESTERS

Ongoing training:

- To develop job skills and job knowledge

- Both area-specific and building-wide

- Opportunities for additional responsibilities (coordinator, training, etc.)

Semester evaluations:

- Regularly track progress toward outcomes of student employment

- Regularly track development of job skills and knowledge

- Discuss successes

- Discuss areas for improvement

3   SEMESTERS

Mid-career interviews:
- Discuss ways to improve and/or individualize the student employee experience
- Personalize the evaluation process
- Aid in the retention of student employees

4   SEMESTERS

5   SEMESTERS

6   SEMESTERS

...

Exit interviews:
- Bring closure to the employment experience
- Gain honest, reflective feedback on outcomes
- Connect experience to individual's future goals

FINAL SEMESTER

EMPLOYEE LEAVES (VOLUNTARILY OR INVOLUNTARILY), OR GRADUATES

J. Rudisille & S. Domachowski
Bowling Green State University © 2008

Continuing the work

Final components for consideration in any student employment program are to define and explain future opportunities for students to experience development or professional growth. This can be done through learning outcomes and student development workshops or meetings. Learning outcomes will vary by organization, but should intend to assist the interaction and learning process between students, faculty, and staff outside of the classroom. "By attending to the educational and social needs of the campus through student employment, students can develop their own values and the ability to make mature and responsible decisions concerning a healthy and intellectually rewarding lifestyle" (Bates & Punsky, 2008, ¶ 2). For more information on learning outcomes, please reference Chapter 4.

Student staff development

Training is an extensive process that should not stop after an initial orientation. Consider holding mandatory staff meetings to create a continuity of training. These could be fairly infrequent, occurring once or twice a year or once a month. They could take place on campus or off site. Content can vary from reminders of job responsibilities, updates on new policies, refreshing a theme, or providing a short lecture on a topic that is learning outcomes-focused.

Another consideration or variation of the mandatory meetings is to offer student staff development workshops. These allow for the specific incorporation and encouragement of student's development. When holding these workshops, it is important to distinguish the difference from regular training. Some institutions (e.g., Syracuse University) establish a committee that includes students with the purpose of coordinating the student employee's development. These groups have an established mission statement and set annual and quarterly goals. The University of Akron offers a mentor program that provides more individualized student development. Some specific topics to consider include resume-building, time management, work ethic, leadership, community service projects, motivation, and initiative.

Organizations should remember to incorporate learning outcomes and encourage personal and professional development (e.g., presenting at conferences and participating in leadership programs such as ACUI's I-LEAD®). The Ohio State University's Ohio Union sets aside a percentage of its student staff development budget specifically for conferences or other sources of professional development.

Recognition and reward

Recognition and reward should be a part of student staff programs, and it would be beneficial to review those topics during the training so that students know how to recognize their co-workers and how they can be rewarded and recognized for their hard work. Recognition could be as simple as acknowledging good deeds for employees who went above and beyond performance once per month at a staff development meeting, or having a celebration or banquet at the end of each term or at the end of the year. At Bowling Green State University, an advisory board of student employees recognizes an official employee of the month, nominated by peers or supervisors based on the employee's job performance and commitment to furthering the Bowen-Thompson Student Union's mission. In addition, a "thank you" system could be in place, either in the form of professional staff recognition or a comment card that customers complete and turn in to recognize excellent service. Even a "Thank you" or "Great job" can go a long way when well-timed and genuine. "Encourage the heart; show appreciation for people's contributions and create a culture of celebration" (Kouzes & Posner, 2002, p. 19).

Advancement and career potential

Many students will prove themselves to be exemplary employees ready for promotion. Most institutions have a standard process for upgrading students' pay grade or position level and adding additional responsibilities. However, even within the prescribed process, employees can be given opportunities for advancement. These might include cross-training students or rotating them into an alternative position, thereby continuing to challenge them while also benefiting the department. Area-specific training also is an opportunity to give more senior student employees the ability to transfer their knowledge to new employees while developing their teaching and interpersonal skills. If senior-level student employees are, in fact, in student manager roles, it is imperative for their own development and skill-building that they have formal involvement in the training process of new employees.

Additionally, high-performing students should be invited to attend on-campus workshops, professional organizations' conferences, and other opportunities for continued education beyond the scope of their daily work. Volunteer leadership might be another avenue in which students can grow. Examples include serving on a departmental governance team, coauthoring an article for a professional publication, or implementing a new technology to optimize operations.

Finally, a career in academe or higher education administration might not be one that students have previously considered. While these students may go on to pursue other professional roles, this path should be presented as an option. This is a conversation supervisors are best positioned to initiate, and often it happens too late. An early investment in students' potential can return benefits during employees' college career and beyond.

Conclusion

Supervising student staff is an amazing, exhausting, and exhilarating experience. Higher education organizations would be hard pressed to operate without student employee support. Being intentional in their learning and development will benefit them, the department, and the entire academy. It is beneficial to the trainer or supervisor, as preparing for training allows time for reflection on where they have been and where the program is going, and it can be reinvigorating to work with both returning and new student employees. Training programs are an important factor in improving students' on-the-job experience and ensuring the success of organizations. Student employee supervisors must be intentional to ensure that students are gaining valuable work experiences that ultimately prepare them for life after college. "By attending to various needs of the campus through their work, student employees are developing their own values and the ability to make mature and responsible decisions concerning a healthy and intellectually rewarding lifestyle" (Smith College Mission Statement, 2003, ¶ 1). Finding balance between academics, personal, and work responsibilities is essential to any path that students choose to follow.

References

Bates, T., & Punsky, S. (2008). Strategic planning initiative: The Campus Center as a learning laboratory, Developing student leaders through the world of work. Retrieved March 1, 2009, from http://www.smith.edu/planning/proposals/pdf/SD5/SD5-12CampusCtraslearninglab.pdf

Baxter Magolda, M.B. (1992). *Knowing and reasoning in college: Gender-related patterns in students' intellectual development.* San Francisco: Jossey-Bass.

Carleton College. (n.d.). Student employee training. Retrieved August 8, 2008, from http://apps.carleton.edu/ campus/sfs/student_employment/training

Chickering, A.W., & Reisser, L. (1993). *Education and identity* (2nd ed.). San Francisco: Jossey-Bass.

Gehrke, S. (2006). Student learning in leadership programs. In S.R. Komives, J.P. Dugan, J.E. Owen, C. Slack, & W. Wagner (Eds.), *Handbook for student leadership programs* (pp. 15–27). College Park, MD: National Clearinghouse for Leadership Programs.

Gleason, P.M. (1993). College student employment, academic progress, and post-college labor market success. *Journal of Student Financial Aid, 23,* 5–14.

Holland, J.L. (1992). *Making vocational choices: A theory of vocational personalities and work environments* (2nd ed.). Odessa, FL: Psychological Assessment Resource.

Jacksonville State University. (n.d.). Library student employee training checklist. Retrieved August 25, 2008, from http://www.jsu.edu/dept/library/graphic/stcheck.htm

Kincaid, R. (1996). *Student employment: Linking college and the workplace.* National Resource Center for The Freshman Year Experience & Students in Transition. University of South Carolina.

Kohlberg, L. (1976). Moral stages and moralization: The cognitive-developmental approach. In T. Lickona (Ed.), *Moral development and behavior: Theory, research, and social issues* (pp. 31–35). New York: Holt, Rinehart & Winston.

Kolb, D.A. (1984). *Experiential learning: Experience as the source of learning and development.* Englewood Cliffs, NJ: Prentice Hall.

Komives, S.R., Lucas, N., & McMahon, T.R. (2007). *Exploring leadership: For college students who want to make a difference* (2nd ed.). San Francisco: Jossey-Bass.

Kouzes, J.M., & Posner, B.Z. (2002). The leadership challenge (3rd ed.). San Francisco: Jossey-Bass.

Kuh, G.D., Kinzie, J., Schuh, J.H., & Whitt, E.J. (2005). *Student success in college: Creating conditions that matter.* San Francisco: Jossey-Bass.

McEwen, M.K. (2003). The nature and uses of theory. In S.R. Komives, D.B. Woodard Jr., & Associates (Eds.), *Student services: A handbook for the profession* (4th ed., pp. 153–178). San Francisco: Jossey-Bass.

Miller, T.K. (Ed.). (2001). *The book of professional standards for higher education* (2nd Rev. ed.). Washington, DC: Council for the Advancement of Standards in Higher Education.

Murrell, K.L. (1994). Empowerment: new concepts and new thinking about power. In D. Cole, J. Preston, & J. Finlay (Eds.), *What is new in organization development* (pp. 177–195). Chesterland, OH: The Organization Development Institute.

Myers, I.B. (1980). *Gifts differing.* Palo Alto, CA: Consulting Psychologists Press.

Palmer, P.J. (1981). *The company of strangers: Christians and the renewal of America's public life.* New York: Crossroads.

Perry, W.G., Jr. (1968). *Forms of intellectual and ethical development in the college years: A scheme.* New York: Holt, Rinehart, & Winston.

Peters, T.J. (1997). The role of the union, student development, and student employment. In A.V. Devaney (Ed.), *Developing leadership through student employment* (pp. 17–28). Bloomington, IN: Association of College Unions International.

Shertzer, J., & Doyle, M.K. (2006). Experiential learning. In S.R. Komives, J.P. Dugan, J.E. Owen, C. Slack, & W. Wagner (Eds.), *Handbook for student leadership programs* (pp. 91–102). College Park, MD: National Clearinghouse for Leadership Programs.

Smith College Mission Statement. (2003). Retrieved Dec. 14, 2008, from http://www.smith.edu/collegerelations/mission.php

Taylor, H.L. (1991). *Delegate: The key to successful management.* New York: Beaufort Books.

Teampedia: Tools for Teams. (n.d.). Retrieved August 8, 2008, from http://www.teampedia.net/wiki/index.php?title=Main_Page

Texas A&M University. (n.d.). Student Employment Office: Training opportunities and workshops. Retrieved August 8, 2008, from https://financialaid.tamu.edu/workshops/Workshop.aspx?View=Students

MEASURING STUDENT PERFORMANCE: USING APPROPRIATE EVALUATION TOOLS

by Jessica Hickmott

Employment on campus allows for a plethora of learning and development opportunities for students (Kuh, Kinzie, Buckley, Bridges, & Hayek, 2006; Perozzi, Rainey, & Wahlquist, 2003). Through measuring student performance and evaluating students' learning and development, these opportunities can be enhanced to help students achieve higher levels of academic success. This chapter details the types of tools to consider when measuring performance and students' gains in learning and development, steps to choosing and validating evaluation tools, and recommendations for implementation.

Measuring performance

Evaluation tools used in on-campus employment situations can focus on a host of measurements, ranging from performance reviews and satisfaction surveys to measuring the cognitive and affective skills that students gain during their employment. Performance evaluations allow for a conversation to occur between the employer and employee around such topics as setting performance goals and identifying opportunities for improvement (Randell, 1973). Performance evaluation templates are readily available and often are incorporated into employment in some capacity. Satisfaction surveys also are useful for employers to indicate whether their employees are satisfied with the work environment and whether customers are satisfied with aspects of the service provided. Although these types of measurements are useful and valuable when measuring student performance, this chapter focuses primarily on those methods of evaluation associated with student employees' learning and development.

Components of evaluation

Choosing an appropriate evaluation tool for measuring student learning and development depends on the goals and outcomes each organization identifies. Once goals and outcomes have been articulated, the next step is to decide which tools will most effectively measure the achievement of the identified outcomes. The following section offers an overview for choosing, designing, and administering evaluation tools.

Who to include in the evaluation process

Each institution will have to determine who will be involved in identifying specific evaluation methods. The individuals who have a vested interest in the process, such as the administration and staff, should have a vital role (Upcraft & Schuh, 1996). Student input also is essential to the process of choosing and designing evaluation tools (Maki, 2004; Palomba & Banta, 1999). Community members, assessment committees, faculty members, and peers can be considered as well (Bresciani, Moore Gardner, & Hickmott, in press).

Administrators

Although upper-level administrators (e.g., presidents, vice presidents, provosts, and chancellors), deans, and directors may not always have direct input on the specific evaluation methods a department decides on, their support of the overall process is essential (Maki, 2004). According to Suskie (2004), administrators provide resources and support for assessment while ensuring that the results of assessment are celebrated and used in the strategic planning process. In contrast to upper-level administrators, directors or deans of a particular department or college may have a more hands-on role in the assessment and evaluation process as they can help discuss whether the chosen evaluation method will accurately measure the intended learning outcome and help to provide an overall view of assessment. Administrators may have an active role in creating a framework for assessing all student employees on campus. Sharing ideas and results with upper-level administrators and directors will allow them to take the role that they deem most appropriate.

Students

When measuring student employees' performance, one of the most integral groups to involve is students. Students can participate in pilot groups to test survey instruments and provide valuable feedback on the wording of questions as well as the chosen instrument's length and design. Students also can be influential in identifying learning opportunities within their position and in highlighting other areas of growth they have experienced that may not have been considered (Roberts, 2006). At the University of North Dakota, student employees explain "two things that they learned during the school year that they feel will better prepare them for employment after graduation" (University of North Dakota, 2008, ¶ 3). Supervisors can then use the information gathered from this student feedback and compare it to the learning outcomes that have already been identified to see if any new themes emerge.

Staff

When designing evaluation tools, the professional staff who work directly with the students will play a fundamental role in the design and feasibility of a chosen tool. The level of staff involvement in the process will look different at each institution. Some institutions may incorporate evaluation tool selection and design into monthly meetings and involve those individuals who work directly with student employees. Other institutions may schedule specific times to focus on assessment and evaluation separate from regularly occurring meetings, or they may form and consult with an assessment committee to assist with the assessment process, to keep initiatives moving along, to increase staff buy-in, etc.

Because student employment programs often span a wide range of departments, staff representatives from each area, with assistance and support of appropriate administrators, may want to form a committee to standardize the measurement of student learning and development across organizational boundaries. At Eastern Michigan University, the Career Services Center staff "formed a committee of students, faculty, and student affairs professionals to develop a list of intentional learning outcomes related to job skills for the on-campus student employment program" (Broughton & Otto, 1999, p. 87). This same committee later identified specific activities in which students would participate to fulfill learning outcomes, and the committee designed the Leap to Excellence Acceleration Program (LEAP) for student employees.

At the University of Rhode Island, an assessment committee created a common set of 24 learning outcomes for student employees and developed rubrics to measure each of the outcomes (Frenzel, Rohland, & Williams, 2007). Rubrics are tools commonly used to quantify documents or situations often considered abstract, such as observations or reflection papers. Regardless of whether a committee is formed specifically to identify common outcomes for student employees and ways to measure those outcomes, it is important to include upper-level administrators, directors, staff members, and students in the process.

Community members

Although community members do not usually supervise student employees, they can provide great assistance when choosing evaluation tools and measuring student performance. Eastern Michigan University used feedback from employers in the community when drafting learning outcomes for student employees (Broughton & Otto, 1999). The university's steering committee then designed activities and programs, as well as evaluation methods, to incorporate the outcomes that employers identified. Community members also can be invited to present at professional development sessions for student employees and can suggest ways to evaluate the material covered in their sessions.

Faculty members

In addition to community members, faculty members can be a valuable resource when it comes to evaluating the learning of student employees. As greater emphasis is placed on assessment and evaluation at almost every institution, faculty members and student affairs staff members alike are considering the ways in which they contribute to student learning and development (Keeling, 2006; Kuh, Kinzie, Schuh, Whitt, & Associates, 2005). As such, faculty members are designing evaluation tools to assess student learning. By developing relationships with faculty members, similarities in learning opportunities may be identified. Faculty and staff can then work together to refine existing evaluation tools or develop new ones for their specific needs (e.g., a rubric examining critical thinking skills gained).

Selecting an evaluation approach

There are many approaches and tools available to measure student performance. However, it is important to decide upon a tool or set of tools that most closely aligns with the values, goals, and outcomes articulated for student employees at each institution. The following sections highlight different approaches to consider when choosing evaluation tools. Other considerations when choosing a tool, such as resource availability, also are discussed.

Methodology

Before discussing specific methodology, it is important to note the difference between research and assessment. According to Keeling, Wall, Underhile, and Dungy (2008), research is conducted to test a hypothesis while assessment "borrows from the principles of research" to make changes and improvements to programs and courses (p. 35). Assessment, therefore, can be considered as a type of "action research" as the results often are used immediately (or quite soon afterward) to make improvements, instead of testing a hypothesis. Research is conducted with a high level of rigor and often seeks to be generalizable to a larger population, whereas assessment seeks to improve students' learning and development—in this case student employees' learning and development—at an individual institution while contributing to the institutional mission. This is not to say that assessment cannot be conducted as research. Often assessment tools, such as benchmarking surveys, seek to be generalizable to a larger population (Bresciani et al., in press). If research methodology frameworks are adhered to when designing an assessment study, that study could be considered research. There are two major approaches to research and assessment: qualitative and quantitative.

Quantitative methodology tends to be specific and often seeks to identify a trend (Creswell, 2008). Results yielded through a quantitative methodology generally involve numbers and can be statistically analyzed, often with the assistance of computer programs. Samples used in quantitative methodology are often large. Quantitative tools include surveys, tests, and other methods of measurement involving numbers, such as a self-assessment tool using a scale. These tools are discussed later in the chapter.

Qualitative methodology often explores the unknown and seeks to understand a central phenomenon (Creswell, 2008). This type of methodology uses words instead of numbers, and themes are identified among the data gathered. Sample sizes can be quite small as qualitative methodology is not often generalizable to a larger population. Qualitative methods include observations, focus groups, open-ended questions, portfolios, and other documents that can be analyzed, such as a reflection paper. These methods are an excellent way to see how individuals "make meaning" of their environment (Upcraft & Schuch, 1996, p. 60). This process can be time-consuming as it is typically done by hand, transcribing interviews or focus group conversations, making observations based on behaviors or situations, or analyzing the content of reports and documents for common themes. Qualitative methods can be used in combination with quantitative methodology in a mixed-methods approach.

Cross-sectional and longitudinal approaches

Cross-sectional studies take a snapshot of what an identified group of students learned at a single point in time. In the context of this chapter, the identified group would be student employees. Cross-sectional studies allow for comparisons within the group based on background variables such as age, gender, ethnicity, etc. Achievement of learning outcomes could be compared based upon these background variables as could grade point averages (GPAs), retention rates, and other similar performance indicators.

Longitudinal studies are much the same as cross-sectional studies except the same variables are observed over an extended period of time. For example, an institution may look at the achievement of student employment learning outcomes using a pre-/post-test design and include cumulative GPA of student employees as another variable. Cohorts of student employees could then be observed over the years and their achievements compared to the other cohorts and to that of the entire student body. This would be a longitudinal study.

Formative and summative approaches

Formative assessment is ongoing. This type of assessment occurs during the activity or program so that changes can be made immediately (Maki, 2004). For example, if student employees are participating in a semester-long professional development workshop series, the evaluation of one session might reveal that students do not feel as though they are learning from a lecture-style approach, and they would like to "do" more. The workshop facilitator could then adjust the teaching style immediately to incorporate a more hands-on approach.

Summative assessment occurs at the end of a process (e.g., course and workshop series) to measure learning over a set time period (Suskie, 2004). Mid-term and final examinations or end-of-course evaluations are kinds of summative assessment. For example, at the end of the professional development workshop series, student employees could write a reflection paper examining concepts learned during the entire series. This type of assessment does not allow for immediate improvement.

Objective and subjective approaches

Objective assessments typically have only one right answer (Palomba & Banta, 1999). There are no gray areas left open for interpretation. Objective assessments include multiple-choice tests, true/false tests, and matching tests, which are components on most standardized tests.

Subjective assessments, however, leave much open for interpretation. This type of assessment includes portfolios, open-ended response and essay questions, and even items scored on a rubric. Subjective assessments give greater insight into a student's ability and how they make meaning of certain situations (Maki, 2004). Subjective assessments do take more time to score, and, unless themes are identified within answers, it is difficult to determine an "average score" for a large group of people. However, rubrics offer a relatively simple way to achieve an average score on subjective assessments such as observations and reflection papers. This is achieved by assigning a number to sections of prose within the rubric. For example, rubrics are often divided into three sections: Needs Improvement, Meets Expectations, and Exceeds Expectations, with numbers corresponding to each section. Most evaluation tools used in cocurricular assessment, including student employment, are subjective. All of the tools described in the following, except pre- and post-tests and some types of surveys, are examples of subjective assessment.

Selecting a tool

After determining the approach that aligns with the goals and outcomes being evaluated, the next step is to choose an appropriate tool. The following sections are divided into those assessment methods that yield direct evidence of student learning and those that gather indirect evidence.

Direct methods

Direct assessment methods have students complete an artifact (e.g., document, test, or rubric) to demonstrate what they have learned (Palomba & Banta, 1999). Direct methods related to student employees discussed in this chapter include case studies, documents, pre- and post-tests, and observations.

Case studies offer a way to analyze student employees' critical thinking, problem solving, and communication skills. During training sessions or professional development workshops, case studies can be utilized to determine how student employees would react to certain situations based on the concepts they have learned. Ideas for case studies can be drawn from topics covered in training sessions such as a session detailing the importance of friendly, effective customer service. This concept could be turned into a case study on its own, or multiple topics could be combined into one case study. Details on a certain topic or situation a student may face would then be put in narrative form, such as having student employees share how they would deal with an unhappy customer. Based on this scenario, prompts could be used to stimulate thoughtful responses, such as "Identify the key issues in this case study and describe in which order and how each issue will be addressed." The students' answers could then be analyzed using a rubric (Huba & Freed, 2000).

Documents that students produce can be used as a direct measure of student learning. For example, a document could be a resume produced after a workshop detailing what should be included when designing a resume, or it might be a reflection paper a student writes about lessons from a three-day training retreat. If students design a presentation for a weekly staff meeting on a topic related to a specific learning outcome, this presentation can be used as a direct measure of student learning. Students may not necessarily design a portfolio during their experience as a student employee (although this would also be a direct measurement of learning); however, documents they produce during their time as a student employee could be used as out-of-class artifacts for a portfolio they are putting together for their degree program.

Pre- and post-tests often are used in measuring student employees' learning and development. This assessment method is a way to determine a program's or experience's value (Suskie, 2004). When pre- and post-tests are administered, it is vital that the tests are exactly the same to accurately measure the learning that occurred over the identified time. As such, pre- and post-tests should be well thought out and pilot tested to determine that the questions are clear and easily understood. An example of a recognized pre- and post-test instrument, while different than what would be used in an employment setting, is the Collegiate Learning Assessment (Council of Independent Colleges, 2008). The Collegiate Learning Assessment looks at entering college students' knowledge using a pre-test given during the first few weeks of school. Then, the test is administered to senior students before graduation (i.e., post-test) to determine the value the institution has added. In contrast to a pre- and post-test that would be used in student employment, the questions on the Collegiate Learning Assessment vary, whereas the pre- and post-test in student employment would have the same set of questions. The Collegiate Learning Assessment also is administered to a set of 100 freshmen and, most likely, 100 different seniors; however, in student employment, the individual student's learning is being measured. Therefore, the pre-test would be exactly the same as the post-test for student employees and would be administered to the same set of students.

The University of Arkansas incorporated a pre- and post-test design after seven learning outcomes were articulated for student employees working in the college union (Burgess & Freeman, 2008). After supervisors explained the outcomes and their purpose, students were given a pre-test asking specific questions about the learning outcomes. In addition to the pre- and post-test method used to assess the learning outcomes, supervisors discussed the outcomes with the student employees during their evaluations and sometimes offered "additional training to further develop any areas that needed improvement" (Burgess & Freeman, 2008, p. 31). At the end of their second semester of employment, students completed a post-test to determine their growth in each of the identified outcomes. These results also were used to refine training and the learning outcomes' focus, if necessary. The University of Arkansas union staff used other methods to reinforce the learning outcomes including required training on areas related to the learning outcomes and optional professional development opportunities offered through other departments.

This combination of multiple assessment methods including observation, pre-/post-testing, and performance evaluation will yield more reliable results on the student employees' achievement of the learning outcomes. When pre- and post-tests are the sole forms of assessment, there is no way to know that the student employee experience on its own contributed to the students' growth (Suskie, 2004) unless conducted as a research study with a control group. Therefore, pre- and post-tests can be more valuable when used with other assessment methods.

Observations are another direct measure of assessment, often used in combination with other measures (Bresciani et al., in press) as described in the previous example. Student employees often gain a variety of skills that are abstract and seemingly difficult to measure, such as communication skills or conflict management. Understanding of such topics can be measured in a pre- and post-test or articulated through a case study; however, many times outcomes such as "communication development" are obvious simply by observation. Without being recorded in some way, this observation cannot be demonstrated to others; therefore, if considered a method of evaluation, observations must be recorded. This can be accomplished through a variety of means including note-taking, rubrics, or criteria checklists (Bresciani, Zelna, & Anderson, 2004). If taking notes, it is best to record them soon after the observation to capture the highest level of detail. Such detail enables more changes in growth and development to be observed throughout the process. Rubrics or criteria checklists will have specific skills for which the observer is looking, and these can be especially useful if multiple observers are being used (see Appendix 15 for an example). There is no set amount of time that is best to have between observations, but observing on a frequent basis may impede the recognition of small changes.

Indirect methods

Indirect assessment methods gather information typically after the learning has occurred. This involves students reflecting upon their learning rather than demonstrating it as it happens (Bresciani et al., 2004). Surveys, self-assessment questionnaires, interviews, focus groups, and performance indicators are discussed in the following paragraphs.

Surveys offer an opportunity for students to reflect upon what they have learned in addition to offering insight into their experiences, background, and interests. Survey formats include those distributed face to face, via e-mail, via mail, online, over the phone, or in interviews or focus groups. Surveys are generally administered to a sample of students to "identify trends in attitudes, opinions, behaviors, or characteristics of a large group of people" (Creswell, 2008, p. 61). Many standardized surveys exist including the National Survey of Student Engagement (NSSE), College Student Experiences Questionnaire (CSEQ), College Senior Survey (CSS), and those surveys conducted by

Educational Benchmarking, Inc. (EBI) and StudentVoice. Although these surveys may not directly measure student learning, when used in combination with other tools, they can be informative. Articulated goals and allotted budget are important to consider when determining which instrument to administer.

If a survey will be developed locally, there are numerous resources available to assist in survey design. These resources include survey software programs and numerous books and websites that can be found easily through an online search. Before choosing any of these programs, the product should be thoroughly investigated to ensure its compatibility with the department or institution's needs.

Self-assessment questionnaires are a type of survey method. These questionnaires are typically locally designed, as they tend to address a student's achievement of learning outcomes. Because of the transparency of self-assessment, accuracy is often called into question as students may inflate reported characteristics such as GPA (Turrentine, 2001). As a result, self-assessments often are used in combination with employee observations examining similar skills. Appalachian State University uses student self-assessment in its evaluation of student employees learning outcomes; however, the university's approach intends to deflect this potential inflation of skills (Plemmons Student Union, n.d.). The Plemmons Student Union has developed the Student Training and Education Program, which not only evaluates employees' learning and development but also provides a framework for students to understand how their work contributes to the overall campus environment and to see the skills they gain during their employment. Through this program, students gain an understanding of the overall process and can clearly see the benefits of accurately filling out the pre- and post-self-assessment tool.

Interviews/focus groups offer a great way to gather detailed, rich data, especially when focused on a specific topic (Bresciani et al., 2004). For example, San Jose State University identified a learning outcome stating that student employees will achieve "well-being, balance, and a healthy lifestyle" (San Jose State University, n.d.). Through interviews or focus groups, students could discuss how they develop balance in their life and describe techniques they use to maintain a healthy lifestyle. Directed questions could ask how their position helps them in aspects of personal balance and well-being as well as how programs or workshops could better facilitate their development in these areas. Conducting exit interviews with student employees also can yield information such as the student employees' thoughts on learning opportunities offered during their employment and what they enjoyed or believe could be improved. These interviews can supplement information gathered through other assessment methods.

Interviews and focus groups can be time-consuming when it comes to gathering and analyzing the data as they are an aspect of qualitative methodology and will often involve transcribing or coding (Schuh, 2008). Individual interviews, while very informative, can be the most time consuming. The interviewee must have a rapport with the interviewer. Most of the time, multiple one-on-one interviews will be held, which will involve more time analyzing each individual interview. Focus groups, on the other hand, allow for many individuals to be interviewed at once, which can save time when compared to individual interviews. The group setting will allow students to reach a comfort level much quicker, and students will be able to build upon what others say. However, peer influence should be taken into consideration during analysis, unless peer influence is what is being observed. To conduct either type of interview according to research methodology, and to gather the richest results, record the interview with a handheld audio recorder and have an observer take additional notes on body posture and reactions that cannot be captured through an audio recording (especially in group interview situations). Following the interview, the information recorded will need to be transcribed; themes can then be identified within the transcribed text. This can be done according to research methodology where open, axial, and selective coding take place (see Creswell, 2008), or through skimming of the text to see key ideas or concepts that multiple interviewees shared. Gathering data from interviews or focus groups can, therefore, be labor-intensive because of the added time it takes for transcription and coding. However, they offer a great way to gather specific, detailed information from students.

Considerations before selecting an approach to evaluation

Performance versus evaluation

Before deciding on an approach to assessing students' learning and development, it is important to distinguish between performance evaluations and the evaluation of learning and development as this can sometimes be seen as a potential barrier. Performance evaluations tend to focus on how student employees perform in relation to the duties assigned as part of their position (e.g., specific position-related skills and customer service). In contrast, evaluation of student learning and development tends to examine the additional skills and behaviors (e.g., oral and written communication skills, public speaking skills, and awareness of and appreciation for diversity) students gain as part of their employment experience. There are multiple perspectives as to how performance and evaluation are connected. Some professionals believe that performance and the evaluation of learning are inherently separate and should be kept that way. Other professionals believe that job performance and learning and development are intrinsically interwoven. The following perspective provides a compromise between the two viewpoints.

Working on campus provides a unique, cocurricular learning environment for students. As such, this presents an equally unique opportunity to measure students' learning and development. However, if traditional performance evaluations are mixed with the evaluation of learning and development, this mix should be approached cautiously as many questions may arise, such as:

- Will the evaluation of learning and development be tied to raises as performance evaluations typically are?
- If a student does not achieve a particular outcome, is it the fault of the employer, the student, or a combination of both?

- How can students' learning and development be measured in an objective way that will not be influenced by employer bias?

Each institution will want to consider these questions before designing an evaluation system where performance and learning are tied. To answer the questions posed above, institutions may want to consider identifying multiple levels of achievement for each learning outcome articulated. Other concepts discussed in this chapter such as triangulation and the use of rubrics to measure subjective areas of learning may be helpful when distinguishing how performance evaluations and the evaluation of learning and development will be tied.

Common challenges

One of the most common challenges cited when engaging in the assessment process is the availability of resources (Banta & Associates, 2002; Bresciani et al., in press; Bresciani et al., 2004; Palomba & Banta, 1999; Upcraft & Schuh, 1996). These resources include cost and time, both of which need to be considered before designing or selecting evaluation tools.

Cost considerations

When designing evaluation tools, it is important to consider the budget available for assessment and evaluation (Bresciani et al., in press). Costs often are associated with standardized instruments and benchmarking surveys as well as with data analysis. If a survey software system is selected, this also will come at a cost. However, it is not always necessary to create an original instrument. Many tools are already developed that have been tested for their validity and reliability; however, as these tools often must be purchased, the organization must choose an instrument aligned with the outcomes being measured (Schuh, 2008). If there is not a nationally normed tool available, colleagues at other universities as well as peers and faculty members at local institutions are valuable resources as they may have developed tools that can be easily adapted (Bresciani et al., in press). If resources are limited, consider using services provided by professional organizations for discussion, networking, or document sharing to potentially yield information on tools that may be available.

Labor-related costs are another essential component to consider when developing the budget for assessment and evaluation. With any method chosen, someone or multiple individuals will need to administer the evaluation tool and analyze the results. Because of this, time allotted toward administration and evaluation is vital to consider as these often are outside of normal duties and will need to be budgeted as labor costs. Whichever method is chosen, the costs of design, implementation, analysis, and labor should be incorporated into the overall budget of the assessment process.

Balancing workload

As mentioned, assessment and evaluation often can add to an individual's workload, at least initially. Because of this, it is important to consider the breadth of the evaluation chosen and to utilize administrative and peer support to help distribute the workload. If multiple, in-depth evaluation approaches are used, this will yield valuable results; however, if each of these approaches is locally designed, creating the tools and validating them can be time-consuming. Designing and administering evaluation tools may require more time on the front end, as meetings may be involved to articulate outcomes and decide on the best approach; however, less time will be needed once the instrument is complete. When selecting a preexisting tool, time will only need to be allotted to refine the tool and analyze the results. For those designing and administering a tool locally, the next section provides information on creating a valid and reliable instrument.

Validity and reliability of evaluation tools

When evaluating student employees' learning and development, the information collected must be both valid and reliable. This means that the results are consistent (i.e., reliable) and that they yield the information the outcome intended to measure (i.e., valid). As such, if an instrument proves to be reliable, it may not necessarily be valid (Banta, 2002). For example, student employees could take a multiple-choice test following training that included questions about teamwork principles; however, this test would not be a valid instrument to measure students' demonstration of teamwork. But the test could partially measure a learning outcome stating that "students will understand and demonstrate teamwork principles" as the test could measure understanding. While not an exhaustive list, the following paragraphs discuss a few ways to strengthen the instrument's validity and reliability.

Pilot testing is one way to check an instrument's validity and reliability. By administering an instrument to a small group of student employees during the design process, instructions and other aspects can be refined to ensure that they are clear and complete and that the instrument yields the intended results. Collecting feedback from the participants and comparing it to the pilot test's results will allow for improvements to be made to the instrument before it is administered to a larger population.

Rating is the process of evaluating or grading—for example, student employees rating their increase in communication skills on a Likert scale or using a rubric to rate students' reflection papers that they compose at the end of a semester. When administering evaluation tools, it is important that everyone is rating or scoring similarly. To achieve this, "norming" sessions can be held. For instance, if a new rubric is created to examine students' reflection papers, those individuals scoring the papers can examine an example of a great paper and one that needs improvement. If the individuals scoring the reflection papers grade the papers similarly, then inter-rater reliability has been achieved. Inter-rater reliability is the "degree to which different individual observers or graders agree in their scoring" (Maki, 2004, p. 93). If those individuals do not score similarly, more discussion can occur about what the different levels on the rubric may look like, or, if needed, the rubric can be altered.

Other reflection papers would then be examined again until all individuals produce similar scores. Achieving inter-rater reliability is one way to increase an instrument's validity and reliability.

Triangulation (i.e., mixed methods) is another process that can contribute to an instrument's validity and reliability; although, it often has many different meanings depending on the type of research being conducted (Bogdan & Biklen, 1998). Therefore, for purposes of this chapter, triangulation means using a variety of methods to ensure the credibility of the data collected. For example, if an outcome is that student employees will gain public speaking skills, conducting a self-assessment before a series of training sessions and one afterward is an excellent way to see how the student employees rate their change in speaking skills. To strengthen the statement that student employment is significantly contributing to students' increase in skills, a supervisor can record observations on a rubric or skills checklist to corroborate the student's self-assessment of skills gained. Or, a group of student employees could design an in-service training session on speaking skills to be used the following year. If indirect assessment methods are used (e.g., interviews and surveys), combining their use with direct assessment methods will allow there to be physical evidence of what students have gained. This will reinforce the indirect methods' findings. Combining data from multiple assessment methods will lend more credibility to the results.

Planning, administering tools, and analyzing data

As there are many steps in the assessment and evaluation of student employees, it may be easiest to gather all of the information concerning the process into some type of plan. This will allow those involved in the process to see how the stated outcomes align with the chosen evaluation methods. The plan also can indicate who will be responsible for gathering and analyzing data as well as provide a place to document the results of evaluations and improvements made with the use of results. Compiling this information in one document will enable easy access to the goals and outcomes articulated for those involved in evaluation and for student employees. Additionally, this document can serve as a reference tool for new employees and others to see what was done in the past and the changes made along the way. The specific details of what is included in the plan will vary based on each institution's needs and articulated outcomes. Planning ahead for the administration of tools and data analysis can make the process flow more smoothly.

When planning for the administration of tools and analysis of results, the following questions might emerge:

- Who will be included in the sample of students?
- Who will administer the evaluation tools?
- How often should student employee performance be measured to gather reliable data?
- Who should analyze the data?
- How should the data be reported?

These questions are answered in the following sections.

Sampling

Sample size will depend on the evaluation tool selected and the conclusions drawn from the data. The more students included in the sample of student employees, the more credible the results become. If those involved in the evaluation intend to conduct the evaluation of student employees with the rigor of research or hope to make the results generalizable, the sample chosen is of great importance, and there are resources available to determine exact sample size required. However, if the results of the evaluation are only being used for improvements within an individual student employment program, it is a greater priority to select a manageable sample size. To answer this question, consulting with an assessment or institutional research professional on campus is advisable. If a truly random sample of students is desired, these professionals usually can identify random samples that are representative of the larger population. If the results are used in performance evaluations or in individual work with students to improve their learning and development, using the entire population may be the best option (Banta, 2002).

Timeline for administration

Administration of the evaluation tool will depend on the method and sample selected. If a survey is administered to a random sample of students, an institutional research professional on campus may select the sample and e-mail the survey to students. If a rubric is used to evaluate student employee presentations, the supervisors may collectively evaluate the presentations or other student employees can be used to score the presentations. Administration will also differ at each institution based on what is feasible and can gather the most reliable results. As such, the timeline for administration depends on the conclusions being drawn. If the evaluation involves tracking a cohort of students through four years at the institution, some type of evaluation may be administered once or twice a year or more frequently, depending on the outcomes selected. To make administration more feasible, the evaluation methods could be incorporated with existing programs such as employee training, performance evaluations, or professional development sessions.

Analyzing and reporting

There are many publications that provide explanations of how to analyze and report assessment and evaluation results (Huba & Freed, 2000; Maki, 2004; Palomba & Banta, 1999; Suskie, 2004; Upcraft & Schuh, 1996). When administering a survey, the results can usually be analyzed by the survey program with which the survey was administered or with the help of an institutional research or assessment professional. If a qualitative method was chosen, which involves finding themes in the data, the supervisors will most likely analyze the data unless another individual has been appointed within the division/area to do so. Rubrics will offer a way to assign numbers to qualitative data; however, if using rubrics to observe change over time, it will be important to record the scores for later comparison. When using multiple evaluation methods, the data can be gathered in a centralized place for future data analysis. The group used to analyze the results can be similar to the group used in selecting and designing evaluation tools.

The way in which the results of data analysis are reported will vary depending on the audience. Within a department, lots of information may be valuable. However, if presenting information to students, administrators, or community members, their different interests should be kept in mind.

Recommendations

With all of the information provided in this chapter and throughout this book, it still may seem difficult to determine where to begin when selecting an approach to evaluate student employee learning and development. This section provides two examples of triangulated approaches that can be employed at an institution of any size or affiliation.

After articulating student employee learning outcomes, deciding how to effectively measure the learning outcomes is the next step. Depending on the number of outcomes articulated, it may not be possible to measure each outcome every year, but the recommended approaches can be adapted to meet various needs.

Approach 1

At new-employee orientation, share expectations with the new student employees. For existing employees, these expectations can be refreshed during annual or semester training sessions. Training should include position-specific expectations as well as the learning outcomes articulated for student employees. Following a discussion of expectations, the students can be given a pre-test examining their knowledge and understanding of position-related information as well as the learning outcomes. Specific to the learning outcomes, students can answer questions about each outcome's meaning and rate their achievement level for the outcome on a five-point scale. When developing the pre-test, it is important that the test be tested for validity and reliability, so the tests should be developed months in advance of employee orientation.

During new employee orientation or department-specific training, students can be given case studies describing situations they may face in their position. If orientation is division- or university-wide, these case studies should be broad, dealing with issues faced in any position. If case studies are completed during a department-specific training, the case studies can be more focused, dealing with individual positions or issues specific to that department. Individually or in groups, student employees can answer questions on how they would deal with the situation described in their case study and then share their responses with the rest of the group. Their responses should be written or typed so later they may be scored. A potential situation for a case study could involve an interaction with a disgruntled customer who is of a background other than that of the student employee. When scoring the case study, a rubric could be used to score the students' interpersonal communication skills as well as their cultural competence based on their answers. Different case studies, or the same one, can be administered to the students again during the next training (if applicable) to determine growth in the relevant learning outcomes.

In addition to the pre-test and case studies, two or three times during the term supervisors can observe students while they are working. A rubric can be designed for the employer to rate the employee on each learning outcome. The supervisor can then discuss with the student employee, during individual meetings or performance evaluations, what they are doing well and areas in which they can improve. At the end of the first semester, results can be compiled from each of the methods described and recommendations made as to how training or student employment as a whole can be improved. The results can be examined again at the end of the academic year, following the administration of the post-test, to draw further conclusions. Depending on how many student employees are retained, the employees' progress could be tracked over time to measure further learning and development gains.

Approach 2

During employee orientation or an initial student employee training session, expectations should be described and discussed with students as in the previous example. Students can then complete a self-assessment questionnaire rating their development related to the outcomes articulated for student employees. During this session or an individual meeting early in the term, supervisors can complete the same questionnaire from their viewpoint. Student employees and supervisors should complete the same questionnaire one or two additional times throughout the term for comparison to questionnaires completed earlier. After the initial meeting, areas for growth and improvement can be discussed in relation to the self-assessment questionnaire and learning outcomes. Additional activities or professional development sessions then can be incorporated to help employees achieve the outcomes. Student employees could even design short presentations related to learning outcomes to present to their peers at staff meetings or professional development workshops. Student employees could then rate each other's presentations on a rubric or checklist related to the outcomes. This feedback could be integrated with information from the self-assessment questionnaires.

When students leave their position, an exit interview can be held to discuss position-related information as well as what the student gained or learned through employment on campus and how learning opportunities can be improved for future students. Notes can be taken during the interview and compared to other information gathered over the period of the student's employment to draw conclusions on the learning gained. Information can then be compared across all student employees annually to see if the learning outcomes are all being achieved or if modifications should be made.

The approaches mentioned can be modified at any institution, and examples can be mixed with other methods articulated earlier in the chapter. They are intended to be examples of triangulated approaches to evaluating student employees' learning and development. Whichever approach chosen, whether one described here or one designed locally, it is important that the approach aligns with the institution's values and the learning outcomes identified.

Conclusion

As the mission and goals vary at each institution so too will the goals and outcomes articulated for student employees. It follows, then, that evaluation methods also will be specialized to best serve each institution's needs. Even so, one overarching goal will remain the same: to contribute to students' overall academic success. As discussed throughout this book, employment has proven to increase students' learning and development. However, conscious efforts should be made to intentionally design programming and opportunities for student employees so that jobs continue to be learning opportunities. Regardless of whether tools originate locally or pre-designed evaluation tools are used, multiple methods of assessment provide a clearer picture of how student employment contributes to students' overall academic performance, engagement, and growth.

References

Banta, T.W., & Associates. (2002). *Building a scholarship of assessment.* San Francisco: Jossey-Bass.

Bogdan, R.C., & Biklen, S.K. (1998). *Qualitative research for education: An introduction to theory and methods.* Needham Heights, MA: Ally & Bacon.

Bresciani, M.J., Moore Gardner, M., & Hickmott, J. (in press). *Demonstrating student success: A practical guide to outcomes-based assessment of learning and development in student affairs.* Sterling, VA: Stylus Publishing.

Bresciani, M J., Zelna, C.L., & Anderson, J.A. (2004). *Assessing student learning and development: A handbook for practitioners.* Washington, DC: National Association of Student Personnel Administrators.

Broughton, E.A., & Otto, S.K. (1999). On-campus student employment: Intentional learning outcomes. *Journal of College Student Development, 40*(1), 87–89.

Burgess, P.L., & Freeman, J.P. (2008, May). Facility professionals develop outcomes-based education for student employees. *The Bulletin of the Association of College Unions International, 76*(3), 30–35.

Council of Independent Colleges. (2008). *Evidence of learning: Applying the collegiate learning assessment to improve teaching and learning in the liberal arts college experience.* Washington, DC: Author.

Creswell, J.W. (2008). *Educational research design: Planning, conducting, and evaluating quantitative and qualitative research* (3rd ed.). Upper Saddle River, NJ: Pearson Merrill Prentice Hall.

Frenzel, G., Rohland, P., & Williams, L. (2007). Student affairs assessment strategies: Connecting learning outcomes to practice. Retrieved August 8, 2008, from http://www.uri.edu/assessment/media/public/page_files/uri/outcomes/student/outcomes/division_assessment/URI_SA_Assessment_Sum_of_6_07_rev.ppt

Huba, M.E., & Freed, J.E. (2000). *Learner-centered assessment on college campuses.* Boston: Allyn & Bacon.

Keeling, R.P. (2006). *Learning reconsidered 2: A practical guide to implementing a campus-wide focus on the student experiences.* Washington, DC: ACPA, ACUHO-I, ACUI, NACA, NACADA, NASPA, NIRSA.

Keeling, R.P., Wall, A.F., Underhile, R., & Dungy, G.J. (2008) *Assessment reconsidered: Institutional effectiveness for student success.* Washington, DC: NASPA.

Kuh, G.D., Kinzie, J., Buckley, J.A., Bridges, B.K., & Hayek, J.C. (2006, July). *What matters to student success: A review of the literature.* Final report for the National Postsecondary Education Cooperative and National Center for Education Statistics. Bloomington, IN: Indiana University Center for Postsecondary Research.

Kuh, G.D., Kinzie, J., Schuh, J.H., & Whitt, E.J., & Associates (2005). *Student success in college: Creating conditions that matter.* San Francisco: Jossey-Bass.

Maki, P. (2004). *Assessing for student learning: Building a sustainable commitment across the institution.* Sterling, VA: Stylus Publishing, LLC.

Palomba, C.A., & Banta, T.W. (1999). *Assessment essentials: Planning, implementing, improving.* San Francisco: Jossey-Bass.

Perozzi, B., Rainey, A., & Wahlquist, Z. (2003, September). A review of the effects of student employment on academic achievement. *The Bulletin of the Association of College Unions International, 71*(5), 15–20.

Plemmons Student Union. (n.d.). S.T.E.P.: Student training & education program. Retrieved August 8, 2008, from studentunion.appstate.edu/files/phatfile/STEP_VT.doc

Randell, G.A. (1973). Performance appraisal: purposes, practices and conflicts. *Occupational Psychology, 47*(3/4), 221–224.

Roberts, D. (2006, April). Students in the assessment process: Part II. *NASPA NetResults.* Retrieved August, 17, 2008, from http://www.naspa.org/membership/mem/nr/article.cfm?id=1530

San Jose State University. (n.d.). Department mission statements and associated learning outcomes. Retrieved August 9, 2008, from http://sa.sjsu.edu/about/dept_mission_statements.html

Schuh, J.H. (2008). *Assessment methods for student affairs.* San Francisco: Jossey-Bass

Suskie, L. (2004). *Assessing student learning: A common sense guide.* Bolton, MA: Anker Publishing Company, Inc.

Turrentine, C.A. (2001). A comparison of self-assessment and peer assessment of leadership skills. *NASPA Journal, 38*(3), 361–371.

University of North Dakota. (2008). Memorial union learning outcomes for student employees. Retrieved August 8, 2008, from http://www.union.und.edu/team/learningOutcomes0809.htm

Upcraft, M.L., & Schuh, J.H. (1996). *Assessment in student affairs: A guide for practitioners.* San Francisco: Jossey-Bass.

APPENDIXES 1–15

STUDENT EMPLOYMENT INTERVIEW ASSESSMENT

1. Tell us a bit about yourself. (e.g. major, family, hobbies, interests, high school experiences, etc.)

Unacceptable   Poor   Fair   Good   Excellent

2. If we were to ask a previous supervisor, what would he or she say was your greatest strength?

Unacceptable   Poor   Fair   Good   Excellent

3. If we were to ask a previous supervisor, what would he or she say was your greatest weakness or area needing improvement?

Unacceptable   Poor   Fair   Good   Excellent

4. How do you deal with stress?

Unacceptable   Poor   Fair   Good   Excellent

5. What does "customer service" mean to you?

Unacceptable   Poor   Fair   Good   Excellent

6. What did you like most/least about your last job?

Unacceptable   Poor   Fair   Good   Excellent

7. What one single quality in others do you aspire to?

Unacceptable   Poor   Fair   Good   Excellent

8. For what kind of supervisor do you like working?

Unacceptable   Poor   Fair   Good   Excellent

9. Why are you interested in this position?

Unacceptable   Poor   Fair   Good   Excellent

10. Student manager candidate only: What kind of supervisor do you feel as though you are becoming?

Unacceptable   Poor   Fair   Good   Excellent

11. Student manager candidate only: You have just been hired as a student manager. You come in your first day for training and, for whatever reason, you find yourself alone in the building with no supervision. You know nothing about emergency procedures yet. The fire alarm sounds. What, out of instinct, would you do?

Unacceptable   Poor   Fair   Good   Excellent

12. SM Candidate Only: You observe a physical fight between two people in the building. What do you do?

Unacceptable   Poor   Fair   Good   Excellent

13. Student manager candidate only: According to the reservation system, the student government has the ballroom reserved from 5–7 p.m. on a particular day. Someone from the university president's office comes to you and tells you that they have the ballroom reserved from 5–7 p.m. There are no administrators around and no one can be contacted. How do you resolve the conflict? (The interviewer should roles play the part of the staff member from the president's office and should be combative and uncooperative).

Unacceptable   Poor   Fair   Good   Excellent

14. What do you think sets you apart from all of the other candidates for this position, and why do you think we should hire you?

Unacceptable   Poor   Fair   Good   Excellent

_____ This person should be considered for employment

_____ This person should NOT be considered for employment

Reason/Comments:

Interviewer: _____   Date Interviewed: _____

Reprinted with permission: Texas A&M University–Corpus Christi

STUDENT REFERENCE REQUEST, FERPA RELEASE, & RELEASE OF LIABILITY

Student Name:_____ ID_____

I request_____
to serve as a reference for me. The purpose(s) of the reference are: (check all that apply)

☐ Application for Employment   ☐ General Reference

☐ Admission to another institution   ☐ Scholarship or Award

Other (Please Specify):_____

The reference may be given in the following form(s): (check one or both options)

☐ Wrtten Format   ☐ Oral Format

I authorize the above named person to provide an evaluation of any aspect of my academic or work performance, whether based on personal observation or on my educational records, and to release information from my educational records, including my grades, GPA, class rank, any information pertaining to my education at other institutions I have previously attended, and any other personally identifiable information. I authorize release of this information and reference or evaluation to:

(Check all that apply)

☐ All prospective employers OR

☐ Specific prospective employers listed here:_____

_____

☐ All educational institutions to which I seek admission OR

☐ Specific educational institutions to which I seek admission listed here:_____

_____

☐ All organizations considering me for an award or scholarship OR

☐ Specific organizations listed here:_____

_____

I understand that under the Family Educational and Privacy Act, 20 USC 1232g: (1) I have the right not to consent to the release of my education records; (2) I have the right to receive a copy of any written reference upon request; and (3) I may, but am not required to, waive my right of access to confidential references given for any of the purposes listed above.

☐ I waive my right of access to references given by the above-named person.

☐ I do not waive my right of access to references given by the above-named person.

This consent shall remain in effect until revoked by me, in writing, and delivered to the above-named person, but any such revocation shall not affect disclosures made prior to the person's receipt of my written revocation.

I release Texas A&M University–Corpus Christi, its employees and the person(s) providing the above-described reference or evaluation from all claims and liability for damages that may result from their compliance with this request.

_____   _____
Student Signature   Date

NEW STUDENT EMPLOYEE CHECKLIST
(paperwork required for new student employees)

Student Name: _____

ID#: _____ E-mail: _____

- ☐ Student Employee Packet (HR)
- ☐ Student Application (HR)
- ☐ I-9 (HR)
- ☐ Social Security Card or Birth Certificate or Passport (copy to HR)
- ☐ Driver's License or Student ID Card (copy to HR)
- ☐ W-4 Form (HR)
- ☐ Political Aid and Legislative Influence Prohibited (HR)
- ☐ Statement of Selective Services Registration Status – Men (HR)
- ☐ Notice to Employees of Worker's Compensation Insurance (HR)
- ☐ Employee Acknowledgement form (HR)
- ☐ Attestation Form (HR)
- ☐ Confidentiality Statement (HR & copy for file)
- ☐ Employee Personal Data (HR & copy for file)
- ☐ Acknowledgement form for General Employee Handbook (copy for file)
- ☐ Hepatitus B Form (copy for file)
- ☐ EPA (copy for file)
- ☐ GPA _____ Date _____ Check By: _____
- ☐ Create Appointment Letter (to student & copy for file)
- ☐ Computer Account Request
- ☐ Shirt Color _____ Size _____ (issue to student)
- ☐ Name Badge
- ☐ Work-Study/Awards Letter (copy for file if applicable)
- ☐ Institutional
- ☐ Direct Deposit _____ Date _____ (HR)
- ☐ CPR Card or Date of Training (for files)
- ☐ Picture for Student Employee Database

Complete Date: _____

Completed By: _____

Sent to HR: _____

     Reprinted with permission: Texas A&M University–Corpus Christi

BUILDING MANAGER TRAINING RUBRIC

Information listed here is meant to supplement the University Center Student Employee Handbook. Once the employee understands an item on the list, the trainer should initial to signify that the area has been covered.

Date/ Trainer	Date/ Trainer	Date/ Trainer	Training Area
			Attire • Shirt/nametag • Closed-toe shoes • Radio • Set-up worksheet and pen • Cell phones are not a part of your attire
			Keys • Which areas keys access (and which areas we do not have keys to access) • Sign-out procedure • Unlock rooms before meetings • Secure rooms with equipment and after meetings • Make sure you have them on your person at all time and don't take them home
			Storage Areas • Know locations and which areas they serve • Understand contents stored in these areas (how many chairs, tables, etc., belong in that particular area) • Learn how to put away all audio-visual equipment (which includes turning off wireless microphones), furniture, and supplies which do not belong in the room. All items must be stored properly and in the correct location so they will be readily available for the next occasion.
			Meeting Rooms • Walk through each meeting room • Understand the standard set-up/configuration of the room • Be familiar with capacities for each room • Learn the room features: marker boards, screens, shape of the rooms, limitations (columns) location of outlets/ports. • Know room numbers and names • Know what set-up options are available (open square, classroom, lecture, rounds of eight, rounds of six, conference)

STUDENT EMPLOYEE EXIT INTERVIEW

DATES CONTACTED: 1 _____ 2 _____ 3 _____ INTERVIEWER: _____

DATE: _____

Employee name: _____ Phone: _____ E-mail: _____

Supervisor: _____ Length of employment: _____

During which of your academic years did you work for UCSA: ☐ FR ☐ SO ☐ JR ☐ SR ☐ GRAD

Work-study? ☐ Yes ☐ No (during last year of employment)

Average number of hours worked per week in the last year:

☐ Fewer than 5 hours ☐ 6–10 hours ☐ 11–15 hours ☐ 16–20 hours ☐ More than 20 hours

Positions held: _____ _____

_____ _____

College major(s): _____

1. What was your initial reason for seeking employment with UCSA? (Check all that apply):

☐ Work experience ☐ Money ☐ Personal referral ☐ Meet people ☐ Other (specify)_____

2. How did your employment with UCSA specifically increase your life skills? (Check all that apply)

☐ Professionalism	☐ Training skills	☐ Creative thinking	☐ Relationship building
☐ Leadership skills	☐ Supervisory skills	☐ Critical thinking	☐ Initiative
☐ Decision-making	☐ Assertiveness	☐ Implementation	☐ Follow-through
☐ Communications	☐ Organizational skills	☐ Financial management	☐ Interviewing skills
☐ Verbal	☐ Customer service skills	☐ Adaptability	☐ Conflict resolution
☐ Non-verbal	☐ Teamwork skills	☐ Tolerance for risk	☐ Tolerance for stress
☐ Written	☐ Time management	☐ Planning	
☐ Other (specify) _____			

4. Did your UCSA work experience provide you with opportunities to gain more knowledge of people whose backgrounds were different than yours? ☐ Yes ☐ No

If yes, how? (Check all that apply)

☐ Improved communication	☐ Acceptance of differences	☐ Opportunities to interact
☐ Understanding	☐ Increased tolerance	☐ Knowledge of cultures
☐ Other(s) (specify): _____		

5. Did your work experience with UCSA complement your academic coursework? ⬚ Yes ⬚ No

If yes, in what way?_____

6. Has your career path or professional goals changed since you began working for UCSA? ⬚ Yes ⬚ No

If so, how or why? _____

7. Rate UCSA in the following areas on a scale of 1–5 (5 being perfect/no change needed):

	Rating:	Ways to improve:
Communication between:		
• Supervisors & student employees	_____	_____
• UCSA administration & student employees	_____	_____
• Peer student employees	_____	_____
Student employee involvement in:		
• Day-to-day operations	_____	_____
Sense of community with:		
• Peers	_____	_____
• Other UCSA staff	_____	_____
Overall work environment	_____	_____

Reason for leaving: _____

May we contact you at a later date? ⬚ Yes ⬚ No

Phone: _____

Permanent address where we might contact you:

c/o_____

_____

Comments: _____

_____

_____

_____

SAMPLE JOB DESCRIPTION:
BOWEN-THOMPSON STUDENT UNION, BOWLING GREEN STATE UNIVERSITY

Audio-Visual Staff

General responsibilities:

The Bowen-Thompson Student Union audio-visual staff member is responsible for setting up and dismantling audio-visual equipment used in meeting rooms and throughout the building. The staff will also provide technical assistance and support during events as requested or as needed. It is important that the audio-visual staff member is familiar with the building, its equipment, policies, programs and services, and the day-to-day schedule of events.

Supervision:

The audio-visual student staff is directly supervised by the audio-visual manager.

Specific tasks and responsibilities:

- Read and interpret room diagrams.
- Place customer service forms in meeting rooms and collect forms at the end of each event.
- Unlock meeting rooms
- Set up/remove room set-ups and change room arrangements, including tables, chairs and stages in accordance with the schedule of events for the Bowen-Thompson Student Union and Olscamp Conference Center.
- Set up and put away basic audio-visual equipment as needed. This includes overhead projectors, simple microphone set-up, monitors/television and other equipment on carts, portable sound system.
- Respond to requests from the event services manager, event facilities services manager, building manager, and student building manager.
- Inspect rooms for damage and cleanliness and document issues to be addressed. Give documentation to supervisor.
- Read and interpret room diagrams with respect to audio-visual set-ups.
- Set up audio-visual equipment for meetings and various functions around the building.
- Troubleshoot audio-visual equipment when there are technical questions or problems related to audio-visual equipment and identify appropriate solutions.
- Serve as on-site audio-visual support for events that take place in the Bowen-Thompson Student Union, and if requested in the Olscamp Hall Conference Center.
- Provide basic instruction on the operation of audio-visual equipment to customers as necessary.
- Clean and maintain equipment; report damages to the audio-visual manager.
- Assist in conducting inventory of audio-visual equipment as requested or as needed.
- Assist with room set-ups and tear-downs, as necessary. Attend staff meetings and training sessions as needed.
- Be attentive to the safety and security of the Bowen-Thompson Student Union and Olscamp facilities.
- Be aware of emergency procedures and trouble-shoot concerns throughout the facility.
- Other duties as assigned.

Reprinted with permission: Bowling Green State University

Basic qualifications:

- General knowledge of audio-visual equipment is preferred.
- General knowledge of computers, presentation software, and audio-visual equipment.
- The ability to work independently, identify resources, and make independent decisions.
- Strong oral communication skills.
- Ability to work in a team environment.
- Ability and interest in learning technology related skills.
- Demonstrate excellent interpersonal skills.
- Flexible hours for availability (including evenings and weekends) when the building is open.
- Positive customer-oriented attitude and professional image.

Transferable skills:

Transferable skills are those abilities that can be useful in many different settings. They can make you qualified to enter into many different fields even though you may not have specific education or experience in that area. Your position will allow you to progressively develop a variety of skills in a supportive environment where you can improve upon your weaker abilities, monopolize on your strengths, learn from your mistakes, and create your own personal character in the work setting. The following list identifies only **some** of the skills that you will develop during your time working with us. The list is not all-inclusive.

- **Leadership:** The ability to motivate others, develop and implement programs, delegate responsibility, and lead by example.
- **Communication:** The ability to listen to others objectively, paraphrase the content of the message, speak effectively, use various forms of written communication through written reports, etc.
- **Planning and Organization:** The ability to identify alternative courses of action, accommodate multiple demands and requests, prioritize, establish goals and follow through on fulfilling these goals, manage time effectively, and predict future trends and patterns.
- **Event Planning:** The ability to effectively plan programs, understanding what it takes to coordinate a successful event.
- **Management and Administrative:** The ability to analyze tasks, identify people and resources useful to the solution of a problem, delegate responsibility, manage time effectively, and successfully complete the formal training needed to do a job well.
- **Interpersonal and Human Relations:** The ability to interact effectively with peers, colleagues and supervisors, the ability to work well in a group, express feelings appropriately, understand the feelings of others, contribute in staff meetings, and share in staff responsibilities.
- **Informational Management:** The ability to problem solve, sort data and objects, compile and rank information, apply information creatively to problems or tasks, synthesize facts, concepts and principles, understand and use organizing principles, evaluate information against appropriate standards.
- **Critical Thinking:** The ability to identify quickly and accurately the critical issues when making a decision or solving a problem, identify problems and needs, identify information sources appropriate to a problem or need, and formulate questions to clarify a problem.
- **Valuing:** The ability to assess a course of action in terms of its long-range effects on the general human welfare, make decisions that will maximize both individual and collective good, and the ability to use ethical thinking and decision-making when solving issues.

STUDENT EMPLOYMENT WAGE SCALE

		1st yr.	160-hrs. raise	2nd yr.	3rd yr.	4th yr./ cap.	Avg.
Level 5	Senior Building Managers	$8.40	$8.65	$9.15	$9.65	$10.15	$9.34
Level 4	Student Managers	$7.90	$8.15	$8.65	$9.15	$9.65	$8.84
Level 3	Office/Marketing/Information Center Coordinators	$7.65	$7.90	$8.40	$8.90	$9.40	$8.59
Level 2	Operations Crew	$7.40	$7.65	$8.15	$8.65	$9.15	$8.34
Level 1	Office Assistants	$7.50	$7.50	$8.00	$8.50	$9.00	$8.19

Students are paid based on the position in which they are working. However, they will receive the salary appropriate to the year(s) of service they have performed. Students must complete at least six months of continuous employment before they can advance to the next salary year.

Mini, verbal evaluations are performed at the end of the first semester. Full, written evaluations are performed at the end of the second semester. Raises will be awarded at the beginning of the first semester every year based on merit as reflected in the most recent performance evaluation.

Exceptional performance may be rewarded by "jumping" a salary year but must be thoroughly documented by the immediate supervisor and approved in consultation with the assistant director and/or the director. A "salary year" is defined as a year(s) of service. A promotion from one level to another level will result in the student's salary raising to reflect both position promomtion as well as a salary year promotion if applicable.

SAMPLE JOB DESCRIPTION
UNIVERSITY OF MINNESOTA STUDENT UNIONS & ACTIVITIES

Student Food Services Attendant

Minimum Skills/Qualifications:
- High school graduate or equivalent; current University of Minnesota student
- Excellent communication skills
- Ability to work independently
- Self motivated
- Flexible schedule
- Must attend mandatory student training sessions offered during semesters
- Previous catering experience and/or beverage restaurant service highly preferred, but not required

Duties/Responsibilities:

Responsibility/Accountability
- On time for shift and required to provide replacement, if cannot work assigned shift
- Adheres to basic policies and procedures and understands staff roles
- Friendly and professional
- Takes responsibility for, and learns from, errors
- Takes responsibility for his/her learning
- Always meets basic expectations
- Customer-focused and driven

Independence/Interdependence
- Seeks instruction from supervisor when unclear of procedures or how to correct errors
- Demonstrates clear and effective communication with supervisors and team members
- Able to work independently
- Adapts behavior appropriately in response to team or organizational needs

Goal Orientation
- Manages time to complete all required and/or assigned duties and tasks
- Able to prioritize work tasks
- Does not all distraction to prevent timely completion of work

Self-Confidence/Humility
- Demonstrates good verbal and nonverbal communication
- Displays positive attitude with customers, with co-workers, and toward work
- Demonstrates the ability to help others adapt to new situations

Resilience
- Accepts instruction and/or constructive criticism from supervisor
- Able to work through problematic experiences by assessing what caused them, what can be done to repair them, and how to avoid them in the future
- Able to apply knowledge in multiple settings
- Able to handle high volume food service

Appreciation of Differences
- Understands and respect the values and beliefs of others.
- Treats all customers, peers, and supervisors respectfully and congenially

Tolerance of Ambiguity
- Able to handle an error or a challenging customer when minimal information is available
- Employs basic problem-solving skills, uses good judgment, and looks to supervisor when needed
- Able to embrace a duty or task without fully agreeing or understanding
- Maintains composure in difficult situations
- Demonstrates a willingness to attempt new tasks
- Able to work under conditions of uncertainty, such as filling in for an assignment other than the one you were hired in

Educate all employees to understand mission and goals so they can provide great service to customers.

SAMPLE JOB DESCRIPTION
UNIVERSITY OF MINNESOTA STUDENT UNIONS & ACTIVITIES

Title: Gameroom Attendant – Entry-Level
Job Code: 2801
Salary Range: $8.00 to $9.50 per hour

Essential Functions:
Attendants report directly to the gameroom managers. Responsibilities include:

45%	Customer service
15%	Food preparation
15%	General cleaning
15%	Stock merchandise
10%	Miscellaneous duties as assigned including trouble-shooting of gaming equipment

Essential Qualifications:
- Current University of Minnesota student enrolled at least half-time(undergraduate student, six credits; graduate student, three credits)
- Ability to serve and interact with customers and guests in a pleasant manner
- Ability to accurately handle money and transactions
- Aptitude toward independent work, responsibility, problem solving, and respect

Preferred Qualifications:
- Experience in customer service
- General knowledge of bowling and billiards
- Mechanical aptitude

Opportunities for Skill Development on the Job:
Students participate in experiences outside the classroom that allow them to develop and demonstrate life skills. These skills and characteristics for success and citizenship are learned and refined during their college years and beyond. The Office for Student Affairs has developed seven student development outcomes that the Student Unions & Activities has incorporated into the student employment system in the unions. Here is a listing of the student development outcomes with some examples of how you can learn or further develop your own skills set.

Responsibility/Accountability
- Arrives on time for shift and attempts to provide replacement, if cannot work assigned shift
- Acknowledges when mistakes/missed deadlines occur and knows when supervisor should be alerted
- Adheres to basic gameroom policies, procedures and understands staff roles
- Attends scheduled orientation and training sessions and work area meetings
- Generally knowledgeable of games and gameroom equipment
- Develops knowledge of menu, food preparation procedures, and food safety rulesDemonstrates correct operation of cash register/point of sale (POS) system
- Able to balance cash register at end of shift
- Always meets basic expectations (e.g., wears T-shirt/uniform, nametag, stays busy, etc.)

Independence/Interdependence
- Seeks instruction from supervisor and asks when unclear of tasks, procedures, or how to correct errors
- Informs supervisor when needed using training and good judgment
- Demonstrates good judgment on when to defer questions, complaints, and issues to supervisor

Goal Orientation
- Makes progress and improvements in job performance as experience grows
- Seeks guidance from senior employees and supervisors when needed
- Responds well to goals and training set by supervisor as needed

Self-Awareness
- Demonstrates good verbal and nonverbal communication skills
- Displays friendly and helpful attitude with customers and peers
- Can separate the demands of the job and customers from personal concerns and ego

Resilience
- Accepts instruction/constructive criticism from supervisor
- Able to work through difficulties when they arise

Appreciation of Differences
- Tolerant of the values and beliefs of others
- Treats all customers, peers, and supervisors respectfully and congenially

Tolerance of Ambiguity
- Able to handle an error or challenging customer when there is no information available
- Employs basic problem-solving skills, uses good judgment in being not afraid to fail, and looks to supervisor when needed
- Can embrace a duty or task without necessarily a personal need to fully agree or completely understand the reasons of the organization or supervisor

The employer reserves the right to change or add duties to this position as long as the changes and/or additions are consistent with the job classification.

PERFORMANCE REVIEW SUMMARY
STUDENT EMPLOYEE PERFORMANCE
AND DEVELOPMENT PROCESS
UNIVERSITY OF MINNESOTA STUDENT UNIONS & ACTIVITIES

Employee Name	
Employee ID Number	
Job Title	
Department	Student Unions & Activities
Work Unit	
Supervisor	

Date of Appraisal		Date of Hire		Appraisal Time Period	

Has the employee passed probation?	☐ Yes ☐ No

Overall Rating	☐ Needs Improvement ☐ Meets Expectations ☐ Exceeds Expectations

I acknowledge that I have discussed this evaluation with my supervisor.	

Employee Comments

Employee Signature		Date	
Supervisor's Signature		Date	
HR Director's Signature		Date	

Performance Standards and Descriptions

Exceeds Expectations
During this review period, the individual performed the job at an excellent level. This category describes the overall performance of dedicated individuals who consistently perform the duties and responsibilities of their positions at a very high level. Efforts result in outstanding customer service, teamwork, quality of work, etc. The individual shows initiative, demonstrates thoroughness, and makes contributions that go well beyond the expected level.

Meets Expectations
This standard reflects an effective employee whose performance ensures the Twin Cities Student Unions & Activities' ongoing success. The individual's overall performance is solid and meets the standards necessary to contribute to the unit. The employee's job performance demonstrates commitment to the performance factors on a daily basis. Staff in this category may exceed expectations or need improvement in some aspects of their work. This is the level at which we expect the majority of staff to perform.

Needs Improvement
During the review period, the individual did not carry out all the assigned duties and responsibilities of the job at the expected level. One or more of the performance factors pertaining to the unit's work are below standard (e.g., teamwork, customer service). While there may be some areas where job performance meets the basic requirements of the position, overall there is a distinct need for this individual to improve performance. During the review process the supervisor will highlight areas of competence as well as areas that need improvement. Immediate attention to improving areas identified as less than satisfactory is expected by means of coaching and training to help meet defined expectations. A performance improvement plan may also be put in place.

List 4–5 major job duties from job description:

1.	
2.	
3.	
4.	
5.	

Performance Review Summary

All employees of the Student Unions & Activities are expected to meet the following relevant performance expectations and standards that support the mission and values of our department. Supervisors are to evaluate an employee's performance on relevant performance factors. Describe for each factor an example using work assigned to the position to support the performance rating. For employees not meeting expectations, develop a performance improvement plan with the employee, document the plan, and actively manage and support the employee's progress.

Performance Factors & Expectations

1. **Customer Service**

☐ Needs Improvement	☐ Meets Expectations	☐ Exceeds Expectations
Supervisor's Comments on Performance		

2. **Responsibility and Accountability**

☐ Needs Improvement	☐ Meets Expectations	☐ Exceeds Expectations
Supervisor's Comments on Performance		

3. **Independence and Interdependence**

☐ Needs Improvement	☐ Meets Expectations	☐ Exceeds Expectations
Supervisor's Comments on Performance		

4. **Goal Orientation**

☐ Needs Improvement	☐ Meets Expectations	☐ Exceeds Expectations
Supervisor's Comments on Performance		

5. Self-Awareness

☐ Needs Improvement	☐ Meets Expectations	☐ Exceeds Expectations
Supervisor's Comments on Performance		

6. Resilience

☐ Needs Improvement	☐ Meets Expectations	☐ Exceeds Expectations
Supervisor's Comments on Performance		

7. Appreciation of Differences

☐ Needs Improvement	☐ Meets Expectations	☐ Exceeds Expectations
Supervisor's Comments on Performance		

8. Tolerance of Ambiguity

☐ Needs Improvement	☐ Meets Expectations	☐ Exceeds Expectations
Supervisor's Comments on Performance		

9. Supervision *(if applicable)*

☐ Needs Improvement	☐ Meets Expectations	☐ Exceeds Expectations
Supervisor's Comments on Performance		

Reprinted with permission: Bowling Green State University

Other Comments

TRAINING SCHEDULE EXAMPLES

Week-long

The Campus Center at Smith College provides an example of a week-long training schedule that took place prior to the start of a new semester.

Day 1 (Saturday): Campus Center manager training
- Team-building
- Goal setting with learning outcomes and core values
- Expectations from supervisors and of supervisors
- Pre-test on the operations manual (i.e., What knowledge are students coming in with?)
- Pre-test review using tour of facility, hands-on approach to answering questions, and policy and procedure overview
- Facility management

Day 2 (Sunday): Campus Center manager training continued
- Building community (outside speaker)

Day 3 (Monday): New student employee training (utilizing Campus Center managers as facilitators)
- Team-building
- Introduction of student employee program, learning outcomes, and core values
- Facility tour
- Facility equipment, policies, and procedures

Day 4 (Tuesday): New student employee training continued
- Fire extinguisher training
- Facility set-ups and technical equipment training

Day 5 (Wednesday): New and returning student employee training
- Off-site ropes course

Day 6 (Thursday): New and returning student employee training continued
- Community building
- Leadership training
- Lunch with campus administrators
- Technical equipment training

Day 7 (Friday): New and returning student employee training continued
- Practice facility setups and technical equipment
- Website overview
- Scheduling
- Shirt distribution
- Wrap-up and evaluations

Three-day

Virginia Tech and Emory University offer examples of shorter, three-day training programs to provide a general orientation with specific position-based training to occur at another time.

Virginia Tech
- Day 1 (8 a.m.–5 p.m.): Breakfast, welcome from director, learning outcomes introduced, overview of retreat, specific skill training (fire extinguisher, blood-borne pathogen), lunch, overview on service and leadership, job exchanges
- Day 2 (7:30 a.m.–5 p.m.): Breakfast, customer service, team-building, icebreakers/low ropes, lunch, high ropes, announcements

- Day 3 (8 a.m.–2 p.m.): Breakfast, communication in a diverse community, sexual harassment, retreat evaluations, lunchtime barbeque

Emory University
- Day 1 (11 a.m.–9 p.m.): Introductions, icebreaker, review mission/goals/expectations/competencies, building tour, learning outcomes assessment, lunch, team-building, dinner, manual review
- Day 2 (8 a.m.–8 p.m.): Breakfast, team-building, emergency procedures, discipline police reviews, customer service, lunch, scheduling, goal setting, dinner, and fun time
- Day 3 (8 a.m.–12:30 p.m.): Breakfast, competency review, learning outcomes, closing, lunch, audio-visual training

Two-part

The Ohio State University's college union provides an example of multiple shorter trainings throughout the year.

Training Part 1
- Students arrive (with their license and ID card, ready to be photographed for student staff directory)
- Icebreaker/introductions
- Name tags
- Take pictures
- "Administrivia" (e.g., shut off cell phones, location of restrooms, etc.)
- Review agenda and expectations for the day
- Organizational traditions
- Paperwork and snacks
- Unveil theme with skit or video
- Team-builder/small-group projects
- Review "Owner's Manuals" and nominate representatives to serve on student staff development committee
- Training on online scheduling system
- Customer service activity
- Closing/dinner

Training Part 2
- Icebreaker/expectations for the day
- Cross training (split into groups and rotate between three area trainings)
- Wrap-up/eat

PEER PERFORMANCE EVALUATION

Student Employee Name:
_____

Date:
_____

PLEASE RATE TO THE BEST OF YOUR ABILITY

	Effectively uses time		Problem and/or conflict resolution		Appearance (shirt and name badge)
	Open to new ideas and suggestions		On time for scheduled shifts		Is a good listener and is genuinely concerned
	Takes time to get to know staff members		Organized and fair in relation to student staff		Models teamwork; willing to help out
	Approachable and visible		Provides specific constructive feedback where needed		Communication (too much or not enough)
	Available; easy to get a hold of when needed		Challenges me with new projects, tasks, & ideas		Leads by example; models good behavior; models Ohio Union mission/vision/values
	Offers support and encouragement				

APPRAISAL VALUES

5	Exceptional	Routinely goes far beyond standard expectations
4	Commendable	Conscientious performance at all times
3	Satisfactory	Performance is equal to expectations
2	Needs Improvement	Not effective or compliant with standards/expectations
1	Unsatisfactory	Unacceptable performance

CONSTRUCTIVE FEEDBACK FOR STUDENT EMPLOYEE:
_____

_____

_____

_____

Your name (optional):
_____

Reprinted with permission: The Ohio State University

STUDENT STAFF SUPERVISOR PERFORMANCE EVALUATION

Supervisor Name: _____

Date: _____

PLEASE RATE TO THE BEST OF YOUR ABILITY

	Consistent with decisions		Keeps meetings to the point		Treats student staff as adults
	Open to new ideas and suggestions		On time for meetings and appointments		Is a good listener and is genuinely concerned
	Takes time to get to know staff members		Organized and fair in scheduling hours		Models teamwork; willing to help out
	Effective in training and providing professional growth opportunities		Understanding of student schedules (class and work); makes scheduling efforts on their behalf		Communication (quality)
	Approachable and visible		Provides specific constructive feedback where needed		Communication (quantity) (1 = Not enough; 5 = Just right)
	Available; easy to get a hold of when needed		Challenges me with new projects, tasks, & ideas		Leads by example; models good behavior; models Ohio Union mission/vision/values
	Offers support and encouragement				

APPRAISAL VALUES

5	Exceptional	Routinely goes far beyond standard expectations
4	Commendable	Conscientious performance at all times
3	Satisfactory	Performance is equal to expectations
2	Needs Improvement	Not effective or compliant with standards/expectations
1	Unsatisfactory	Unacceptable performance

CONSTRUCTIVE FEEDBACK FOR SUPERVISOR: _____

_____

_____

_____

_____

Your name (optional): _____

Reprinted with permission: The Ohio State University

PERFORMANCE REVIEW

Name: _____   Title: _____

Supervisor Name: _____   Date:_____

Ohio Union staff members are expected to meet the expectations of their position. Your performance contributes to the overall success of the Ohio Union. The purpose of this review is determine how you are progressing and performing in the following areas: learning outcomes, Ohio Union values, job knowledge, attitude, customer service, and attendance. This evaluation and conversations with your supervisor may lead to incentives. Please make additional comments in the spaces provided.

Learning Outcomes:
Based on the progress made in developing skills/learning outcomes selected with supervisor.

Chosen Outcomes:_____

How are you progressing in these outcomes? What experiences could your supervisor offer you to help you develop your chosen outcome? Please use the space below to reflect on these questions and your progress this quarter.

Ohio Union Values: As part of the Ohio Union staff, everyone is expected to live the Ohio Union values as they interact with customers, clients and each other. While we realize you may not be able to use all these values everyday, please choose 2 or 3 and let us know how you use these as a student staff member. Then choose 1 or 2 that you would like to use more often and how you can achieve that.

Service – I provide the highest quality service and seek to be an active partner in my community.

Inclusiveness – I celebrate individual differences and seek to learn more about others.

Tradition – I look to the past to learn about our history and seek to transfer this information to others.

Involvement – I create opportunities for others to be involved.

Teamwork – I know that my individual contributions are important, but I seek to collectively pool efforts with fellow staff members for maximum gains.

Discovery – I consider the union as a laboratory for learning and practicing new things.

Personal and Social Development – I am willing to explore opportunities and participate in challenging and supportive activities to foster my personal and social development.

Job Knowledge:
Understands job responsibilities.

Needs Work	1	2	3	4	5	Excellent

Shows initiative by checking with supervisor or looking for tasks to keep busy during shift.

Needs Work	1	2	3	4	5	Excellent

Demonstrates ability to perform assigned tasks.

Needs Work	1	2	3	4	5	Excellent

Demonstrates ability to work well without direct supervision.

Needs Work	1	2	3	4	5	Excellent

Attitude:
Shows pride in job.

| Needs Work | 1 | 2 | 3 | 4 | 5 | Excellent |

Shows respect for authority and peers.

| Needs Work | 1 | 2 | 3 | 4 | 5 | Excellent |

Is understanding of others knowledge and abilities, and works as a team-player.

| Needs Work | 1 | 2 | 3 | 4 | 5 | Excellent |

Uses positive verbal and non-verbal skills.

| Needs Work | 1 | 2 | 3 | 4 | 5 | Excellent |

Customer Service:
Acknowledges and greets all clients and guests with a smile.

| Needs Work | 1 | 2 | 3 | 4 | 5 | Excellent |

Shows respect for all clients and guests.

| Needs Work | 1 | 2 | 3 | 4 | 5 | Excellent |

Makes every effort to provide clients and guest with all information/assistance/equipment requested.

| Needs Work | 1 | 2 | 3 | 4 | 5 | Excellent |

Attendance:
Shows up on time dressed for work.

| Needs Work | 1 | 2 | 3 | 4 | 5 | Excellent |

Makes every attempt to contact supervisor in advance if unable to work or is going to be late.

| Needs Work | 1 | 2 | 3 | 4 | 5 | Excellent |

Makes every attempt to cover his/her shift if unable to attend work.

| Needs Work | 1 | 2 | 3 | 4 | 5 | Excellent |

Volunteers to cover empty shifts, closings, and/or flips.

| Needs Work | 1 | 2 | 3 | 4 | 5 | Excellent |

GENERAL COMMENTS:

EXAMPLE STUDENT EMPLOYEE LEARNING OUTCOMES EVALUATION RUBRIC

	1 **Insufficient Performance –** Performance is below expectations	2 **Basic Performance –** Meets minimum standards with need for improvement	3 **Good Performance –** Often performs above standard expectations	4 **Exceptional Performance –** Consistently achieves and models performance above expectations
EMPLOYEE GROWTH & DEVELOPMENT				
Manages time effectively to increase productivity	Can focus and complete one task at a time; shows a low level of motivation to complete job tasks; regularly works on non-job-related tasks while on the clock	Can focus and complete more than one task at a time; shows motivation to being productive and efficient when completing job tasks; completes all job tasks before working on any non-job-related tasks	Is proficient in multitasking; shows commitment to being productive and efficient when completing job tasks; rarely works on non-job-related tasks while on the clock	Consistently provides high customer service while completing multiple tasks at one time; consistently models high levels of productivity and efficiency when completing job tasks; uses work time to complete or initiate job-related tasks
COMMUNICATION SKILLS				
Communicates clearly and appropriately when speaking	Can speak to others in person and on the phone with some reservations; communication is often not clear or focused; language used is limited, inaccurate, or includes slang or jargon	Can speak to others in person and on the phone with basic confidence; communication is clear but does not always flow smoothly; language used is accurate and free of slang but not always relevant	Demonstrated and consistent confidence when speaking to others in person and on the phone; communication is clear, appropriate, accurate, relevant, and well-organized	Actively invites and engages others in relevant, appropriate, and purposeful communication when speaking in person and on the phone

PROBLEM SOLVING				
Exercises good judgment when setting priorities or dealing with critical issues	Is aware of basic support network when dealing with critical issues requiring judgment; uses resources to locate basic information, but needs assistance in synthesizing concepts; is reluctant to make independent decisions	Can make recommendations based on basic information sources and limited experience; can determine basic priorities when working through critical issues; requires assistance from supervisory personnel to resolve issues	Maintains composure and solves problems with little or no supervisory assistance; sets priorities in tasks and process steps; initiates action in problem solving, seeks alternative solutions; knows when to seek additional help from co-workers or supervisor	Prioritizes information, concepts effectively when responding to complex issues; works independently in problem solving; may assist other less confident/ experienced co-workers

CITIZENSHIP AND PARTICIPATION				
Works all schedule shifts	Understands absence policy; has had two or more missed shifts during this evaluation period; does not make an effort to follow appropriate procedures for absences and/or shift replacements	Has had one missed shift during this evaluation period; follows appropriate procedures for absences and/or shift replacements; regularly requests shifts off	Has had no missed shifts during this evaluation period; follows appropriate procedures for absences and/or shift replacements; makes effort to fill shifts for co-workers	Has had no missed shifts during this evaluation period; communicates appropriate procedures for absences and/or shift replacements with others; regularly fills shifts for co-workers

ABILITY TO SERVE CUSTOMERS				
Professional and pleasant attitude when working with customers	Demonstrates a pleasant attitude in interactions with customers; smiles and makes eye contact; serves as the building host; welcomes customers and visitors	Shows enthusiasm in welcoming customers and works well with staff	Takes initiative in speaking with customers; provides leadership for other staff and models customer service behaviors; displays courtesy and customer service skills	Serves as a university representative and reflects the university image through customer service

INTERPERSONAL SKILLS				
Demonstrates high-quality interactions with peers, colleagues, and supervisors	Is timid when interacting socially with others; shows little motivation to relate to peers	Is respectful and courteous when interacting socially with others; has developed work relationships with several peers and supervisor	Is genuine and pleasant when interacting socially with others; has developed work relationships with many peers and several student and professional staff members from other areas	Is compassionate and encouraging when interacting socially with others; consistently initiates interactions to build relationships with other staff members
Appreciates and works well with a diverse population	Interactions are of a clearly different quality when working with co-workers and/or customers who have characteristics unlike their own	Demonstrates effort to interact at a consistent quality with all co-workers and/or customers, regardless of differences; demonstrates appreciation for diverse perspectives	Interactions are of consistent quality when working with all co-workers and/or customers; recognizes the needs of diverse populations	Actively seeks opportunities to learn from and interact with people different from self; advocates for services and procedures necessary to meet the needs of a diverse population

Adapted from:
Bowling Green State University. (2008). *Bowen-Thompson Student Union student employee evaluation rubric: Information center.* Bowling Green, Ohio.

ABOUT THE EDITOR

Brett Perozzi has been a scholar-practitioner at five universities throughout his career. Perozzi is currently the associate vice president for student affairs at Weber State University, a public institution of 22,000 students located 30 miles north of Salt Lake City. He most recently served as the executive director of student engagement at Arizona State University and has also worked at Indiana, Texas Tech, and Colorado State Universities.

Perozzi received a Ph.D. from Indiana University and a master's degree from the University of Arizona, both in higher education administration. He has taught in the higher education graduate programs at Indiana, Colorado State, and Arizona State, and served as a faculty member for graduate student international study programs. Perozzi's research interests are student employment and international education.

ABOUT THE CONTRIBUTORS

Kathleen Boyle, Ph.D., is an assistant professor in the department of leadership, policy, and administration at the University of St. Thomas and the director of the master's degree program for leadership in student affairs. Prior to this, she was a visiting faculty member at Indiana University, coordinating the master's degree program in higher education and student affairs. Boyle also worked for several years as a practitioner in student affairs.

Sebastian Contreras Jr. is the associate director of the Norris University Center at Northwestern University. He earned a B.A. in psychology from the University of Iowa and an M.S. in student affairs in higher education from Colorado State University. Previously, Contreras was the assistant director of the student leadership institute at DePaul University. His professional experiences in higher education have included work in leadership development, training and education, college union administration, student activities, and residence life.

Linda Croston received an honors bachelor degree in social science in 2004 from University College Cork. She also has a postgraduate degree in management and marketing. Throughout her academic studies, Croston was employed as part of the Student Centre information desk team and also as a student manager. In 2005–06, Croston traveled part of the world and upon her return, was appointed to the position of assistant facility services manager of the Student Centre at the University College Cork.

David L. Grady is the associate vice president and director of University Life Centers at the University of Iowa. He also holds an adjunct assistant professor appointment in the university department of counseling, rehabilitation, and student development. He earned a Ph.D. from the University of Texas at Austin, an Ed.M. from Harvard University, and a B.A. from Mississippi State University.

Jessica Hickmott is the student affairs assessment coordinator at Weber State University. Her current research interests include assessment in higher education and competencies of student affairs professionals. She received her master's in postsecondary educational leadership with a specialization in student affairs from San Diego State University.

Janelle Kappes serves as the senior coordinator for transition and parent programs at Arizona State University, where she implements programming for new students and their families. Additionally, Kappes serves as a faculty associate in the master's in higher and postsecondary education program. She completed her doctorate in educational leadership and policy studies at

Arizona State University, and her research interests include underrepresented students in higher education, student assessment, and evaluation.

Jonathan S. Lewis has served since 2007 as the assistant director for the Reynolds Club and Bartlett Hall at the University of Chicago. In this role, Lewis oversees event planning, audio-visual services, operations, and facility management for the university's 108-year-old college union. Prior to that, Lewis served for five years at the Norris Center at Northwestern University, where he also received his master's degree in higher education administration and policy.

Larry Lunsford is the associate vice president for student affairs and the university ombudsman at Florida International University. He is also an assistant professor in the College of Education. Lunsford co-authored "The First Year: Making the Most of College," which is used in a required course for all first-year undergraduate students at the university. He has a bachelor's degree in communications from the University of Tennessee, a master's in college student personnel administration from Indiana University, and a Ph.D. in higher education administration from the University of Pittsburgh.

Jerry Mann is the director of the University Center at The University of North Carolina at Charlotte. Formerly the director of the union and student support services at University of California–Los Angeles, Mann spent 25 years there before moving. He has a bachelor's degree in business from California State University, Northridge and an M.B.A. from Loyola Marymount University. Mann is a true believer in student governance, and he also enjoys travel, music, reading fiction, watching college basketball, and riding bicycles.

Sara Punsky McGuire is the assistant director for work and leadership at Smith College. She attended Edinboro University of Pennsylvania where she received a bachelor's degree in speech, language, and hearing while working at the University Center. She received her master's in educational leadership from Central Connecticut State University, where she was a graduate intern at the union. After graduate school, McGuire worked as the assistant director of the Campus Center and student activities at Amherst College for two years.

John V. Moore III is finishing doctoral work in higher education and student affairs and in inquiry methodology at Indiana University. For six years, he has worked at the Center for Postsecondary Research as a research analyst on multiple projects such as the national survey of student engagement, the beginning college survey of student engagement, and the College Board student survey. Moore's interests also include identity development theories, the relationship between theory and methodology, and factors associated with student persistence.

Andrew O'Brien is the former CEO of campus life at Monash University in Australia; he has also served as president of the Australian Campus Unions Managers Association and as an ACUI regional representative. In 2004, O'Brien was recognised as the Customer Service Institute of Australia's CEO of the year. After 25 years of working in student affairs, in 2007, O'Brien established Organisations that Matter and now spends his time consulting higher education, industry, and government in the fields of vision, strategy, people development, customer service, and relationship management.

Denny Olsen is the senior associate director of Student Unions and Activities at the University of Minnesota, where he's been responsible for finance, activities, facilities and retail. His 26-year career also includes serving as the assistant director at the University of Washington. Olsen has a master's degree in counseling and student personnel from Minnesota State University, Mankato. His interests include building renovation, student employment development outcomes, organizational change, and event programming.

Ryan D. Padgett is a doctoral student in the higher education program and a research assistant at the Center for Research on Undergraduate Education at the University of Iowa. His research interests include student access, college choice, first-year college experiences, and persistence in higher education, particularly on diverse student populations.

Nadesan Permaul is the director of the Associated Students of the University of California Auxiliary. The ASUC was established at Berkeley in 1887. The auxiliary oversees ASUC operations. Permaul has a B.A., M.A., and Ph.D. in political science from the University of California, Berkeley. He has been an administrator on the campus since 1979 and began teaching in rhetoric and more recently political science. He is also past president of the California Alumni Association.

Melanie Rago serves as the senior director at Campus Philly, a nonprofit organization focused on growing greater Philadelphia's college-educated workforce by attracting, engaging, and retaining college students. Rago also is a doctoral student in higher education and student affairs at Indiana University. Her research interests include working students and leveraging data in student affairs. Prior to Campus Philly, Rago worked for the Project on Academic Success at Indiana University.

Z. Paul Reynolds holds a bachelor's degree in secondary education from the University of Toledo. He went on to become the assistant manager of student life at the University of Pennsylvania. While at Penn, he received his master's degree in higher education and also completed coursework toward the degree of Doctor of Education in Higher Education. Reynolds moved onto Texas A&M University–Corpus Christi in 2002 and served as the assistant director of the University Center and Student Activities. In 2008, he was appointed the associate director of the Bone Student Center and Braden Auditorium at Illinois State University.

Debbie Santucci, a Ph.D. student in higher education and student affairs at Indiana University, serves as a project associate for the Center for Postsecondary Research and the National Survey of Student Engagement, as well as a graduate research assistant for the National Institute for Learning Outcomes Assessment. Santucci has a master's degree in higher education and a bachelor's degree in marketing (with minors in communication and dance) from Arizona State University. Her main research interests include professional and organizational development, assessment and evaluation, and organizational theory.

Eve Scrogham is an assistant director at the Ohio Union at The Ohio State University, where she has worked since 2002, after receiving her master's degree in higher education. She received her bachelor's degree from Purdue University, where she majored in communications and health studies. Scrogham enjoys training for endurance events that raise money for good causes, listening to audio books, and being crafty when time permits.

Maggie Towle is the director of Student Unions and activities at the University of Minnesota, where she provides oversight for three union facilities, student activities, campus-wide programming, and a $15 million budget. She led the $72.5 million renovation project of Coffman Memorial Union on the Minneapolis campus. She has 28 years of experience in the profession. Towle has an master's in human development from the University of St. Mary's. Her interests include building renovation, student development, organizational change, and administration/management.

Printed in the United States
147850LV00003B/1/P